Gendering Talk

Gendering
Talk

ROBERT HOPPER

Michigan State University Press • *East Lansing*

∞ The paper used in this publication meets the minimum requirements
of ANSI/NISO Z39.48–1992 (R 1997) (Permanence of Paper).

Michigan State University Press
East Lansing, Michigan 48823-5202

Printed and bound in the United States of America.

08 07 06 05 04 03   1 2 3 4 5 6 7 8 9 10

LIBRARY OF CONGRESS CATALOGING-IN-PUBLICATION DATA
Hopper, Robert.
Gendering talk / Robert Hopper.
p. cm.
Includes bibliographical references.
ISBN 0870136364 (pbk. : alk. paper)
1. Sex role. 2. Communication—Sex differences. 3. Communication and sex.
4. Man-woman relationships. 5. Interpersonal communication. 6. Conversation.
HQ1075 .H67 2002
302.2 21
2002014110

Conversation by Henri Matisse, courtesy of The State Hermitage Museum, St. Petersburg.

Book and cover design by Sharp Deslgns, Lansing, MI

Published with the support of University Cooperative Society, University of Texas, Austin.

Visit Michigan State University Press on the World Wide Web at: *www.msupress.msu.edu*

. . . gender is a kind of imitation for which there is no original;
in fact it is a kind of imitation
that produces the very notion of the original
as a consequence of the imitation itself.

—*Judith Butler, "Imitating and Gender Insubordination"*

There is nothing the matter with speech
Just because it lent itself
To my uses

—*W. S. Merwin, "In the Winter of My Thirty-Eighth Year"*

Contents

Acknowledgments

ROBERT POURED HIS HEART AND SOUL INTO THIS BOOK. IT WAS HIS DREAM TO SEE it published. The dream has become a reality thanks to the dedication of Rod Hart and Leslie Hope Jarmon of the University of Texas and Sandy Ragan of the University of Oklahoma. Rod and Leslie shepherded the work through the publication process and Sandy performed the editorial chores. These activities no doubt required enormous amounts of time—and with no hope of ever receiving any help from the author. Robert was a lucky man to have had friends like these. Rod, Leslie, and Sandy, thank you so much for your labor of love. I would also like to thank Marty Medhurst and the Michigan State University Press for their generous support of the project.

There is a tall, skinny angel in heaven who is thrilled to see *Gendering Talk* become a real book. Many thanks to you all.

Kay Hopper

Transcript Symbols

no	Italics shows vocal stress of a sound.
no:	Colon shows a stretching of a sound.
<no	Arrow shows a high-pitched sound.
no-	Hyphen shows a sound suddenly cut off at end.
no?	Question-mark shows a sound ending with rising pitch.
no.	Period shows a sound ending with falling pitch.
n(h)o	Shows laugh token embedded in a word.
hhh	Shows audible breathing (¡hh is an in-breath).
(1.5)	Shows a pause timed to nearest tenth of a second.
[no [yes	Brackets show two sounds by different speakers spoken at the same time.
*	scratchy or gravelly voice
UTCL	University of Texas Conversation Library
◄	Arrow indicates particular focus on that utterance in the discussion.
SDCL	San Diego State University Conversation Library

Gendering the Conversation

CONVERSATION IS HENRI MATISSE'S TITLE FOR A PAINTING COMPLETED ABOUT 1909, in the fortieth year of the artist's long life. Matisse wrote that this work is a study in the color blue, but it is also a study in gendering talk.

The pictured figures face one another: The artist himself stands in pajamas, and a woman, presumably his wife, sits across a window from him. The interior of their room is monochrome dark blue, a deep, rich, depressed color that contrasts with the bright colors visible through the window. Matisse frequently included colorful windows in his paintings. In this painting the bright window separates the deadpan spouses.

This is a picture of a prosperous midlife marriage. This woman and man remain in their sleeping clothes when the riot of color in the window between them suggests that the sun is well up in the sky. Yet these partners do not look out the window. They look straight, unblinkingly, at one another, opposing each other across the window. The man stands upright in straight, stark stripes of blue and white. The seated woman appears as rounded dark curves. Her eyes and forehead bear a dark smudge. Her right hand is visible; his is in his pocket.

The figures face each other eyeball to eyeball across the bright window. Perhaps the window grillwork connecting the estranged bodies of husband and wife spells the French word *non*, but probably that is a forced interpretation. Still, the painting does reflect opposition, a contest of wills such as occurs with an accusation or an unwelcome announcement. At such a problematic moment partners seek explanations for their stiff, careful discomfort: "Here we go again."

At couple crises, gender is particularly available to explain problems. How and why we gender the talk in our lives, a topic in Matisse's painting, is also the subject of the book you are now beginning to read.

Matisse sold *Conversation* to a rich Russian ninety years ago. My parents were babies then, cars and radios were novelties. The wiring of telephones and electronic lights was in its first generation. That time may now be seen as the cradle of modern consciousness, yet the painting was created before two world wars, the Holocaust, television, the Soviet Union, rock music, the baby boom, LSD, or the silicon chip. Still somehow this painting continues to ring true today. It points to our implicitly gendered conversation performances. We are still going about gendering talk.

Gendering talk is a phrase with two meanings. It refers to certain features in talk that are strongly saturated with gender, for example, my use of the word "woman" to describe a character in Matisse's painting. The sense that some talk seems more gendered than other talk is communicated by emphasis on my title's first word—*gendering* talk. To use the word "woman" is to infuse gender into the human conversation. Such gendering action may be implicit or subliminal. To say "woman" is not necessarily to think about gender. Gendering talk creates social problems because there are so many ways that gender creeps into talk, and we employ them so often.

A second sense of this phrase, pronounced gendering *talk,* refers to the ongoing, taken-for-granted project to gender the world of social experience. Talk is not the only thing we gender: We also gender clothing, jewelry, room decor, career paths, public restrooms, household chores, and above all, sexuality. Yet gendering talk binds together our many disparate social senses of sex difference, sexuality, and stereotype. The consequence is a world in which the difference between men and women is taken for granted, as is sexual pair-bonding, as is a mythical battle between the sexes which from time to time propels us into these stymied conversations with a member of the opposite sex.

Why do we say *opposite* sex? Well, it is argued, men and women are quite different from one another, and this difference leads women and men to communicate differently—to speak different languages—and hence to misunderstand each other. Men and women face each other numbly and grimly before the world's colorful window. "You just don't understand," each of us rails at the opposite other. The prototype case, the person who understands us least, is a spouse at midlife. How can this be? Did God Almighty invent marriage to introduce me to one person completely different from me?

I wrote *Gendering Talk* after many years of married conversation with Kay, to whom I gratefully dedicate this book. At certain problematic moments, Kay has seemed to represent much that differs from me. The marriage conversation manufactures a special kind of social lens, a fun house mirror that stretches the notion of sex differences. Writers of self-help books about male-female differences concentrate on examples of conversations between members of midlife married couples. Many of these authors, John Gray and Deborah Tannen, for instance, write at length of their own frustrations in married midlife—the age of Dante when he became lost in the woods, the age of Matisse when he painted *Conversation.*[1] Midlife marriage makes a prototype case that men and women act differently. Even Matisse's title, *Conversation,* suggests that the painting takes up a topic more general than a certain conversational moment at midlife marriage. The title suggests that experiences in marriage can be taken as indicators of communicative problems—gender troubles that evolve out of gender differences.

Marriage partners affect not only each other but also their societies. Parents teach to children their own special preoccupation with sex differences, mostly by example. This social preoccupation is present to some degree at every age of the life cycle. This week (in early 1998) Kay and I eagerly await sonogram evidence of the sex of our unborn first grandchild. Of any expected or recently born child we ask, "What is it?" which means, "Is it is a boy or a girl?" Friends and relatives ask this question to know what color gift to buy and how to greet the child. To a boy child I may say, "Hey slugger," delivered deadpan from deep in the throat and accompanied by a tummy tickle. To a girl child it is more likely I will say, "Hello sweetheart" in a high pitch and accompanied by a gentle knuckle dimpling the cheek.

The belief in sex differences is elaborated and buttressed by myths of romantic love between a man and a woman—myths that frame many adolescent struggles. Any understanding of gendering talk must take this mythology as a central social fact. I discovered the importance of talk during adolescence by noticing my conversational failures at early courtship. This discovery of conversation led quite directly (if accidentally) to my life's vocation:

thirty years as a college teacher of speech communication. I have taught more than fifty semester courses about speech and gender to students at the University of Texas at Austin. During this time, I have launched a dozen scholarly attempts to describe the communicative differences between men and women. Each of these attempts has failed.

As a social scientist I have slowly and grudgingly become convinced that men and women are more alike than different and that our experience of male-female differences is an artful, cultural construction, a trick of the ear, something we all believe in, regardless of the facts. As a member of our culture I believe in sex differences, too. However, in comparative studies I have failed to unearth substantial male-female speech differences. I conclude that women and men do not actually talk so differently from one another. Rather, men and women listen and talk similarly: We all listen to women differently than we listen to men. Sometimes we talk differently to a woman than to a man. We all talk differently about men than about women. We all talk differently to a sexual partner than to anyone else (whatever our sexual preference). We make gender in the social world by practices of gendering talk.

Many writers suggest that gender troubles result only from male-female differences. John Gray has sold millions of books claiming that men and women are so different from one another as to hail from different planets. Others suggest that patriarchal traditions divide males and females, as well as members of different races and social classes. Yet such generalizations do not help us much unless we describe, in detail, how ordinary people communicate to make gender salient to any particular moment.

Men and women are not from separate planets; instead, we are co-performers of gender in the social planet we all inhabit. Let us listen carefully to each other, with that special attention we might lavish upon poetry being read aloud. Let us not be so sure what the problem is. The problem has many parts and a long history.

• • •

Gender hangs around us like a communicative albatross. We slouch toward possible male-female political equality, while at the same time we fear that communication between the sexes is biased and troublesome. We struggle to communicate with intimate others. Sometimes we believe the problems stem from communicating with a differently gendered other. We worry about sex discrimination in employment and discrimination against those of unpopular sexual orientation. We worry about sexual harassment and sexual violence. Sometimes we fret about the political correctness of gendered language.

Whatever our politics on matters of gender—feminist, traditionalist, or gay rights activist—each of us routinely encounters gender in everyday social interaction. Naming practices illustrate how often gender is marked in talk. We gender the names for occupations from priest to president. We gender most of our personal given names (Tom, Sallie). We gender our terms for intimate relationships (mother, son, girlfriend).

Most humans believe that males and females are pretty different, but our theories about gender remain a patchwork of partially contradictory folklore and inconclusive research. In our confusion we follow different standards of sexual politics within different settings. In matters of public professions, Western laws and customs increasingly ask us to turn a blind eye to sex and gender. However, in matters of sociality and intimacy, *vive la différence!* Many of us attempt to enact egalitarian scripts in our careers, yet abandon notions of sexual equality or similarity when we pair up to dance, flirt, or start a family.

We may momentarily forget gender, only to find that it crops up unexpectedly, like a neighborhood dice game, to affect a plan or to transform a social setting. "We have been engendered," writes social historian Donna Haraway.[2] This wording suggests that being infused with gender is something that has happened *to* us. Yet who are the actors in this gendering? Gendered scenes and actions always happen here and now. However, gendering talk unfolds so obviously, so smoothly, that we seldom even notice our own actions.

Even our understandings of communication itself are gendered. We hold two partial understandings of how communication works: monologue and dialogue. We associate those notions with myths about masculine and feminine talk.

In a monologue view, communication is the travel of information from a source to a recipient. The monologue view, which grows from the study of writing, characterizes precise achievements of command and control, grammar, computer programming, and scientific reports. Effective monologue is accurate (high-fidelity) communication, in which an information source expresses a clear meaning that a recipient understands as accurately as possible. Communication problems occur when message flow is distorted or stopped or when sender and receiver differ in code.

Monologue is associated with masculine gender, getting the right answer, and dominance. Monologue is the primary understanding most educated people hold about communication. In this view gender troubles are consequences of male-female speech differences.

A dialogue understanding of interpersonal communication is difficult to formulate in (monologic) writing. Effective dialogue occurs over time, through interaction of more than one participant, in listening with care, in keeping the conversation going, in opening possibilities, in letting more than one speaker contribute to the direction of events, and in building community.

Consider the first moments of a telephone conversation: "Hello," "Hi Pat," "How are you," and the like. These utterances show modest content but are saturated with the dialogic demands of relationship and culture. The telephone opening sets implicit ground rules for more content-laden talk that follows. Therefore, the telephone opening is a very important phase of an encounter, even though it has little content. Dialogue carries the stream of consciousness; dialogue works the amorphous gel of both cultures and human relationships. The concept of social interaction as dialogue within a network of relationships is associated with feminine gender.

Monologue views of gender trouble in talk emphasize male-female differences that distort clarity; dialogue hearings emphasize that men and women are all in the same boat, trying to solve problems. In monologue each individual speaker should be assertive and clear in each speaking turn. Effective dialogue entails each speaker listening carefully and responding appropriately within evolving goals and outcomes.

In a monologue view, men's and women's different language patterns create puzzles akin to intercultural communication. The sexes are doomed to gendered separateness unless we become facile translators or unless men's and women's languages converge. In a dialogue hearing, we may be unable to calculate either the extent of male-female language differences or their importance. We can, however, engage optimistically in the communicative tasks of mutual understanding, support, intimacy, and politics.

These two notions, monologue and dialogue, must be repeatedly sharpened on each other. Neither notion by itself explains human speech. An effective communicator must be able to operate in both monologue and dialogue modes. I lean toward dialogic explanation, in part to balance the dominance of monologue in the history of thought. Yet I also question the gendered stereotyping of monologue and dialogue and try to uncouple this dichotomy of communication forms from oversimplified assignment to gendered categories.

· · ·

This book is a series of sketches describing how we mark gender in talk, how we cause gender troubles, and how we conceptualize these troubles in talk about male-female differences. Chapter 2 considers gender as social performance. Chapters 3 to 6 take up gendering talk in the formation and development of pair-bond sexual relationships, especially these intertwined issues:

- Flirting
- Sexual violence
- Couple formation

Flirting and sexual violence are kissing cousins out of which couples (and eventually families) form and which emphasize the performance of male-female difference within each sexual couple. Therefore, these performances of sexual coupling are important carriers of the belief that men and women differ.

Speakers also support beliefs in gender differences within the tiny details of everyday talk—not just the talk between women and men but all social interaction. This everyday performance of gender differentiation is the topic of chapters 7 to 9.

- How we talk about women and about men
- Male/female differences in speech style

The discussion of male-female language differences appears rather late in the book, partly because those issues remain unresolved but also largely because earlier chapters explain phenomena that are commonly chalked up to male-female differences.

It is necessary to examine all of these varying issues about gender in talk in order to make progress with any of them. Many writers explore only a single manifestation of gender trouble: sexist language, sex differences in talk, powerless language, sexual violence, courtship customs, family communication patterns, or employment discrimination. I have often struggled to keep such issues distinct from one another—only to discover that, in lived experience, they mush together again. Although I treat these issues in separate chapters here, there are numerous cross-references between chapters, and the analysis grows more comprehensive as each topic is added to the mix. The book concludes with three chapters that put these varied issues back together and offer some perspective on our gendered futures.

One limitation of the present volume must be admitted at the outset. I have been limited by my own experiences and education to writing about conversation practices of North American, middle-class, Anglo heterosexuals. I welcome amendments and contrastive studies that include other social classes, ethnicities, and sexual preferences.

The focus in this book is everyday talk, the primary carrier of gendered practices. The approach is to study details of speech patterns in everyday life and in popular culture. Most of the analyses to follow are based on examples of communication events. *Naturally occurring speech events* that have been audio or video recorded provide the best evidence of how we talk. These examples have been transcribed to show details of timing and emphasis. Here is an example used in chapter 2 to illustrate sexual innuendo. (The colons in midword indicate that the speaker stretches out a sound. See the list of transcript symbols at the front of the book.)[3]

[1] UTCL D8:2 (Phone call)
Cara: You queer: what're you doin
              (.) ◀ (a pause)
Rick: Uh: I dunno what're you doin you queer bait

Almost as useful as tape-recorded talk is that gathered as *field notes,* or written records of speech events made from memory soon after an event. About half of these field notes I recorded myself. The balance were recorded by undergraduate and graduate students completing a course in speech and gender. Here is one student's field note showing sexual innuendo:

[2] Field note (at work in restaurant)

Shelly: Hey Derrick, can I have a bun?

Derrick: Do you want the left or the right?

Field notes make it possible to record personal or sexual talk that might not turn up in electronic recordings. In addition to these records of natural speech, I also use dialogue examples from *fiction,* especially films. In example [3] a rich man reacts with disbelief when a hooker says her rate is one hundred dollars an hour. She counters with sexual innuendo:

[3] Film: *Pretty Woman*[4]

He: Hundred dollars an hour (.) pretty stiff

                  (While he is driving, she puts one hand in his lap)

She: No, no:. But it's got potential.

Of course, a film is not life, and therefore I advance no argument supported only by fictional examples. (I use fictional examples, mostly from films, as samples of everyday talk. I do not intend to analyze mass media content or public politics.)

Occasionally, I also employ less reliable forms of evidence, such as self-reports, interview data, or hypothetical examples. These examples lose the sense of dialogue, and one should be suspicious of descriptions based only on these kinds of evidence. In this book I risk mixing all these kinds of examples to make this treatment comprehensive. For example, the analysis of flirting (chapter 3) relies on film examples but confirms the analyses in examples from naturally occurring talk and field notes.

• • •

We perform gender in talk. We make, in everyday interaction, the differences that seem to gender our lives. In addition to this, men and women may also speak differently. Evidence remains sketchy on this point, and I cannot firmly deny this possibility. Even if this is so, however, our task is to understand the interactive gendering talk that misleads us into thinking that difference is our *only* problem. If we learn to understand the range and variety of gendering talk, we might yet discover that women and men inhabit a single, slowly improving planet.

❷

....

The Arrangement
between the Sexes

....

We accept, as a cosmic joke, the separate ways of men and women, their different levels of foolishness. At least we did back in the year 1936.

—*Carol Stone*

THIS SEGMENT FROM CAROL STONE'S FICTIONALIZED MEMOIR, *THE STONE DIARIES*, states (in the present tense) the incredible power of gender. However, her second sentence disclaims this power by putting it in the past tense, as something believed in many decades ago. Stone's ambivalence points to this oddity: Gendered communication patterns do have some mysterious staying power, even when we believe they are changing.

How much has gendering talk changed during the past couple of generations? Most U.S. college students believe that sexist practices are on the wane. I believed this thirty years ago. Penn State undergraduates in the 1930s reported similar sentiments to sociologist Willard Waller, who wrote that the formal code of courting practices was "derived chiefly from the usages of the English middle classes of a generation or so ago."[1] Most students in the 1930s followed norms from their parents' generations, though they believed that these norms no longer applied to them.

I first read Waller's essay in 1965 when I chose courtship communication as a topic for an undergraduate research project. I chose the topic because I had noticed that I acted oddly whenever I flirted or considered going on a date. I was surprised to read that college courters in the 1930s professed up-to-date, egalitarian sexual values, and yet they acted much as their grandparents had done. Most college students today claim that they are more liberated than were people of the past generation. How much has really has changed in our flirting and dating talk since the 1930s?

Certainly some things have changed. The ratio of women to men in college has changed, and more college women now cherish ambitious career plans. Yet many courting practices remain stable. When Waller asked college women in the 1930s whether they could ask men on dates, they answered yes, they could. However, none had actually done so. Is that much different from women's values and actions of the 1990s?

[1] Field note (female best friends)
Kit: I'm worried that he hasn't called.
Sue: It's only been two days.
Kit: I know, but I want him to call me.
Sue: He's probably freaking out
Kit: Maybe. If nothing else, at least I got some.

Kit poses as a modern woman, especially in joking that she has obtained sexual gratification from this male, even if the relationship may not continue. Kit worries mainly that the man may not care for her enough to call. She confides her worry to her pal, who mentions encouragingly that "It's only been two days." The man might still call. Neither woman suggests that it is time for Kit to call this man. Here is what happens when a woman does make such a call:

[2] Field note
Lee: Guess what, Fay. I called him today!
Fay: Already?!
Lee: Well, yeah.
                         (three-second pause, Lee looks at Fay)
Lee: Why, is that bad? Should I not have called him?

As in [1], two college women discuss calling a man. In [2] the worried woman, Lee, has already placed the phone call. Her friend's response to this news is a question, "Already?!" indicating surprise at hearing the announcement. In her second utterance, Lee seems less sure of herself. Following a long pause she seeks reassurance for having called. When this contemporary woman telephones a man, her friend withholds support for the decision. Lee's optimism is chastened across this brief encounter in which her friend says only one word.

Another comparison point between past and present gendering practices is Waller's description of a "rating and dating complex" through which 1930s students (often members of social fraternities and sororities) seek "class A dates." A class A date belongs to the best clubs, drives a car, dresses well, and knows how to dance. Certainly much has changed since the era of Andy Hardy movies. Fraternities and sororities no longer enroll a majority of students at most state universities. Many young people claim there is a less status-conscious social scene at today's universities. Yet consider this 1996 encounter:

[3] Field note
Ed: I have a sister who goes to UT
Lisa: Oh what sorority is she in?
Ed: She's an A D K.
Lisa: Eeew!
Ed: Excuse me. They're not bad there.
Lisa: They're bad everywhere.

Lisa's first question about a person she's never met presumes that the sister is in some sorority. Ed's answer confirms that the sister is, in fact, a sorority member, and he names the group with its Greek letters (disguised here). Lisa's disgusted response to the sorority's letters seems immediate and involuntary, like a noise made over spoiled food. Ed protests this response ("Excuse me"), but his defense of his sister's group is local and understated ("They're not bad there"). Lisa utterly rejects Ed's defense of his sister's social station and pronounces the group to be subpar everywhere.

Class A date constraints are illustrated in this conversation at a high school for deaf students. (The field worker translated from American Sign Language.)

[4] Field note

Mandy: Who are you asking to the dance on Saturday?

Alice: I think I might ask Brian.

Mandy: Who's Brian?

Alice: You know Brian from our algebra class.

Mandy: Really? Why? He's track two.

Alice: I was just teasing, I wanted to see your face.

Mandy asks Alice about her plans for a dance. Alice phrases her choice tentatively ("I think I might . . ."). Mandy does not recognize the boy's name at first, and then she questions Alice's choice based on his academic standing. Alice then claims that she was only teasing. Alice may be trial-ballooning a potential social partner, but her peer's questioning of her choice based on the boy's standing leads her to back away from the idea. Alice's stance toward going out with Brian may have evolved across this short encounter.

Somehow flirting and dating practices are already on the culture's table as each new cohort comes along to enact them. Old norms are reminted for each new generation. Present-day colleges still sport a social scene dominated by heterosexual flirting, thrill-seeking, dancing skills, and double standards.[2]

One text that helps us compare gendered interaction across recent decades is the 1937 film *The Women*. In the film, a well-to-do woman learns (from a manicurist's gossip) that her husband has been unfaithful to her. Her mother advises her to do nothing to show that she knows about the husband's affair. The mother also confides that her own husband (the heroine's father) had also been unfaithful in his time. Here is a portion of the dialogue:

[5] Film: *The Women*[3]

Daughter: I love him so much.

Mother: And he loves you baby so take my advice, keep still; keep still when you're fairly aching to talk. It's about the only sacrifice, spoiled women like us ever have to make to keep our men.

Daughter: And what if I don't want him under those terms?

Mother: But Mary

Daughter: Oh Mother it's all right for you to talk of another generation

> when women were chattels and did as men told them to but—
> but this is today, Stephen and I are equals.

Speaking in the same era in which Waller published his essay on college dating, this movie heroine takes a position that I hear from students in the 1990s: Things have changed. Maybe our mothers encountered sexist double standards, but current generations have resolved these problems!

Undoubtedly, many gendered practices have changed for the better. Some nineteenth-century women encountered legal battles because they refused to change their surnames at marriage. It was just over eighty years ago that the United States adopted women's suffrage. There has been progress toward social equality of the sexes. Yet this 1930s movie mother strikes a timeless note: Thirty-something male adulterers have been on the prowl for many centuries. This activity emerged in the mother's generation, and it still emerges now. Each generation, at university as at midlife, finds itself reenacting modes of flirting and romance that are decades out of date, compared with most of the rest of our lives.

How do gendered interaction practices, such as those in flirting, gain such staying power? Sociologist Erving Goffman's essay, "The Arrangement between the Sexes," poses the problem as follows: "How are very slight biological differences . . . identified as the grounds for vast social consequences?"[4] How is it that sex, a biological fact of fluctuating importance, is elaborated by social practices into such a variety of gendered practices?

A short answer is through gendering talk. Members of speech communities live within gendered arrangements that last longer than the lives of individual humans because there are many day-to-day speaking practices that stabilize these arrangements. These speaking practices are institutional (bigger than personal preferences) and reflexive (self-regenerating).

Goffman writes that these reflexive gendering practices relate courtship (practices by which males ogle at and sexually pursue women) to courtesy (practices by which women are treated as "precious, ornamental, and fragile," and therefore in need of protection).[5] Courtship and courtesy reinforce one another. Both include motives for males to closely watch any female and for females to groom and position themselves to elicit male gazes that carry both protection and attraction.

A second cluster of reflexive gendering practices happens in home socialization, where sex-biased distribution of chores, food, and liberties occurs. Such double standards are noted in ordinary talk:

[6] Field note

Chuck: Last night I washed a bunch of my clothes, and my red shirt bled all over my other clothes!

Mary: Didn't your mother ever teach you to wash colors together on cold, and whites on hot?

Chuck: No, my mother never expected me to learn, she did all of my washing and ironing until I left for college.

Certainly there are families in which both parents make a concerted effort to equalize children's homemaking skills, but Mary presumes that Chuck's mother bears primary responsibility for laundry instruction. Chuck does not challenge Mary's presupposition of maternal laundry responsibility but only agrees that mom did not teach him. In this story gendered laundry practices are indicated without becoming a focus of attention. This is a very general principle, which critic Judith Butler describes as follows: "Gender is a construction that regularly conceals its genesis."[6]

Consider the North American practice of hiding one's naked body from members of the opposite sex by use of sex-segregated rest rooms. As I choose a sex-appropriate public rest room I only experience myself responding to a familiar situation—not as performing gender. Yet I perform gender at this moment whether I think about it or not. Each gendered performance in everyday life connects to other gendered performances. The gendered body in a great many of these performances is the sexual body.

SEX

The word "sex" carries double meaning:

- a categorical variable (*the female sex*), and
- acts of sexuality (*Jan and Leslie are having sex*).

In every culture, "infants at birth are placed in one or in the other of two *sex classes*," and this "sex-class placement is almost without exception exhaustive of the population and life-long."[7]

Sorting not only ourselves but other humans using the male-female contrast is an ongoing project from (and even before) birth. Female-male also serves as "a prototype of social classification,"[8] or provides a frame upon which we build many social rules, customs, and distinctions. When we fail to perform such classification, we may react strongly:

[7] Field note (night on a city street)

Fran: What is she doing?

Elise: Is she drunk or what?

Fran: Too many margaritas

Elise: Oops, it's a man, ha ha.

Fran: I hate it when I do that

[8] Field note (pre-med students at interview)

Pat: Are you nervous?

Sandy: Yes, I am (.) I don't even know if it's a woman or not. You can't tell. I hate that.

In each of these cases, actors experience difficulty judging the sex of another person. In each case the person expresses irritation that the project of classifying others by sex has become problematic. The sorting task on this variable, sex, is a taken-for-granted preoccupation in everyday social life. Most Americans can discriminate the sex of most telephone strangers, even though no single acoustic criterion (pitch, intonation contour, etc.) makes this classification easy.[9]

Sex (in the sense of this sorting task) is a dichotomous variable: male-female. The vast majority of us consider ourselves to be lifelong members of either the male or female category. Exceptions seem only to prove the rule.[10] We experience sex as a static characteristic with just two values and high test-retest validity. If you are filling out a questionnaire and come to this choice, with no further instructions:

☐ M

☐ F

you easily choose one (and only one) of these items to classify yourself or another. You grow frustrated if such classification seems ambiguous or mistaken.

We use this classifying system to understand the things people do (e.g., she's wearing too much makeup; he dresses so well). Most of us hold gendered standards for judging much that men do and much that women do. A man who is described as a "good cook" cannot necessarily cook as well as a woman to whom the same label applies. Gendered double standards are routine. Most of us believe men and women are quite different. In fact, it seems easier to conceptualize sex differences than anything else related to sex. Often the concept of sex differences drives other aspects of gendering from our attention:

Sex appears as an independent variable in a large percentage of social psychology studies. If there were just one hundred such studies in a year (using the standard .05 confidence level), then five studies would reveal sex differences by random chance alone. There undoubtedly are some actual male-female differences: Males and females differ in average size, upper-body size and strength, body shape, and construction of genitals. There are some different hormones, in most cases. Yet biologists tell us that among animals we humans are only weakly dimorphic. Male and female humans are more alike than, say, female and male luna moths, cardinals, or gorillas. Most of the male-female differences humans have noticed do not affect speech and language skills. Neither male nor female humans are in principle more verbally intelligent or more able to perform as social actors. The average vocal pitch difference between men's and woman's speech has few intrinsic consequences. That we grow skilled at distinguishing men's and women's voices indicates our piety toward sex more than it indicates sex differences in speech patterns.

● ● ●

Most humans become sexually active, that is, we learn when and how to perform sexually. Sex-sexuality punning may hold in many languages. In fact, almost everything that may be said about sexuality is a pun: *mistress, queer, making love, doing it, aroused, climax, beating it, intercourse, sleeping with.* We must resort to medical Latin to avoid such ambiguity.

Sleep is one of those words with a primary nonsexual meaning but one in which sexual uses become almost irresistible. Recently, a friend whose wife was undergoing radioactive medical treatment reported at lunch with a group of men that her physician had advised him "not to sleep with my wife for a couple of weeks." My friend prepared himself a space in the guest room. His friends laughed at his interpretation of *sleep* as resting, rather than sexual contact.

Systematic ambiguity or pervasive ambiguity is also used to describe the sexual state of self or sexual partner as *excited, hard, frigid, or turned on.* Sexuality words are cuckoo terms that move into the nests of existing words and get their progeny by accident. Talk about sexuality takes place in a lexical underground that allows us to deny or disguise it.

[9] Field note (college siblings)

Brad: I got some last night.
Sue: You got some of what, Brad?
Brad: A chick. She's on the soccer team and she lives upstairs.
Sue: Did you use protection?

At first Sue shows she cannot understand what Brad is saying, but when Brad supplies "a chick," she understands what he means by "got some." The words "sex," "intercourse," "sexuality," and the like do not appear in this dialogue, but the words "got some," "chick," and "protection" show among them a collaborative performance of discussion about sexual activities. Sexual interpretation is so commonplace that it may pop up unintended and unexpectedly, as in this telephone encounter:

[10] Field note

Annie: Is Jay around?
Mary: Yeah, but he's on another line, can you hold on for a minute?
Annie: Sure.
Mary: Actually, never mind, he's getting off.

Annie:	(laughs) You might want to be more careful in choosing your words.
Mary:	Why?
Annie:	He's getting *off*!
Mary:	Oh, oops!

Annie catches Mary making an unintended sexual pun and teases her about it. It is difficult not to speak of sexuality by accident. Whose mind is in the gutter?

Sexual puns provide pratfalls to every non-native speaker. Anthropologist Nigel Barley reports these problems in his interaction within an African speech community.

> I would meet a Dowayo and greet him . . . "Is the sky clear for you?" "The sky is clear for me, is it clear for you?" "The sky is clear for me too," which had to be gone through for each person you were greeting. . . . A shift of tone changes the interrogative particle, attached to a sentence to convert it into a question, into the lewdest word in the language, something like "cunt." I would therefore baffle and amuse Dowayos by greeting them, "Is the sky clear for you, cunt?" [At the end of one interview] I rose and shook hands politely, "Excuse me," I said, "I am cooking some meat." At least that was what I had intended to say; owing to tonal error I declared to an astonished audience, "Excuse me. I am copulating with the blacksmith."[11]

The very language subtleties that baffle a foreigner provide a native with resources for off-record pursuit of either flirtation or sexual violence.

In recent decades scientists have interviewed people about the facts of human sexual enactment. Thick textbooks now treat this subject. Kinsey's informants shocked 1950s readers by reporting that they practiced sanctioned acts (homosexuality, masturbation). In the 1990s a randomized population of interview subjects showed lower estimates of these controversial practices. These investigators, like most of us, frame questions to collect male-female contrasts.[12]

Educated readers have grown used to scientific claims about sexuality. How we use these claims is another matter. Virtually no ordinary human learns sexual performance practices from these studies. We learn sexuality from semi-informed others who use ambiguous vocabulary in preference to scientific jargon and develop motives to falsify or distort what they tell each other.

My own evolving sexuality has seemed learned. When I was eleven, two of my brothers astonished me with the news that I would become sexual. My first female sexual partner gave me instructions without which our activities would have been even more futile. My choices of sexual objects and partners have been more affected by concerns of fashion (blatant heterosexuality, interest in forbidden thrills) and of safety (diseases, pregnancies, jealousies) than by any sex drive. For the most part I have treated sex acts as social arousal experiences, as intoxications. I have learned how to experience sexual euphoria, followed by a period of depressive relaxation. Sexual adventuring, like substance abuse, can leave a participant to depend on the high. Addicts may manipulate others in attempts to repeat peak experiences.

Recurrent sexual enactment can come between sexual partners. Repeated sexual experiences may lead a lover to an unrealistic belief that one's partner shares similar sensations and feelings. Also, sexual enthusiasm may be simulated.

These inadequate reflections on sexuality in social interaction indicate a range of memories and media events. How do these issues show up as gendering practices in social interaction?

GENDER

Gender is in principle social, while sex (the variable) is biological. The sex classification words are *male-female;* but gender is indexed in the terms *feminine-masculine.* Each of us embraces gender in many ways. Yet gender, unlike sex, cannot easily be expressed as a variable. Gender is continuous, not a dichotomy (like sex). One can act a little bit feminine but not a little bit female. Social activity may be highly masculine (football), not especially masculine (walking), or rather unmasculine (needlepoint). Things that are not masculine may be feminine: (makeup) or not especially gendered (coffee). Women may do or say masculine things without changing gendered customs. For instance, women who are expert car mechanics or math geeks do not change gender stereotypes; neither do men who are skillful with babies or sewing. Such individuals are conceived as gendered exceptions, and stereotypes remain stable.

Psychologist Sandra Bem conceives of gender (at least gender of the self) as a *pair* of continuous variables: high to low masculine and high to low feminine.[13] Please complete the self-rating scale (*at right*) called the Bem Sex Role Inventory (BSRI).

Your M score on the BSRI indicates the degree to which you perceive yourself in terms of traditional masculine attributes. Your F score is a self-rating on traditional feminine attributes. Though median scores fall around 100, the main information in your scores comes from comparing your F and M scores.

- If your M score exceeds your F score by more than ten points, your perceptions of your gender orientation shade toward traditional masculine norms.
- If your F score exceeds your M score by more than ten points, you perceive yourself in terms of traditional feminine norms.
- If your scores are quite close together, this indicates that you value masculinity and femininity about equally; the BSRI classifies your self-reports as *androgynous,* or enacting the best of both masculine and feminine identities.

Looking at the words that comprise the M and F scores helps us to think about how we perform gender in the world. However, the precise application of this conceptualization to our gendered communication patterns remains problematic. Social psychologists have rarely succeeded in using the BSRI to predict language use.

Fashion in the 1990s prefers use of the term "gender" to describe everything about language that might vary by sex or express gendered identity. Since all language is social, this terminology seems reasonable, but it leads to some odd usages. For instance, if a study of male and female language is based primarily on sex as a variable (e.g., do women use more color adjectives than men?), I prefer the term "sex" to "gender." Psychologist Mary Crawford writes:

TABLE 1. BSRI (SIMPLIFIED)

Directions: Indicate by writing numbers from 1 to 7 in the blanks below how true of you these various characteristics are. That is: Mark a 1 if the characteristic is never true of you; mark a 4 if the characteristic is true of you about half the time; mark a 7 if the characteristic is always true of you.

_____ Self-reliant	_____ Yielding
_____ Defends own beliefs	_____ Cheerful
_____ Independent	_____ Shy
_____ Athletic	_____ Affectionate
_____ Assertive	_____ Flatterable
_____ Has strong personality	_____ Loyal
_____ Forceful	_____ Feminine
_____ Analytical	_____ Sympathetic
_____ Has leadership tendencies	_____ Sensitive to the needs of others
_____ Willing to take risks	_____ Understanding
_____ Makes decisions easily	_____ Compassionate
_____ Self-sufficient	_____ Eager to soothe hurt feelings
_____ Dominant	_____ Soft-spoken
_____ Masculine	_____ Warm
_____ Willing to take a stand	_____ Tender
_____ Aggressive	_____ Gullible
_____ Acts as a leader	_____ Childlike
_____ Individualistic	_____ Does not use harsh language
_____ Competitive	_____ Loves children
_____ Ambitious	_____ Gentle
_____ TOTAL = M	_____ TOTAL = F

Calculate your total score in each column before reading on.

The (re)conflation of sex and gender has become ludicrous. New sex difference studies, virtually identical to those published two decades ago, are now labeled studies of "gender differences." A lengthy report on National Public Radio discusses selective abortion based on the *gender* of the fetus. . . . [S]uch "gender differences" are the old [sex] differences dressed up in a new label. They are still seen as fundamentally residing within the individual and divorced from their social contexts, and they are as readily biologized as ever. Ironically, a feminist usage intended to theorize the social construction of masculinity and femininity is now enlisted to obscure it.[14]

These problems come about in that when one begins to see a problem in terms of sex differences, it becomes difficult to recast the problem in any other terms. To paraphrase an old maxim: To the extent we conceptualize gender as difference we all think alike and nobody thinks very well. Conceptualizing gender as difference also seems to postpone consideration of issues of power. Gender has not been easy to conceptualize, yet it remains the most important and ubiquitous term in the triad of sex, sexuality, and gender.

To deepen our thinking about gender we must go beyond variables and consider how we perform gendering in everyday conversation. Judith Butler argues that "gender is instituted through the stylization of the body and, hence, must be understood as the mundane way in which bodily gestures, movements, and enactments of various kinds constitute the illusion of an abiding gendered self. . . . [This is] a performative accomplishment."[15]

The performance of gender is woven into the performance of everyday social interaction. Butler seems optimistic about individual actors being able to subject gender performances to stylistic control.

The performance of gender is a theme in Ursula LeGuin's science fiction masterpiece *The Left Hand of Darkness.*[16] This tale takes place on a planet on which people experience sexuality during only a few days of each twenty-six-day cycle. At all other times they know virtually no sexual (or gendered) enactment. They are androgynous except when sexually aroused. Here is an Earthling anthropologist's report:

> For 21 or 22 days the individual is *somer,* sexually inactive. . . . And on the 22nd or 23rd day the individual enters *kemmer,* estrus. . . . A Gethenian in first-phase

kemmer, if kept alone or with others not in kemmer, remains incapable of coitus. Yet the sexual impulse is tremendously strong in this phase . . . [and] when the individual finds a partner in kemmer, hormonal secretion is further stimulated . . . until in one partner either a male or female hormonal dominance is established. The genitals engorge or shrink accordingly, foreplay intensifies, and the partner, triggered by this change, takes on the other sexual role. . . . Normal individuals . . . do not know whether they will be the male or the female, and have no choice in the matter. The culminant phase of kemmer . . . ends fairly abruptly, and if conception has not taken place the individual returns to the somer phase within a few hours. If the individual was in the female role and was impregnated . . . this individual remains female. . . . With cessation of lactation the female re-enters somer and becomes once more a perfect androgyne. No physiological habit is established, and the mother of several children may be the father of several more.

The impact of these matters goes beyond sexual behavior to other aspects of gender relations. During kemmer, "[E]verything gives way before the recurring torment and festivity of passion. What is very hard for us to understand is that four-fifths of the time these people are not sexually motivated at all."[17]

Gethenian society and politics show gender equality, since everybody partakes in both sexes during mating experiences, and in neither for the rest of the time. This world knows no word for rape. This fiction shows how sex, sexuality, and gendering practices entwine with each other. A feature of this fantasy is that both Earthlings and Gethenians view each other as sexual perverts.

LeGuin's fiction celebrates a reformist view that at some times and places (e.g., during a job interview) all humans could enjoy gender-free social equality. LeGuin suggests that people become sexually differentiated consequent to their engaging in sexual activity. Can we learn to act androgynously in everyday life? If we could, would we wish to? Many people seem unwilling to restrict sexual performances to private occasions in the presence of a consenting sexual partner.

GRAMMAR AND GENDER

Gender is also a category in grammar. In language theories "gender" refers to classification systems for nouns and pronouns.[18] Most languages have several such classification systems based on distinctions such as singular-plural, animate-inanimate, and masculine-feminine. Linguists conclude that the function of such systems is to help track speakers' referents across multiple mentions of the same referent. For example, in the following story, which Lana tells her sister, Marie, there is one main male character of interest, Tom. Notice how Lana traces Tom's actions throughout the story by repeated use of the gendered pronoun "he." Consider how difficult it would be to trace Tom's actions across multiple events and characters in the story without the convenience of the gendered pronoun.

[11] UTCL Marie's Family

Lana: After there we go to the Elbow and Tom and I danced and everythin:g and then he di- he held my hand we were gettin' off the floor

Marie: Yay:

Lana: So I was like oh well maybe

Marie: Uh hm

Lana: And then, because I had to entertain other people I couldn't concentrate my get up effort

Marie: huh huh

Lana: And then we go down to Boggles. We all see people we know, then he goes off and then: I see him talking to a cute perky blonde.

Marie: er ur::

Lana: So I was like forget it.

The masculine pronouns in this story clearly indicate Tom and would not do as references to "other people" (which also differs in number). The gendered classification system helps a listener to track the story.

Gender as a category appears in numerous European languages. The term springs from the Latin stem *gener-*, meaning race or kind. The notion of gender serves as a prototype for classifying people and things. In English and German, gender-classified words adhere closely to concepts of sex, sexuality, sexual difference, generation, and so on, while French and Spanish uses seem more varied. One way that gender appears in language is in grammatical gender agreement. In English, for example, third-person singular pronouns (*he, she*) are marked for gender. In Spanish the third-person possessive pronoun is gender-neutral *su;* however, every common noun in that language is marked for grammatical gender, as are articles (*el, la*) and some other pronouns. Spanish adjectives have masculine and feminine forms that should match the article and noun in the same sentence or utterance. It seems that no two languages mark gender in exactly the same ways.

It is difficult to determine the ideological importance of gender classifications in the grammar of languages. Using gender as a primary noun classification system in a language seems to indicate some sense in which classification of people (and other things) by sex is a primary ideological focus in the speech community. In certain cases, as, for instance, the English "generic *he*," such classification seems to strengthen some sex-unequal modes of talk. However, there is no evidence that languages that lack noun classification by gender (e.g., Hungarian, Turkish) are associated with more egalitarian speech communities than are languages with gendered systems of noun classification.

Contemporary males do not force grammatical gender constructions upon women. Though grammarians usually have been men, very few native speakers learn language from grammarians. Rather, each current woman and man putters away intermittently and somewhat mindlessly at the construction of gender as she or he speaks a native (or acquired) language. The performance of grammatical gender, like that of social gender, fosters a natural appearance—as customs we follow rather than something we do or perform.

SEXISM

Gender is a contested ideological term, especially in its associations with the words "sexist" and "feminist." Feminists began the practice of labeling certain acts as sexist if the acts unfairly discriminated male and female on that ground alone. Thus, it would be sexist practice to refuse to hire any woman as an airline pilot. It would be sexist to call your two female teachers by their given names and your two male teachers by *mister + surname.*

Sexist practices occur when an actor (or actors) discriminates according to sex when other criteria might be more appropriate, useful, or fair. The question thus becomes: What are the appropriate circumstances for female-male discrimination? Within such discourse the term "sexist" will remain contested so long as we continue to experience an undersupply of female power in politics, the media, and scholarship.[19]

U.S. courts have applied two criteria in judging claims of sexist discrimination: (1) Was actual harm done?, and (2) Was the offense done intentionally?[20] These tests may be appropriate for court cases, but they are too limited when we are trying to understand the detailed accomplishments in gendering talk.

Consider a hypothetical instance in which a male boss says to his fifty-two-year-old secretary: 'Hey, girl, get me some coffee.' Some listeners would be angered by this use of "girl." Others would not even notice it. Is the harm significant? Is the offense intentional? These questions usually cannot be answered, but the pattern of usage is clear (using a term that can mean young female to refer to a person at middle age). The usage occurs within a direct order from an authority to a status subordinate. My goal in this description is not to blame or punish individuals, only to show social practices for gendering talk. Reconsider this example:

[9] Field note (college siblings)
Brad: I got some last night.
Sue: You got some of what, Brad?
Brad: A chick. She's on the soccer team and she lives upstairs. ◀
Sue: Did you use protection?

Brad's term "chick" derisively describes the individual with whom he claims to have shared a sexual encounter. This person is not named. Also, the phrase "got some" trivializes the sexual encounter as having been mere thrill seeking. Perhaps such usage does harm, though the primary harmed person may never learn about it. Perhaps there is social harm done, in that the parties allow this sexual slurring and do not object to it. Is the harm intentional? We cannot know. Unless one plans to sue, there is really no point in knowing.

We can only rarely establish intention or harmfulness in gender-biased talk, but we can show that a message pattern formulates men and women unequally and unfairly. Such messages need not show intent to act in a biased fashion or perceived harm. Such usages need not be by a member of an advantaged class to a member of a disadvantaged one. These stipulations make it possible to distinguish gender-biased talk on textual grounds.

Gender bias in talk is like other forms of prejudice, especially those described as racist. Both sexism and racism discriminate against a substantial subset of humanity. Often the discrimination seems accidental. Furthermore, both sexism and racism are kinds of unfairness of which few people wish to be accused.

Additionally, sexism and racism operate together, along with classism, as a multiple-whammy complex whose consequences include unequal social and career opportunities. It has been a theme among 1990s feminists that class, race, and gender troubles appear on one interactive grid that is not yet adequately characterized. That task cannot be completed in the current work, but it must be kept before us.

There are historical as well as conceptual affinities between sexism and racism. The history of movements toward women's political equality in the United States has been intertwined with the civil rights quests of African Americans and other ethnic minorities. Nineteenth-century U.S. feminists made political capital by working on behalf of the emancipation of slaves— that is, against institutionalized racism. These feminists were aware that the emancipation of slaves might also be linked to the emancipation of women.[21] Similarly, the women's movements that sprung up in the 1970s—around such causes as equal employment, the Equal Rights Amendment, and the term "Ms."—unfolded in a social environment conditioned by the civil rights controversies of the 1960s.

The word "sexism" seems saturated with the racist analogy. The *-ism* suffix (which to be sure occurs also in Buddhism and Fascism) emphasizes this connection. I endorse a sexism-racism analogy so long as we keep it provisional and make explicit that it is an analogy, not a bland fact. Moreover, sexism runs into complications that seem different from those of racism. Racism is nurtured in racial separation, and the most recommended cure for racism may be intergroup communication. There is partial segregation among males and females: in clubs, public rest rooms, locker rooms, corporate board rooms and secretarial pools; however, men and women are not residentially isolated from interaction with each other. Therefore, intergroup communication alone cannot be the solution to the problem of sexism, no matter its effectiveness with the problem of racism.

Another way that sexism contrasts with racism is that most clear-thinking, educated U.S. citizens now wish to put racism behind us in most facets of professional and public life. Many people would also like to banish racism from most parts of social life. Where racist taboos are strongest they align with sexual practices—for example, interracial marriage.

In contrast to this cautiously tolerant racial politics, most of us (including homosexuals) choose dating, romance, and life partners by first excluding one sex from consideration. We maintain such sexist practices in our social and private lives at the very same time that we try to transcend these practices during the professional day. We aim to defeat the cancer of sexism in our right hand but to nourish the tumors closest to our hearts. Such purposes require clever social engineering, resilient humor, and patience.

We experienced four hundred years of racial slavery. In the 150 years since slavery's legal end, there has been some modest progress against racism. Sexual inequality is more ancient than these versions of racism, however. We are unlikely to correct all of these problems in one generation. We can, however, conceptualize some of the larger tasks entailed in the quest for social equality between the sexes. We can then measure our progress and chart the costs of change.

Suspend your judgment for the moment about what has changed and what has not in regard to the arrangement between the sexes. I request this suspension of disbelief because our widespread belief in positive change toward sexual equality works in tandem with our belief in sex differences to keep us from examining the real problems of gendered conversational performance that cause us so much difficulty and heartache. There is a terrain to be learned, a vocabulary to be savored. If you are willing to read slowly, think along, and examine the details in your own life, you may decrease your own suffering due to practices of gendered talk, and become a more effective speaker and listener in every facet of your experience due to the skills you learn in these exercises in gendering talk.

3

....

Flirting

....

A boy came up the street and there was a girl.
"Hello," they said in passing, then didn't pass.
They began to imagine. They imagined all night
and woke imagining what the other imagined.
They were together. They kept waking together . . .

— *John Ciardi*, For Instance

THE FIRST LINES OF THIS POEM BY JOHN CIARDI PICTURE A LIFELONG MALE-FEMALE
pairing's first moments. The scene was a "street," a place where we exchange
greetings "in passing." Yet in this instance something extraordinary happened—these two persons "didn't pass." They imagined something common
and "imagined all night." They "kept waking together," indicating a sexual
relationship. Yet how did these partners begin to imagine and enact such a
relationship? What happened? The poet remains silent at just this crucial
point. How did these two people communicatively construct a mutual flirtation? How do any of us, as social actors, accomplish the first scene or two of
an incipient courtship?

Interpersonal relationships are made of talk and related actions. By the
way people speak to each other they show who counts as a friend, a stranger,
or a loved one. We speak differently to loved ones than to casual friends, and
most often we do not speak to strangers at all. Our interaction patterns constitute and indicate the states of our interpersonal relationships.

Some writers distinguish between two dimensions of messages: content and relationship.[1] Message content includes meanings, topics, and facts that can be deciphered with reference to a dictionary, grammar, or encyclopedia. Content is associated with the notion of monologue and with masculine stereotypes.

Relationship messages, more difficult to analyze in writing, emerge in dialogic interaction. Relationship patterns emerge over time as humans interact. Some relational communication is nonverbal, but a surprising amount is also verbal—without being very content-full. We make relationships with the forms of our interaction. Consider the first few seconds of this phone call:

[1] Schegloff[2]

Ida:	Hello
Carla:	Hello Ida?
Ida:	Yeah
Carla:	Hi, this is Carla
Ida:	Hi Carla.
Carla:	How are you.

These speakers take about five seconds to start an encounter. During this time they exchange little content, but they indicate some patterns in their relationship. These speakers address each other and recognize one another on the basis of first names. The partners seem willing to speak to one another but do not gush with enthusiasm. Their business is not especially urgent. This telephone opening shows telephone partners who are generic acquaintances. Compare this to the state of affairs shown in this shorter telephone opening:

[2] UTCL D10.3

Jim:	Hello
Sue:	Hey.
Jim:	Hi::::.
Sue:	Are you ready yet?

These partners easily identify one another from voice cues alone. They need not give each other their names in order to recognize one another. The caller,

Sue, in saying "Hey" shows recognition of the answerer's voice from hearing just "Hello." Further, Sue proposes that Jim should be able to identify her voice after hearing just the word "Hey." By answering with "Hi," Jim confirms that he does recognize Sue. No names need be exchanged because these parties are familiar with each other due to either close relationship or recent contact.

The opening of a telephone call displays and coordinates relationship expectations for the talk that follows.[3] Telephone openings, like all human greeting routines, carry slight content but are saturated with relational communication. Relationship talk is dialogic. Speakers use relationship talk to build commitment and accessibility. Consider this list of terms for relationship states, in order of increasing intimacy:

- Stranger
- Acquaintance
- Friend
- Intimate

Relationship states are established and changed in conversational interaction, but what is established is somewhat unique in the case of flirting. The contrast between flirting and other conversational interaction can be shown by how we act toward strangers.

Whenever I am in a public place, such as a park, I scan the social horizon in order to sort strangers from acquaintances and to show strangers a stance of civil inattention: I look away from others while passing by.[4] I act as if to ignore others, yet this is a pretense. I do notice that others are present. I do not bump into other people, and I carefully time my glances so we do not gaze at each other simultaneously. I do not usually speak to strangers, and do not gaze at strangers for too long, or at the wrong time. If I gaze too long at a stranger then I may appear to be staring or ogling—which is rude or even menacing.

Yet an ogle may indicate flirting. Erving Goffman writes:

> [T]he male's assessing act—his ogling—constitutes the first move in the courtship process. . . . The female adorns herself in terms of received notions of sexual

attractiveness and males who are present show broadcast attention to females . . . and await some fugitive sign that can be taken as encouragement.[5]

Of course, ogles may be aimed at women who do not adorn themselves. Furthermore, women may adorn themselves for multiple reasons, not only to attract stares. Many men practice such ogling, and many women prepare their bodies so as to merit appreciative staring. The question of sexual gazing encompasses not only the ogle but also the primp. Consider this instance in which two women sit in a public dining space:

[3] Field note

Penny: Do you see that guy with the black hair over there?

Kerri: I think so, he's kind of cute.

Penny: Well he has been looking over here for the longest time. Do I look okay?

Kerri: You might want to fix your bangs a bit.

These women react to an ogler's attention by checking whether the target's appearance can bear scrutiny. Penny notices that the male's gaze has been trained in her direction and asks Kerri for a critique on her appearance. Kerri responds by suggesting an area for improvement. The point is that staring, a violation of the normal civil inattention we owe to strangers, may also be taken as a sign of flirtatious interest.

Communication with new acquaintances also contrasts with flirting practices in uncertainty reduction.[6] As I start talking to most any new acquaintance, I am uncertain about how the other will act. Due to uncertainty about the other, most talk in first encounters consists of low-risk items: introductions and stereotyped, predictable talk. Topics such as occupation or hometown are likely. With a new acquaintance I would be unlikely to tease the other, or to make a wisecrack or an off-color comment. Yet these are the very things that flirters do. Flirters violate norms of civil inattention and uncertainty reduction precisely to show one another that they are flirting. Flirting partners must achieve alignment in the view that their interaction is different from that of an ordinary friendship or collegial relationship. Flirting is kissing kin to rudeness.

Amy Grant's song-video "Baby Baby" illustrates the distinctiveness of flirtation in public places—and its difference from the norms of civil inattention and uncertainty reduction. This video begins with a series of three men who approach a woman (Grant), ogling and speaking to her as she walks down a public street. The walker blows off the first two without breaking stride; that is, she offers only a greeting in passing, though each of the comical men seems to indicate willingness to stop and co-imagine something. Grant just smiles and rolls her eyes as she keeps going. She seems amused by the attention of each man who chases her. Yet the third man who approaches her does something unusual—he brings a dog and a funny hat into the encounter. Contact. This unusual activity gets the pair started on a special kind of imagining.

Much in the initiation of a love story is marked by something unusual that happens. For example, many romance novels begin with the heroine suffering amnesia or being disinherited. This something unusual marks the moment. As Grant's song puts it:

[4] Song: "Baby Baby"[7]
Stop for a minute, Baby I'm so glad you're mine
And ever since the day you put my heart in motion
Baby I realize there's just no getting over you.

Note the puns on "baby." Grant apparently wrote this song for her infant even though it was marketed through video as a love song. The lyrics locate a pivotal moment in the love story, a moment when there occurs a thrilling turning point in perception of the other, the start of falling in love. The organ that this poet describes as "set in motion," the heart, is the organ of the valentine.

This song, like many flirtation stories, evokes the myth of the love potion. You drink something, you feel funny, then you fall in love with the next person you see: Tristan and Isolde, for example, or the classic pop song "Love Potion Number 9." In Shakespeare's *Midsummer Night's Dream*, Puck administers a potion to an unsuspecting sleeper, who literally falls in love with an ass—which is the first thing she sees upon waking. This fiction capitalizes on the well-known fact that courters may fail to see the obvious shortcomings of the partner.

Candidate flirtation partners create events that fit love potion mythology. In a classic Disney cartoon, an owl warns Bambi and his pals that love is about to happen to them:

[5] Film: *Bambi*[8]

All of a sudden you run smack into a pretty face. Whoo! You begin to get weak in the knees. Your head's in a whirl. And then you feel light as a feather, and before you know it, you're walking on air. And then you know what? You're knocked for a loop. And you completely lose your head.

The owl's language emphasizes the individual as a disoriented recipient of a force: "You're knocked for a loop." This phrase obscures the individual's performance of flirting, substituting language about something that happens to the individual:. You suddenly feel intoxicated, you feel "weak in the knees. Your head's in a whirl . . . you feel light as a feather." This is the love potion notion of courtship initiation. One gets intoxicated. In Bambi males are passive, while the females act by preening gestures and gaze. The female animals in Bambi wear lots of mascara. The males experience eye flashes and feminine giggles as a drug: Their eyes enlarge and lose focus as the preening female approaches.

In art (let alone life!) the participants in a possible romance must perform this disorientation within social interaction. Anticipatory socialization, such as the owl's warnings to Bambi and friends, may provide categories by which we can identify turning points in our lives. Anthropologist Mary Catherine Bateson writes that at such potentially pivotal moments we say:

"I must be in love," "Oh, this is an orgasm," "This is a midlife crisis," "This is sea sickness." We are provided with the labels, the culturally-constructed labels, long before we encounter the realities. . . . [9]

When we do discover that someone is staring or saying something outrageous, we may either flee or flirt. A long stare or an unusual comment signals danger. The flirtatious benefit of such activities is actually tied to a marked social violation.

A popular song from the early 1980s anticipates meeting a "tough cookie" who breaks hearts.

[6] Song: "Hit Me with Your Best Shot"[10]
Well you're a real tough cookie with a long history
Of breaking little hearts like the one in me
That's okay let's see how you do it
Put up your dukes, let's get down to it
Hit me with your best shot . . . fire away

In this song, the courted other is addressed as if entering a fistfight ("put up your dukes"). References to love are not tender ("breaking little hearts"), although this is a song about a meeting of two potential courters. Flirtation is portrayed in this lyric as a fight among bantering adversaries. Flirters use lexical ambiguities to create sexual innuendo—for example, "do it."

Flirters may fight and they may clown, but they may not act as normal folks do. Flirters do not pass by but instead act aroused or combative. Flirters use startling language to mark that something unusual is unfolding. Flirters create sexual innuendo through off-record but repeated bantering ambiguities. Social psychologists Ellen Berscheid and Elaine Walster claim that two things are necessary to start a courtship:

- Something quite unusual happens, such that individuals become physiologically aroused; and
- The participants in the interaction develop an explanation that this arousal might be due to falling in love.[11]

An unusual event arouses the body. In Bambi the hero trips over a rock just after he encounters his future mate. Yet in most literary examples preromance is accomplished with words, especially bantering words. The book (and movie) *Love Story* begins with a service encounter between rich-boy Oliver and sharp-tongued underdog Jenny. Oliver approaches the library desk:

[7] Fiction: *Love Story*[12]
Oliver: Do you have *The Waning of the Middle Ages*?

Jenny:	Do you have your own library?
Oliver:	Listen, Harvard is allowed to use the Radcliffe library.
Jenny:	I'm not talking legality, Preppy, I'm talking ethics. You guys have five million books, we have a few lousy thousand.
Oliver:	Listen, I need that *@#* book.
Jenny:	Would you please watch your profanity, Preppy. ◄

Imagine how often we would go to the library if we were normally greeted like this. Oliver asks for a book, and the librarian refuses! Just two utterances into their first encounter, these partners are arguing. In the fourth utterance, she calls him an insulting name, "Preppy." He curses in his insistent response. She responds with meta-talk (talk about talk, see arrow) that does not answer Oliver's sentence, but criticizes his use of profanity.[13] Jenny also repeats the prior insult term, "Preppy." Something unusual has happened here. This unusual event in no way needs to be pleasant. In principle, it could be intoxication or a car wreck. Jenny hits Oliver with her best shot. The interaction shifts abruptly from library business to a duel of profanity and insult.

Antagonistic insult is a common thread in the initiation of many fictional romances. The literary standard for hostile preromantic banter is Shakespeare's *Much Ado about Nothing*.

[8] Fiction: *Much Ado about Nothing*[14]

Benedick:	What, my dear lady Disdain! Are you yet living?
Beatrice:	Is it possible Disdain should die, while she hath such meet food to feed it as signior Benedick: Courtesy itself must convert to disdain if you come in her presence.
Benedick:	Then is courtesy a turn-coat. But it is certain, I am loved of all ladies, only you excepted: And I would I could find it in my heart that I had not a hard heart, or truly I love none.
Beatrice:	A dear happiness to women: they would else have been troubled with a pernicious suitor.

Beatrice and Benedick speak to us across four centuries as bantering young people who have a strong reaction to each other—a reaction that seems (to them) to be the very opposite of amorous emotions. Their friends know they are in love before Beatrice and Benedick do; and this experience is quite commonplace in art and in life. An extreme case is the contemporary comedy *When Harry Met Sally.* These two antagonists banter so fiercely that the viewer quickly figures out they are in love. The meandering plot of the film chronicles how Harry and Sally discover what the audience member knew ten minutes into the story.

A similar sort of banter introduces the featured couple in the film *Clueless.*

[9] Film: *Clueless*[15]

Josh: Hey, who's watching the Galleria.

Cher: So, the flannel shirt deal is that a nod to the crispy Seattle weather or are you just trying to stay warm in front of the refrigerator.

Josh: (pokes her) Oh, wow, you're filling out there.

Cher: Wow your face is catching up with your mouth.

Each utterance is an insult. Strong language flies both ways, and he touches her aggressively.

An unusual event that triggers a love story is shown in this example from a film biography of Patsy Cline:

[10] Film: *Sweet Dreams*[16]

Charlie: Hey I want you to get your coat (1.5) I wanna drive you someplace for a drink, (1) I want us uh dance awhile, (1) I want us to get to know each other a lot better.

Patsy: You want a lot don't you

Charlie: Yeah I do, Baby

                   (0.5)

Patsy: hih hih Well, huh people in hell want ice water. That don't mean they get it. (She walks away.)

Charlie approaches Patsy after she sings at a country dance hall. He throws a come-on line at her. She responds with a blunt put-down as she walks away. Later Charlie and Patsy get married.

In *The Presidio* a male detective, Jay, rings the doorbell of an unfamiliar house. Nina answers the door and looks him up and down like a searchlight. He stares. There is a very long silence. Finally, she speaks:

[11] Film: *The Presidio*[17]
Nina: Say something
                    (0.4)
Jay: What
Nina: That's a start
                    (1)
Jay: I'm inspector Jay Austin, San Francisco Police Department. We're here-
Nina: You didn't do that right
Jay: I didn't
Nina: No, you're supposed to show me your I.D.

This is certainly an unusual communication event. Jay and Nina, strangers to one another, stand at the door, look at each other, and do not speak. Silence is unusual at the start of a doorway encounter between strangers. If you ring a doorbell, you are responsible for talking first: You knock, someone answers, then you talk. It is therefore Jay's responsibility to talk when Nina opens the door. Yet he does not talk. Finally Nina says, "Say something," meta-talk that indicates Jay's failure to speak. This utterance prods Jay to introduce himself with his job description and full name. Nina interrupts Jay to say that he is not doing his job correctly.

The bantering creation of sexual innuendo is not limited to literature. Consider this real-life telephone call as an event in which the partners create an unusual situation and turn the situation toward the playful pursuit of sexual innuendo.

[12] UTCL D8:2 You queer
Rick: Ye::ss? heh heh heh
Cara: Rick?
Rick: Yes?
Cara: You queer, what're you doin

(0.4)

Rick: U:h I dunno what're you doin you queer bait

This telephone opening includes a pair of initial inquiries, to which are added the word "queer." Queer is an unusual thing to call someone in a telephone opening and has a secondary meaning referring to a homosexual. The response, "queer bait," suggests not only a return of an insult but also an ironic suggestion that there could be a sexual match among these parties.

Since telephone openings between casual acquaintances are usually rather structured, any variation can provide a startling event to start a round of flirting. Consider the word "lovely" in this caller's first speaking turn:

[13] Field note

Libby: Hello?

Frank: Yes, uh, is the lovely Libby McDonald there? ◄

Libby: What? Excuse me!

Frank: Libby, hey this is Frank Sigman

Libby: Oh, sorry! I thought you were some creep giving me a harass-
             ing call.

Frank: (laughs) No, what are you doing?

In this telephone opening, Frank asks to speak to Libby McDonald, using her full name. This shows Frank is at best a casual acquaintance of Libby's. Yet Frank adds the extra phrase "the lovely" before Libby's name, which marks his request as unusual. Libby's response shows that she is startled and probably offended: "What? Excuse me!" After Frank introduces himself, also by his full name, Libby explains that this opening had sounded like harassment to her. Later in this phone call, Frank asks Libby on a date.

Frank may suggest his flirtatious intentions by referring to Libby as "lovely." A similar road toward flirtatious innuendo seems to be at work in this example.

[14] Field note

Fred: Who's that beautiful girl in that great sports car?!

Shirley: (lightheartedly) Shut up and get in the car!

Fred: You mean I get to ride with the beautiful girl?
Shirley: Fred, you're crazy.

Fred offers a courtly compliment, which Shirley brushes aside with a mock-rude retort. This creates an unusual event, and Fred's persisting to repeat the compliment marks a flirtatious intention.

Ordinarily, people first meeting each other talk about the least risky things—the weather, a job, or a hometown. These are safe topics when uncertainty is high. Flirting may start when something outrageous marks the talk as unusual.

· · ·

Two things must happen to start a flirtation: something unusual and something to point toward sexuality or romantic interest. In *The Presidio,* Nina asks Jay a nervy question about why he left the military. She pursues this question by guessing that he left because of problems with her father. His response is to switch the topic to her looks ("You're very pretty"), and a round of sexual innuendo follows.

[15] Film: *The Presidio*[18]
Jay: You're very pretty
                       (4)
Nina: Is it hard?
                       (1)
Jay: Is what hard
                       (2)   (she turns head in double take, smiles)
Nina: Being a policeman
                       (0.4)
Jay: O:hhhh yeah. hh
                       (3)   (audience laughs here)
Nina: Inspector Austin are you flirting with me
Jay: Gee I thought it was the other way around

Jay and Nina's small talk leads quickly toward the touchy subject of his career under her father's supervision. Jay switches from this topic, evading her question by delivering a compliment: "You're very pretty." Nina's next utterance, "Is it hard?" seems disjunctive in response to the compliment "You're very pretty." Nina is apparently ignoring the compliment to return to her prior topic of Jay's career in law enforcement. ("Is it hard" being an MP or policeman?) Yet there is also a possible sexual pun: If "it" can be read as relevant to his compliment or to the pursuit of romance, it makes possible a perverse reading of her question. Jay exploits this possibility in his next two turns. First he asks "Is what hard?" This repair-initiation indicates he has had some trouble interpreting the prior utterance. Jay asks her to specify the referent of "it."

Nina smiles but responds straight, "Being a policeman." This specifies the referent of her "it" as his career. The primary literal meaning of the main question-answer pair here is routine. ("Is it [being a policeman] hard?"— "Yeah.") Meanwhile, however, the repair sequence has called attention to possible alternative interpretation(s) for "it." Jay's question-answering utterance, "O:hhh yeah. hh," is produced with a profound sigh that seems over-built as an answer to a question about his career. What other "it" could be "hard"? One possible understanding is that she has responded to his compliment by asking if he is sexually aroused ("You're very pretty"/ "Is it hard?"). The sound contour of the sighed "oh yeah" could indicate that he is sexually aroused.

This interpretation is not just in my dirty mind. The next events in the episode show that both audience members and these fictional participants interpret the moment this way.

[15] *The Presidio*, detail[19]

Jay:	O:hhh yeah. hh
	(3) (audience laughs here)
Nina:	Inspector Austin are you flirting with me

The notation on the second line of the transcription here (audience laughs) is not in the film but shows the audience response each time I have played this video in a public lecture. Listeners laugh; then afterward they remember having laughed at this juncture and trace this humorous response to the ambiguous word "hard." The fictional characters also note this ambiguity. Nina asks whether he is flirting.

How do these flirters create sexual innuendo? One speaker uses a word with a possible sexual meaning, then the other party responds to the sexual subtext. This cumulativeness of innuendo across turns is illustrated in this musical comedy song:

[16] Song: "The Tennis Song"[20]

He: I may lack form and finesse but I warm up in a jiff

She: It's not exciting unless the competition is stiff . . .

He: This game commences with love

She: Well I think love is a bore . . .

Both: One thing I'm positive of, it's time for someone to score.

This example shows how multiple iterations by alternating speakers make the innuendo game obvious and transparent. The resources for such turns may vary. Some are tennis terms that may be applied in other domains—for example,, "love." Some items may have wide application to sex or flirting—for example, "stiff," "score." Others become available by a combination of stretched semantics and possible tennis relevance—for example, "warm up in a jiff." The important thing is not to be immensely clever but rather to continue to forward the relevance of flirtation. Observers may supply appreciation to assist the creation of sexual innuendo.

[17] Field note

Marie: I take it you're a feminist?

Trey: Ma'am, I've been called a lot of things before, never been sad-
           dled with that one.

Marie: Well you might try being saddled sometime. The smell of
           leather, the sting of a whip.

Others: Mercy!

Marie sort of calls Trey a feminist. Trey sort of denies the charge by saying he's never been "saddled" with the feminist label. Marie free-associates from saddle to "leather" and "whip," which are used as signs of S & M sexuality. Others indicate that they hear that sexual innuendo has been created.

Who starts a round of innuendo is usually indefinite. Consider this

more extended example, which occurs right after the marked telephone opening in example [12] above. Rick and Cara repeat the word "pumping" several
times, neither party accepting responsibility for starting this repetition game.
Each accuses the other. Cara accuses Rick of starting it by asking "what could
that mean?" Rick responds: "I thought that's what you meant."

[18] UTCL D8:2 (You queer.)

Rick: What're you guys doin
                (0.3)
Cara: Well- um we've been looking for: apartments all da:y and no:w
               (.) we're cooking (sounds like "kicking")
Rick: You're- you're punting
Cara: Cooking
Rick: Kicking
Cara: Cooking.
Rick: Cooking huh huh
Cara: Ye::s.
Rick: Oh ho ho ho
Cara: Pumping, we're pumping. hhh huh huh huh huh, what could
               that mean ◀
Rick: U:h I don't kno:w u:h (0.3)
Cara: Huh?
Rick: U- You got me heh heh heh
Cara: You're the one that said the word, Right
                (0.3)
Rick: Well 'at's what th- I thought that's what you said though ◀
Cara: Oh really

Who started this round of innuendo? Cara says the word "cooking" with a
North Texas accent that makes the word sound a bit like the word "kicking."
Perhaps Rick is making fun of Cara's accent when he apparently says "punting," which Cara later indicates she heard as "pumping." Both people subsequently accuse the other one of having said the word "pumping" first.

Interactive performance of sexual innuendo is illustrated early in the
film *Pretty Woman*. We join this encounter when the participants have known

each other for about fifteen seconds. It is evident that she works as a prostitute. He has asked for directions and she has offered to show him to his des-
tination. They drive toward his hotel and he asks about her fees. She responds
that she charges a hundred dollars an hour.

[19] Film: *Pretty Woman*[21]

He: Hundred dollars an hour (1) pretty stiff

           (3) (While driving she puts one hand in his lap)

She: No, no:. But it's got potential.

           (music begins—he turns his head in double take)

In this scene the ambiguous word is "stiff." These two people are having an
unusual encounter. He casts his inquiry about her prices in hypothetical
mode: "What do you girls make now?" The event is unusual for him, in that
he has asked for directions, not for the sexual services of a prostitute. She has
stepped out of work role to show him directions. He is perhaps only bargaining hypothetically, but she remains all business. His "pretty stiff" utterance is a claim that her price is comparatively high. Yet she chooses to react
to "stiff" as a pun about the state of his sex organ. She displays her hearing
of this pun by placing her hand knowingly on his crotch. This act also serves
as a bid for his patronage (a free sample of the goods). His double take shows
that he hears the sexual meaning.

Many words referring to human sexuality have other dictionary meanings. Some of these words are obvious in their sexual freighting (words like
"come" or "mistress," for example), but the words "hard" and "stiff" are not
listed in dictionaries as having such meanings. Actors create sexual innuendoes with them anyway, and next speakers show by their actions that they
have constructed something sexual of these words.

Sometimes, flirters indicate possibilities by denial of interest in
courtship, as marked in *Love Story*.

[20] Fiction: *Love Story*[22]

Oliver: What makes you think I went to prep school?

Jenny: You look stupid and rich.

Oliver: You're wrong, I'm actually smart and poor.

Jenny:	Oh no preppie, I'm smart and poor. (stares at him)
Oliver:	What the hell makes you so smart.
Jenny:	I wouldn't go for coffee with you. ◄
Oliver:	I wouldn't ask you.
Jenny:	That is what makes you stupid.

Jen caps her round of insults with: "I wouldn't go for coffee with you," which denies interest in romance. In fact, immediately after this scene, these two people do have coffee together.

Shakespeare's Beatrice and Benedick also deny interest in falling in love, shortly before their friends entrap them into expressing such sentiments to one another.

[21] Fiction: *Much Ado about Nothing*[23]

Benedick:	. . . truly I love none.
Beatrice:	A dear happiness to women: they would else have been troubled with a pernicious suitor. I thank God, and my cold blood, I am of your humour for that; I had rather hear my dog bark at a crow, than a man swear he loves me.
Benedick:	God keep your ladyship still in that mind! So some gentleman or other shall 'scape a predestinate scratched face.
Beatrice:	Scratching could not make it worse, an 'twere such a face as yours . . .

Denial that one is flirting is commonplace in fictional love stories. Here is a real-life example that follows a very similar pattern. Rick and Cara have been repeating the word "pumping" (example [18]) and accusing each other of starting this game. After several repetitions of the troublesome word, Rick asks whether the term "pumping" is intended as a sexual reference. This gives both parties a chance to deny such intentions.

[22] UTCL D8:2 You queer

Cara:	What does that word mean
	(0.4)
Rick:	Pumping?

Cara:	Pumping
	(1.2)
Rick:	Puppy? or pumping.
Cara:	Pumping. Isn't that what you said?
Rick:	Pumping?
Cara:	Yeah
Rick:	Sexually heh heh heh ◄
Cara:	Is that what you meant hah
Rick:	No not at all. Heh ◄denial
Cara:	Oh, huh huh
Rick:	Is that what you meant?
Cara:	No. not at all. huh heh heh heh. ◄denial

An example with a similar theme occurs when two women engage in a round of kissing:

[23] Field note
Sue: I can't have sex with you on the first date.

The field worker who reported this event (who was the woman kissing Sue) reported the following observations:

> The use of the word "date" to describe the events of the evening was defining it in an entirely new light for me . . .
>
> Sue had been the aggressor at every stage, so her exclamation that sex could not occur seemed odd.

Sue's statement denies her willingness to "have sex" at the present time—which she frames as a "first date." She seems not to discourage the possibility of sexual engagement at a later time.

Consider this thought experiment: You go to a movie or something on what might be a first date, and you have a good time. As you say goodbye one of you says something to deny romantic interest: "You're clearly not the type I get involved with," or "I couldn't have a physical relationship with you." That is the experimental treatment. In the control condition of this experiment you experience the same encounter: the same movie, the same chat over root beer, the same walk home, the same goodbye, but delete this denial of interest. Question: which is more likely, scene one or two, to begin a courting relationship?

The denial of relationship makes a subsequent romance more likely than the scene with no such denial. In order to deny interest one would have to consider the possibility of such a relationship. To say to someone, on scant evidence, "I'm not interested in you," entails that the speaker has considered the issue.

To summarize: These flirtations follow a two-stage template: First there is rude language or meta-talk to stop the interaction on a dime and to indicate that something unusual is happening. Next, flirtation is interactively forwarded as a frame to explain this marked interaction as possible courtship. The parties either create sexual innuendo or show interest by denial of interest in a romantic relationship.

These patterns appear in numerous fictional and real-life flirtations. This is not the only pattern or maybe not even the most common pattern for initiating courtship. Yet this scenario provides a central possibility, a mainstream, competent way to flirt.

The sense of playful banter that flirting partners sustain throughout comes so much to our attention that we should explore the connection between precourtship banter and other sorts of play—which has been much studied among children and animals. The following play-related phenomena may be noted in many of the segments discussed above—but most especially in the real-life "pumping" episode:

- The acts become fictionalized, they do not denote what such acts ordinarily denote.
- There is sustained repetition.
- The parties repeatedly engage in shared laughter.

Cara talks about a class she is taking, and play bubbles up after she brags that she will get a high grade. Sexual innuendo emerges around repetitions of the word "know:"

[24] UTCL D8:2, You queer

Cara: Yeah, I'm gonna get an A in the class. For sure (0.2) eh huh hah hah hhhh
Rick: Why. Do you know the instructor heh heh
Cara: No. Instructor's a lady
Rick: Oh- well do you know her
Cara: Do I know her
Rick: Yeah
Cara: I mean I know her,
Rick: O:h hh Oh you know her. hih
Cara: But I don't know her. huh=
Rick: You don't- hah hah
Cara: You know hih hih hih
Rick: I wouldn't know ho

Rick suggests to Cara that she plans to get an A in a class because she knows the instructor. This casts an innuendo that Cara may exploit a personal connection to gain this high grade. Cara forwards that analysis in her next utterance when she suggests that Rick's suggestion is invalid because "the instructor's a lady." Since the instructor is a lady, she suggests, Cara wouldn't be giving her any (sexual?) favors. The two parties then indulge in word play through multiple repetitions of "know."

Just a few minutes later in this same phone call a climactic moment begins in a possible preinvitation to eat but escalates into four rounds of a rhyming game on the verbs "run," "eat," "go," and "come":

[25] UTCL D8:2, You queer

Rick: Have you had dinner yet
(0.4)
Cara: No I haven't [Have you.
Rick: [I- I'm so hungry,
Cara: Are you starving?
Rick: Ye:s
(0.3)
Cara: Have you ate today?

(0.4)

Cara:	Eaten
Rick:	heh heh [heh huh
Cara:	[heh heh I said eated
Rick:	No I- I- I already eated
Cara:	You already eated?
Rick:	Yes
Cara:	What did you eat at hih
Rick:	But I'm going to go- I'm gonna go- ran now hah hah
Cara:	You gonna go ran
Rick:	I'm gonna go ran
Cara:	nh hah hah hah hah @#*# you. hah hah hah hah
	(off phone) He's gonna go ran now eyahuh huh hih huh huh huh huh [Leave me alo:ne.
Rick:	[And the- and then- and then I'm gonna- and then I'm gonna go:ne to a movie hhh
Cara:	Gonna gone to a movie?
Rick:	Gonna gone to a movie.
Cara:	hih hnh hnh hnh Are you gonna gone to a movie?
Rick:	Yeah, You want to comed? No.
Cara:	I want to came.
Rick:	Want to come.
Cara:	hnh huh You want to came hah hah heh heh hah hah Leave me alo:ne.

Each of these four repeated verbs, "eat," "run," "gone," and "come," is repeated in four variants, most of which show conjugation errors. This makes a doggerel poem of four stanzas, with a refrain, "Leave me alone," after the second and fourth stanzas:

[26] UTCL D8:2 You queer, simplified

Cara:	Eaten, I said eated
Rick:	No I already eated
Cara:	You already eated?
Rick:	Yes

Cara:	What did you eat at
Rick:	But I'm gonna go ran now
Cara:	You gonna go ran
Rick:	I'm gonna go ran
Cara:	He's gonna go ran now Leave me alone.
Rick:	And then I'm gonna gone to a movie
Cara:	Gonna gone to a movie?
Rick:	Gonna gone to a movie.
Cara:	Are you gonna gone to a movie?
Rick:	Yeah, you want to comed? no
Cara:	I want to came.
Rick:	Want to come,
Cara:	You want to came.
	Leave me alone.

The repetition structure in this passage indicates a game to forward the verb-error series.[24] Yet the interaction also forwards innuendoes about dating and sexuality.

- The first, third, and fourth stanzas ("eat," "movie," "wanna come?") can be heard as dating preinvitations: (going out to dinner, going to a movie and coming along.)
- The fourth repetition ("come") transparently associates to sexual intercourse.
- The climactic line "leave me alone," a canonical response to pestering, could also serve as a denial of interest in courtship. If you leave me alone we won't become dating partners.

These sexual innuendoes are forwarded within the verb play series. The repetitive play shows that something sexual is going on. In these ways real-life flirtation resembles the flirtation in popular fictions.

In fiction, and in real-life flirtation, interaction partners make something unusual happen (using meta-talk, confrontation, profanity) and then align to indicate that the something might be romantic attraction (sexual innuendo based in serial ambiguities). These scenes show a turn-by-turn playfulness promoting mock indications of mutual flirtatious consent. Each of these features marks flirting discourse as exceptional. This marking provides opportunities for romantic imaginings to be constructed. Unfortunately, such activity also creates opportunities to cross the divide between sexual attraction and violence—which is the topic of the next chapter.

4

Hey Baby,
You Bitch

THERE IS ONE UNDENIABLE SEX DIFFERENCE IN SOCIAL BEHAVIOR: MEN SEXUALLY harass, assault, and rape women, whereas women rarely do comparable acts. Our society seems to have learned the lesson that these are violent crimes. Unfortunately, some performances of sexual violence also bear troubling relationships to flirtation.[1] This chapter examines some social interaction dimensions of rape and sexual harassment as problems of monologic communication. This is not a comprehensive description of sexual violence, which would include discussions of female mutilation, infanticide, and more. I sketch only those aspects of sexual violence that seem most similar to "normal" flirtation. By most contemporary estimates, such events constitute a majority of sexually violent events.[2]

We begin with an oddity about sexual requests and responses to such requests. In ordinary conversation the recipient of any offer or invitation is obliged to respond with acceptance or rejection.[3] Acceptance is likely to be quick and clear:

[1] UTCL A10
Mel: Wanna go to Kerbey? (a restaurant)
Pat: Sure.

However, refusals often get mitigated and delayed. An indefinite response to a request or invitation usually indicates refusal.[4] In [2] a mother's direct question about a possible visit to a friend stimulates her daughter to say, "I don't know," meaning "no."

[2] UTCL F1.1

Mother: Are you going down to visit June?

(0.8)

Daughter: I don't know.

This mother asks a question, and her daughter gives a delayed "maybe" response. This is the usual way we indicate refusal. Refusal is usually performed by pausing and saying "maybe," not by saying "no."

However, in a man's sexual offer to a woman, this expectation is flip-flopped; a woman's "no" may be heard as "maybe." This point is illustrated in the title of a contemporary pop song: "Maybe I Mean Yes."[5]

[3] Song: "Maybe I Mean Yes"

When I say no I mean maybe

Baby don't you know me yet?

Nothing's worth having

If it ain't a little hard to get . . .

When I say no I mean maybe

And maybe I mean yes.

Does this lyric's first line encourage a resisting female to doubt her intentions? Maybe she does not really intend to say no; or maybe a woman's no—at least in response to a sexual invitation—means maybe.

The song's second line is: "Baby, don't you know me yet?" "Baby" is ambiguous, meaning either a very young person or a special lover. The ambiguity of the term "baby" also appears in this report of a violent assault:

[4] Field note /self-report

As I began to fall asleep, I heard someone in the dark room. . . . I tried to speak with control, truly feeling scared. . . ."Mike, what are you doing in here?" He sat down on the side of the bed, pulling me close to him. I remember struggling to push him away. I pushed on his chest, but it was like trying to move a brick wall. My wrists in his hands were forced above my head as he began to kiss me hard on the mouth. "I want to make love to you, baby. You are just so sexy." Then I blacked out. . . . But I knew that he had made love to me against my will.

Amy's narrative depicts the assailant, at the very time he is forcing himself on her, speaking the endearment: "baby" to invalidate and minimize resistance. Even in this confessional narrative of a rape, Amy uses the euphemism "made love," illustrating her continuing difficulties in categorizing this horrible event.

In the song about ambiguous female resistance the full line in which the word "baby" appears is:

> "Baby don't you *know* me yet?":
> When I say no I mean maybe
> Baby don't you know me yet?

"Know" is a homophone of "no," the syllable of resistance. "Know" also carries sexual undertones: St. Joseph, for instance, took Mary as his wife, but did not know her until later. The singer, who notes that her "no" might mean "maybe," could be heard to taunt her "baby" that if he doesn't yet know her in this carnal sense then his come-on is timid or slow.

Perhaps this song lyric asks only for a date, not explicitly for sexual consent. It does not refer to harassment, assault, or rape. However, this lyric does assert the principled ambiguity of a woman's "no" to an offer of a date or an amorous embrace. This singer taunts the person addressed as "baby" to be more forceful in forwarding amorous advances.

The song's next lines make a maxim: "Nothing's worth having if it ain't a little hard to get." This makes out the speaker as a woman playing hard to get. She resists his advance and yet she encourages the man to overcome this resistance.

Overcoming resistance to a woman's "no" is a theme in the narratives of sex offenders, who often depict their victims as saying no. However, offenders hear this "no" as a stimulus for persuasion or coercion.[6]

[5] Therapy A8:13.59

Alfred: She said no at first then I said something to convince her into having sex.

Alfred reports that his victim said "no," but he treated this "no" as "maybe," and therefore a stimulus for him "to convince her into having sex." Alfred's wording carefully suggests persuasion: He convinced her when he "said something." Alfred does not report what he said (or did) to "convince her." This is a significant omission, since the seriousness of Alfred's offense may depend on the degree to which he coerced her. Here is one therapist's description of rapists' coercive techniques:

> The rapists we work with at the Institute very often are *excellent* at getting women into situations where they're confused, where they don't have the supports they ordinarily have, where they are afraid to resist, and the rape doesn't occur *instantly,* it may occur two or three or four hours into the relationship after they really intimidated her so that from their point of view she has agreed.[7]

To a man bent on sexual coercion, a sexual encounter is seen as "a process of a woman's 'no' becoming 'yes' as a result of a man's persuasion."[8]

That rapists treat a woman's resisting "no" as an occasion for persuasion or coercion can be observed in survivors' accounts of sexual violence and harassment. Here is part of a college student's conversation with her best friend:

[6] Field note

Sara: I don't understand how you can't remember anything about your first time.

Lora: I was drunk and I was fifteen. I didn't know what was going on. I said no but it happened anyway.

Sara: You don't remember anything else?

Lora: Not really. I remember when I got home my boyfriend called and I told him and he cried.

Sara: Did you tell him you were raped?

Lora: No. I didn't realize it was rape until I was in college.

Just as startling as a rapist's denial that resistance is final is this victim's three-year denial that she had, in fact, been raped. In commenting on this narrative, Lora observed:

I couldn't believe that I didn't recognize that event in which I lost my virginity was acquaintance rape. I separated myself from the event before I got home that night and I tr[ied] to pretend that I had a choice even though I was ignored when I said no. I finally had to face the truth when I compared my experience to rape victims who did not know their attackers. I still do not remember what happened between "no" and my arrival at home. I wonder if it's better for me to not know.

Lora's recollections parallel Amy's in the futility of resistance and in the assault survivor's forgetting critical moments of the rape itself. Survivors and perpetrators forget different parts of the offense event. Perpetrators forget the coercive preludes to criminal acts. Survivors sometimes forget the penetration and intercourse.

Each victim in these narratives waited some time before applying the word "rape" to her experience. Lora's recollection helps us to understand such lengthy denial and also to notice the role of postevent interaction in reframing what happened. Once a survivor figures out what happened, this new definition is framed as what has happened all along. Memories of the offense may evolve in this process.

Denial and the reframing of the event in subsequent interaction also constitute major themes within a collection of harassment narratives from academics.[9]

[7] Narrative #30, p. 385
I left believing I was somehow wrong; at the time it didn't even occur to me that he could be wrong. Nearly a decade passed before I defined what had happened as sexual harassment. I wonder if he ever recognized it as that.

[8] Narrative #33, p. 388
When Anita Hill went public, the incidents from my past came back all too vividly—I understood intimately how someone could go years without telling anyone about such events, how shameful and painful they are to remember, why a woman would be reluctant to file a complaint.

[9] Narrative #6, p. 364

For the next ten years I felt the whole thing was my fault because I had had sex with him and did not tell him right off to leave me alone. I can understand now that by setting me up in his house alone, by giving me more alcohol to drink, by approaching me with no clothes on outside of his bathroom, and by coming on to me, he immobilized me.

In each of these instances both the passage of time and new insights from interaction with others have contributed to memories of the harassing events. How such revelatory interaction might occur is shown in this overheard encounter:

[10] Field note

Jan:	So how did your date go last Saturday?
Sue:	It was fun! Really fun! (laugh) But I hope I didn't mess things up.
Jan:	How do you mean?
Sue:	I stayed at his apartment.
Jan:	You slept there? Did you sleep with him? (astonished)
Sue:	Well, I didn't plan on it, but one thing led to another and, you know. He really forced me into it. I think it was borderline rape

Sue's account of her actions shifts during this short scene. At first she foregrounds her hopes for the relationship: "I hope I didn't mess things up." When Jan's meta-talk probes for details, Sue admits: "I stayed at *his* apartment," which implies sexual activity. Jan picks up on this innuendo and returns a stronger one: "Did you sleep with him?" Jan sounds astonished as she asks this question. In her next utterance Sue's account shifts to align with Jan's apparently negative reaction. She first denies premeditation ("Well I didn't plan on it"), then accuses the man ("He really forced me into . . . borderline rape"). Did Sue say "no" during the event? How, if at all, did Sue's date-attacker experience the resistance she claims (in her last utterance) to have offered?

When a man proffers coercive sex, he treats a woman's resisting "no" as ambiguous. Furthermore, a woman's resistance may take forms more subtle than overt disagreement or outrage. Communication researchers Michael

Motley and Heidi Reeder approached this problem by asking college students to respond to a hypothetical scenario:[10]

> You and a [male/female] are alone on your first, second, third, or so, date. The two of you begin to get physical. The physical intimacy progresses—maybe a little, maybe a lot. At some point [you say/she says] what is indicated below.

Each subject evaluated the meanings in a list of women's statements designed to show either direct or indirect resistance:

- Women's direct statements of resistance:
  — 'Please don't do that'
  — 'I don't want to do this.'
  — 'Let's stop this.'
- Women's indirect statements of resistance:
  — 'I can't do this unless you're committed to me.'
  — 'I'm seeing someone else.'
  — 'I don't have any protection.'

The women responding to this questionnaire interpreted all of these statements as saying "no." Males responded differently to the direct statements than to the indirect ones. (See figure 1.)

Male respondents misinterpreted indirect female resistance messages. In this experiment, "I can't do this unless you're committed to me" was interpreted by the males as "She wants to go further, but wants me to assure her that I'm committed to her." Likewise, males interpreted "I'm seeing someone else" as "She wants to go further but wants me to be discreet so the other guy doesn't find out."

Motley and Reeder claim there is miscommunication between women who intend to resist sexual advances and men, who interpret indirect resistance as inviting negotiation. Women who intend to resist sexual advances should use friendly but direct language. Men should realize that women who resist indirectly should still be heard as saying no. These recommendations treat interaction between males and females as intercultural communication. Yet how much of the problem is a problem of misunderstanding?

FIGURE 1. MALES' AND FEMALES' INTERPRETATIONS OF FEMALES' RESISTANCE MESSAGES

(A higher number indicates greater willingness to be persuaded.)

	FEMALES' RATING	MALES' RATING
Women's direct statements		
Please don't do that	1.1	1.2
I don't want to do this	1.2	1.2
Let's stop this	1.1	1.4
Women's indirect statements		
I can't do this unless you're committed to me	2.0	3.5
I'm seeing someone else	1.7	3.2
I don't have any protection	1.8	3.2

Motley and Reeder treat sexual resistance as a one-moment encounter. However, a physically arousing sexual encounter is likely to last for at least several minutes, perhaps much longer. A number of a actions occur, with each act building on prior acts to indicate possible consent. Consenting sexuality is achieved through a series of actions over time. Repeated pursuit in the face of resistance seems crucial to legal definitions of rape and sexual harassment. Clarence Thomas sexually harassed Anita Hill not by asking for a date, but by *repeatedly* approaching her over a period of weeks, and after repeated refusals.[11]

When women resist sexual assaults, attackers treat resistance as ambiguous and open to further persuasion. This problem is complicated by flirtation-related ambiguities in male attack or harassment.

Consider a continuum of sexual violence, with assault and rape at one extreme and ogling at the other. Along this continuum are acts as varied as lewd remarks, forcing a physical agenda in the face of a dating partner's resistance, or a professional's sexual "joking." Each of these acts may be packaged ambiguously as flirtation.

The relationship between heckling and violence is described in sociologist Carol Gardner's report on male remarks to women on the public streets of Philadelphia.[12] Targets of these remarks class them with rape as uninvited harassment. However, men who make such remarks describe them as playful flattery.

> This disparity may in part be explained by the *double-entendre* nature of many remarks. . . . The characteristic sexual freighting of male-to-female street speech reproduces this ambiguity: It supplies a respectful semantic line that presumes the female is inaccessible and a disrespectful semantic line that presumes she is accessible.

The ambiguity of street remarks links sexual harassment (disrespectful line) to flirtation (respectful line). This ambiguity makes it difficult to respond to such remarks, and many women try to act as if nothing were happening. But this often leads to stronger remarks:

[11] Field note (strangers on street)
Guy: Say, baby
Girl: (Says nothing, looks forward, and continues to walk past him.)
Guy: (Turning as she walks past.) Say bitch, I'm talking to you.
Girl: (Her face is fuming as she walks away from him.) Asshole (she
             mutters under her breath)

When the target of this utterance tries to ignore "Say baby," the heckler switches to a disrespectful line: "Say bitch, I'm talking to you." The woman continues walking and shows anger on her face, but her verbal response is muttered under her breath.

The ambiguity of men's approaches to women may occur outside street remarks. A male stranger may approach a woman to offer help or protection (respectful line), but if his offer of help is rebuffed, the man may switch from helpfulness to abuse.

[12] Field note
Man: Can I help you with that?
             (pause)
Woman: No, I have it, thank you.

Man:	Really, a little thing like you shouldn't have to carry all that.
Woman:	(nervously) That's really okay, I have it.
Man:	(angrily) Fine lady, I was just trying to help. You don't have to act like a bitch.

This man's initial helpful offer and the first refusal are marked as polite, though the man does violate civil inattention in speaking to a stranger. The second offer remains polite but adds an air of condescension: "a little thing like you." After the second refusal the man switches to disrespectful language: "bitch."

[13] Field note

Bum:	Ma'am do you have any spare change?
Me:	No, sorry.
Bum:	(under his breath, to his buddies) That's okay, I wouldn't have expected anything from you, you little bitch.

[14] Field note

I wasn't even side-by-side with the truck when I noticed that the driver was practically hanging out the window, trying to get a better look. . . . As I passed him, he started yelling out the window: "Hey, baby." . . . I kept driving, looking straight ahead, never acknowledging him. As I looked back in my rearview mirror, I noticed that the same guy who was giving me a compliment, although a repulsive one, was now sending me an obscene gesture.

The word "compliment" indicates some sense of the respectful line, even in a distasteful, harassing act. Yet the compliment sours into abuse in the event's final gesture.

Veiled ambiguities of unsolicited compliments keep alive the possibility that the approach need not be heard as harassment. Consider this extremely respectful packaging of a street remark:

[15] Field note

| He: | Pardon me, I hope you don't find this offensive, or take this the wrong way, but you have great legs. |

She:	(embarrassed giggle) Thank you.
He:	Whatever you do to stay in shape, keep it up (walks away)

This male politely asks pardon to speak, then offers two disclaimers before delivering a clear (if ludicrous) compliment. He then walks away, showing his intention not to threaten. The recipient of this remark finds the incident flattering. She writes: "I even enjoyed going home to tell my boyfriend about it. I think I was sort of bragging." The compliment flavor seems to her to override the act's inappropriateness, shielding the man from counterattack as he makes an unsolicited remark about the woman's looks.

In some instances a man pursues a sexual line despite being ignored or actively resisted. Such pursuit in the face of being ignored is shown in a tape recording of three males driving around in a jeep, occasionally heckling passersby. When a heckled woman responds angrily, these men offer both respectful and disrespectful accounts for their actions.

[16] UTCL A12

Tom:	Look at that
Harry:	*Oh* oh *ya* Bill.
	(0.4)
Dick:	*U*h ha hah. We're talking some [legs there
Tom:	[Oh man she's got a bik- she's got her little swimsuit on under there
Dick:	Huh huh ha
Harry:	Hold on hold on let her run past
Dick:	[Okay
SHE:	[What's your problem
Tom:	Huh?
SHE:	What's *your* problem
Harry:	We think [you're really cute ◄
Tom:	[You upset at us ◄
	(0.4)
Dick:	*Huh* hah
Tom:	Come *on*, don't get upset just- you should be flattered
	(0.5) (motor noise)

Dick:	Huh hah hah hah hah
Tom:	What a bitch.

This woman talks back to her tormenters. Her repeated "What's your problem?" is a demand for them to explain their heckling. In response two men speak at once, illustrating respectful and disrespectful lines (see arrows). One heckler responds with a compliment: "We think you're really cute," indicating that the staring and talk is intended as a compliment (respectful line). At the same moment another heckler retorts "You upset at us?" implying that the woman's protest is out of line. The relationship between these two utterances (spoken in overlap in the same conversational slot) associates sexual harassment and flirtation. Subsequently, the disrespectful heckler applies the term "bitch" to the woman who talked back.

Ambiguous terms ("baby") and ambiguous lines of action (respectful/disrespectful) connect street remarks to both violence and flirting. These ambiguities also occur in sexual assaults. In the film *Thelma and Louise* the heroines stop at a country bar. Harlan, the rapist-to-be, comes to their table and speaks to them in the style of a street remark: (a) violating civil inattention, and (b) inviting sexual innuendo. Harlan's utterance advances both a respectful and a disrespectful line. One of Harlan's recipients (Louise) responds to harassment, while the other recipient, Thelma, responds to flirting. The two hearings occur in speech overlap.

[17] Film: *Thelma and Louise*[13]

Harlan:	Now what are a couple a kewpie dolls like you doin in a place like this.
Louise:	[h h h Mindin our own business Why don't you try:.
Thelma:	[Uh we left town t'ave a weekend cause we wanted to try and have some fun.

Harlan asks a direct question to strangers. That question contains a belittling compliment on the women's appearance: "kewpie dolls." Each woman responds instantly. Louise tells the intruder to get lost; but Thelma (who has just taken her coat off to reveal bare shoulders) says that she and her friend are out to have fun. Harlan's intrusive approach is heard by one recipient as harassment and by the other recipient as flirting.

A rough pickup line provides ambivalent arousal. How does such an episode become flirtation or sexual violence? How do parties figure out and indicate their evolving intentions for the episode? I once went with fifteen people from my workplace to a country bar much like the one pictured in *Thelma and Louise*. I noticed a married male in the crowd hug dancing with a young colleague. I wondered whether there could be romantic attachment playing out between those two. Later, when I danced with this woman, she said, "Help me, I'm afraid of that man." I said, "Huh?" She said, "He asked me to dance and he won't leave me alone." I replied, "It looked like you were dancing pretty close with him." She snorted: "I have no choice, he holds me so tight it hurts. I don't know what I can do. He could ruin my career. Please help me get out of this room safely." I was shocked, because from watching them dance, I had guessed that the scene was consensual. Such flirting/ assault ambiguity protects violent men, puts women at risk, and promotes underreporting of sexual assaults.

Consenting sexual encounter is interactive dialogue. In acquaintance rape pursuit becomes monologue. A rapist puts forward a (perhaps deniable) request for sex, yet interprets resistance as maybe or yes. An attempted acquaintance rape is represented in the comedy film *Tootsie*. John, an actor who works with Dorothy (Dorothy is actually a man in disguise), coerces "her" to grant an audience in her apartment. The conversation goes like this:

[18] Film: *Tootsie*[14]

John:	Dorothy
Dorothy:	Yes
John:	I want you
Dorothy:	I beg your pardon
John:	I've never wanted a woman this much
Dorothy:	Oh please John please perhaps another time
John:	Don't turn me away it'll kill me
Dorothy:	Not you personally I don't wanna get involved emotionally at this time

John:	Then I'll take straight sex (lunges)
Dorothy:	(wrestling) I don't wanna hurt you
John:	I don't mind

          (Dorothy's roommate, Jeff, enters, the combatants separate)

John forces himself upon Dorothy abruptly and repeatedly. Dorothy resists repeatedly but John's pursuit does not waver. Dorothy never intends to communicate anything to John except no. However, John takes no as maybe, even though such interpretation requires fantastic semiotic leaps. The viewer can scarcely believe how this guy misreads Dorothy's resistance. This comedy works, in fact, because just this type of idiotic situation is all too possible in real life.

    Tootsie also depicts the aftermath of John's assault, which is still in progress when a new person enters. Then both John and Dorothy conspire to deny the obvious.

[19] Film: *Tootsie*[15]

          (Dorothy's roommate, Jeff, enters; the combatants separate)

Dorothy:	Holy shit (nervous laughter) John Van Horne, Jeff Slater. Jeff Slater, John Van Horne
	(1)
Jeff:	How do you do
John:	How do you do
	(0.5)
John:	I'll be going
Dorothy:	I think it's best
	(1) (John walks toward the door)
Jeff:	Gee I hope I haven't uh-
John:	No I hope I haven't (1) I want you to know for the record Jeff that ¡hhh nothing happened here tonight
	(4)
Jeff:	Thank you, John
	(3)
John:	Sorry Dorothy
	(1)

> I didn't understand, I I'm really sorry
>
> (0.4)
>
> Please don't talk about this
>
> Dorothy:　My lips are sealed

The first speech act that happens after Jeff enters is an introduction, one of the most commonplace speech acts available. We hear nothing like 'Thank God you came in,' or 'Throw this bum out,' but instead the assailant and victim collaborate in the introductions. Dorothy and John collaborate to deny that a sexual assault has occurred.

The attempted rapist says to the man whose entrance stopped the crime: "I want you to know nothing happened." John claims that technically no sexual act has occurred: Dorothy would not test positive for sperm, she has not been exposed to sexually transmitted diseases, she could not get pregnant, one could not charge him with more than assault. Also, John implies his (false) conclusion that Jeff is the victim's boyfriend, a male whose turf would be stepped on by a man raping or seducing Dorothy. John has shown no respect for Dorothy's autonomy to resist a sexual advance, but he shows respect for the female property of another man. One phrase serves all these uses: "nothing happened."

For cases as diverse as John and Dorothy and Amy's narratives our culture has fashioned the elastic, contested term "acquaintance rape." In *Thelma and Louise,* Harlan and Thelma meet perhaps less than an hour before the assault, and they spend that time drinking and dancing in a public place. They are acquaintances, though this is their first meeting. Thelma tries to escape Harlan's clutches as she becomes sick from alcohol. She goes to the parking lot to be sick, which leaves her vulnerable to Harlan's rape attempt. Example [20] shows how both Thelma's resistance messages (R) and Harlan's feigned-courtship talk builds sexually suggestive innuendo (S).

[20]　Film: *Thelma and Louise*[16]

Harlan:　How you feelin now darlin ◄S

Thelma:　Think- I think I'm startin to feel a li'l better

Harlan:　Yeah (1) startin d- feel pretty good to me too ◄S

　　　　　(0.6)　◄R

<table>
<tr><td></td><td>You know that (pulls her closer)</td></tr>
</table>

Thelma: I think I need to keep walkin ◀R

Harlan: huh huh Wait a minute- wait a minute- wait a minute, where you think you're going

Thelma: I'm goin back inside ◀R

Harlan: Oh no no

Thelma: Ughhh, Harlan!

Harlan: What

Thelma: Hey quit it stop it stop it stop ◀R

Harlan: Thelma- Thelma listen to me listen. I'm not gonna hurt ya okay, I just wanna kiss you, alright

Thelma: No, no ◀R

Harlan: Come on, come on, come on

(kiss)

Harlan: Damn you are adorable ◀S

Thelma: Alright let me go now come on ◀R

Harlan: We're not going this moment

Thelma: Let me go, I mean I'm married, come on ◀R

Harlan: Well that's okay I'm married too huh huh hah

Thelma: I don't feel good ◀R

               I been sick

(struggling)

Harlan: Listen I said I'm not gone hurt you, alright, relax.

Thelma: Harlan stop it please I mean it uh wait don't I mean it ◀R

Harlan: huh hah huh

Thelma: Louise is gonna wonder where I am ◀R

Harlan: Go *@#* Louise. *@#* Louise

(Thelma slaps Harlan) ←R

Harlan: Hey, (Harlan slaps Thelma repeatedly.)

               Don't you ever *@#* hit me, *@#* bitch

Thelma: Harlan- Harlan [please

Harlan: [You hear me

Thelma: Harlan please d- don't [hurt me Harlan please Aw:: Aw:::::oh

                                                                    ◄R

Harlan: [Shut up. Shut the *@#* up. You hear
            me, shut up.

Thelma: Please- please don't hurt me Harlan. Aw::::uhh ◄R

This is a more graphic and violent scene than the one in *Tootsie,* yet some thematic elements recur, including the mixture of direct and indirect resistances and the futility of both. It is the failure of Thelma's dozen or so resistance statements that shows this event to be attempted rape. Harlan reveals himself to be a control junkie, a man of monologue. Thelma unsuccessfully attempts to introduce dialogic response.

When Thelma hits Harlan, he gets more violent and his language turns from simulated compliments to disrespectful violent insistence. Resistance turns "hey baby" into "you bitch." After Louise stops the rape, the assaulting male asserts that he sees the activity to have been consenting sexuality.

[21] Film: *Thelma and Louise*[17]

Harlan: Alright heh heh just calm down we're just having a little fun
            that's all

Louise: Looks like you got a real *@#* idea of fun.

Thelma: (crying) come on- uhhh huh huh come on-

Louise: Turn around (talking to Harlan)

Thelma: (crying)

Louise: In the future, when a woman is crying like that she isn't having
            any fun

Harlan's "we're just having a little fun" claims that this event was consenting sex. Louise (unlike Jeff, who interrupts John and Dorothy) does not let Harlan's denial stand. Louise speaks for the viewer and for an evolving society: "In the future, when a woman is crying . . . she isn't having any fun." Louise argues this minimal future standard for sexual dialogue: that a male sexual partner has an obligation to interpret as resistance a woman's crying during sexual acts. A similar issue about crying and a woman's resistance to sexual assault is raised in a therapy group for sex offenders:

[22] Therapy A3 b, simplified

Alfred: She did not resist she laid there till I was finished . . . [Near the end] she cried.

Ethan: You saying though she didn't resist but then again you say she uh cried.

Alfred: She cried and laid there just hoping I'd be done, this is what I'd say.

Ethan: Well I say that's resistance. If she was crying she don't want this

This therapy moment turns on understanding that crying counts as resistance. What are the boundaries of resistance and consent? In enactments of sexual violence, monologue takes over from dialogue. Failure to achieve consent evolves into resistance-and-pursuit cycles. Rape, like consent, must be achieved over multiple consent-relevant moments. How many moments add up to full consent? The dialogue view is that it takes an indefinite number of consent moments—the more the merrier. Interactive consent is something to celebrate. However, the legal definition of rape sometimes fails to protect women who have consented to some degree of physical intimacy. In *Thelma and Louise* the attempted rape of Thelma is preceded by Harlan's public sexual pursuit and by her returning his advances. Then Thelma says no, repeatedly. Yet Harlan is not engaged in dialogue. When Louise stops Harlan's rape attempt, then subsequently kills him, she argues that she and Thelma cannot confess to this slaying because people had seen Thelma and Harlan together, dancing and partying.

Resolutions to these problems are distant. We as a society increasingly criminalize rape, but this provides little deterrent. These problems have a long history. Throughout much of human social time—tens of thousands of years—much human sexual activity, if we could get into a time machine and observe it, might fit the 1990s North American definition of rape. Yet at the time of occurrence some of these acts might have been described differently. Provocative critic Camille Paglia writes that "sexual intercourse, from kissing to penetration, consists of movements of barely controlled cruelty and consumption."[18] Nature does not decree that sex should be a pretty spectacle, nor always enacted within romance. One theme of civilization is to lessen suffering due to violent sexual assault.

In a film re-creation of prehistoric life, *The Quest for Fire,* a woman becomes, by current standards, a rape victim.[19] Three men and the woman are gathered around a fire. The men, who have rescued the woman from cannibals, are returning to their tribe with fire coals they have captured. (These people have the skills to maintain hot coals, but they cannot start a fire.) The woman lies by the fire, fidgeting in discomfort. She moves her leg and scratches herself. One man, who is gnawing on a piece of meat, sniffs the air, throws away his food, and moves toward her. He pats her leg three times, and then he moves to initiate sexual contact. Certainly this is not dialogic sexual invitation-consent, although he does warn her of his approach.

When the assault begins, the woman cries out and pummels the attacker with her hands. The other men disattend the event, staring at the fire. The woman escapes her attacker's grasp and scrambles to the leader of the group to beg his protection. The boss drives off the other guy. Mere seconds later the rescuer himself rapes the woman. Nobody aids the victim. This event does not get reported to the police, nor does the abused woman flee into the night. Instead, she settles by the campfire and resumes life as usual.

The Quest for Fire enacts scholars' guesses about social life among partly civilized people. In the film this woman eventually mates with the man who raped her, a chilling ideological precedent. She teaches him the advantages of consenting sex performed face to face. She also teaches him how to start a fire, how to use superior weapons, and how to use derisive laughter. The film suggests that these technologies develop together as civilizing processes. Today these sexual civilizing processes remain incomplete, imperfect, and laced with violence. Consider the mercurial heroine, Christine, in *The Phantom of the Opera,* who alternates between passion and horror at her dark suitor's attentions. A related theme is that of women who are bored with nice guys they date. Here is a middle-class teen from the Midwest describing a nice boy with whom she is friendly.

[23] Senchea, 1998[20]
He is just a cool guy. But he's not like attractive, but he's just really nice and he's funny and he's cute. But no one's like, oh you know, find him sexually attractive or anything. . . . I just feel really bad for him, cause he's like a

good quality guy, like what you'd look for in a boyfriend, like that really cares about the girl. . . . It's too bad.

High school girls criticize boys who are overinterested in sex as "users," but they are still uninterested in people who are too polite. Here are two college women discussing a recent date in terms that equate nice with dullness, or lack of chemistry:

[24] Field note

Fran:	Hey, how was last night
Sandy:	Oh, you know.
Fran:	What'd you think of your date?
	(pause)
Sandy:	It was okay. He's no guy I'd wanna go out with again
Fran:	Why? Was he a jerk?
Sandy:	No (pause) he was nice but-
Fran:	I understand

Sandy is not enthusiastic about her date, but admits that the man was "nice," and certainly he was not a jerk. Possibly he was not exciting, or interaction with him seemed too predictable. Her friend's empathic response is immediate: "*I understand.*" The description of a male date as "nice" gets a similar response in this instance:

[25] Field note

Marlene:	How'd it go?
Paula:	Oh, good. We had a real good time.
Marlene:	You don't sound too thrilled.
Paula:	Oh yeah, it was fun.
	(pause)
Marlene:	Well- that's good
	(pause)
	You like him then?
Paula:	Yeah. Yeah. I don't know. He's- ya know- too nice.
Marlene:	OH! Yeah.

Marlene wrote about this example:

> Paula and I had had this conversation before . . . sometimes after her dates, sometimes after mine. In every case, these post–nice guy conversations were very short, very downbeat. . . . Had the date been completely "successful," Paula would have volunteered . . . details. . . . Her hesitancy of answering . . . resulted precisely from the inability of the romantic female fantasy to encompass the nice guy. My response was immediate recognition, "*OH.*"

To Marlene and Paula "nice guy" signifies dull date. They find little to say about a nice guy. Yet a date with a mysterious, unpredictable, or even vaguely menacing stranger would be a story worth sharing. Healthy women may feel attraction to the darker sides of sexuality—and this shows one more association between sexual violence and flirting.

The Other Side of the Fault Line

We rarely hear perpetrators' stories about sexual violence. We hear victims' laments, as we should, but sexual violence will continue as long as certain men perpetrate it. Curtis LeBaron and I have been studying therapy groups for convicted sex offenders, both to hear these men's stories and to examine the course of their therapy.[21] Statistically, sex offenders have poor prospects to avoid committing repeat offenses. Therapy talk indicates the assailant's side of the story and shows some aspects of these men's course of therapy.

At the beginning of each therapy session, there occurs a check-in moment in which each client says: "My name is _____, and I am a sex offender. I am still capable of committing an offense. My deviant outlets include . . ." and the offender makes a list. Usually masturbation is on this list, as is pornography. Another common item is *dissector*, which is staring at one part of another person's body. Dissector is ogling. Sexual criminals are required to stop ogling in order to prevent themselves from repeating sex offenses. Why is it a problem to look at part of a woman with desire?

These cognitive therapists teach each man to observe himself as he is about to start ogling or to become sexually aroused at an inappropriate time—and to get himself to do something else. Is ogling really that serious a problem? Perhaps not for everybody; but neither does a single drink of whisky seem so serious for everybody. Yet for some people one drink brings an alcoholic binge. The disorder in both cases is one of lost self-control at an early point of arousal. The sexual offender must train himself to ask: Am I acting out something that might be unsafe?

It is dangerous for sex offenders to ogle because sex offenders are sometimes ineffective in reading and adapting to others' feedback, although most offenders are such accomplished manipulators that this hypothesis seems too simple.[22] Dialogue sexuality relies upon interacting over time, repeatedly checking for consent. Much assault and rape happens when dialogue is cut off. So, to prevent repeat sex offenses, these men must learn to curb some aspects of what, for some people, seems part of normal sexuality. Seen in these terms the dilemma of the sex offender is not entirely alien to the dilemma of any person who wishes to court some edge of exciting danger in sexual experience.

It is only the probability of this danger leading to criminal actions that separates the sex offender's problem from that of other oglers—or from the "normal" consumer of visual pornographies. Some critics suggest that "normal" sexuality is largely rape.[23] In this view, men are out to score as often as possible and are willing to be violent in pursuit of this goal. Women deny their own sexual urges at the same time as they learn to associate sexual thrills with violence. In such a world, pornography reflects the violence of normal sexual acts.

One of the sex offenders' therapists suggested to me a link between pornography and rape, a link that social scientists have explored. Sex offenders are usually consumers of pornography, and these cognitive therapists try to persuade each offender to give up pornography because it encourages fantasizing about inappropriate sex practices. One therapist suggested that I might find a connection between the talk in the therapy group and the text in a pornographic magazine that he handed me (it had been turned in by one of the clients). Here is a passage I found:

> Suddenly those old torrid images started to fill my head. Images of getting it on right then and there. Of being taken roughly in hand and ravaged someplace within earshot of the picnic.

I was startled out of my reverie when I felt a real hand grip my upper arm. When I turned, it was John, pulling me away from the crowd. I knew what was up—and delighted. Without a word, John guided me around to the back of the locker rooms, leaned me up against the wall, lifted my shirt up and mauled my . . .[24]

This female narrator is subject to a rush of desire. A real man knows when she wants him. When she enjoys sex, there is no consent-related interaction; rather, she is grabbed roughly (monologue). She knows what is up, and she is pleased at the combination of danger and unbridled desire. The language in this pornographic passage indicates rough lovemaking: She longs to "be taken roughly in hand and ravaged"; she is grabbed by the man and "mauled." The only thing that distinguishes this sexual encounter from criminal trespass is that the activity pleases the woman. Therefore this passage may be dangerous reading for a sex offender who craves sexual excitement and who distrusts, or habitually misreads, sex partners' dialogic feedback. We can see in this passage the persistent rape myth that certain women secretly crave borderline sexual assault.[25]

There are fortunes being made in pornographic magazines, videos, and 900 phone calls, and there are millions of supposedly civilized people, mostly men, who use pornographic publications and films as recreation. The story of pornography, like the story of sexual assault, is seldom told from the standpoint of the person who consumes pornography. One exception to this silence is Scott MacDonald's essay "Confessions of a Feminist Porn Watcher."[26] MacDonald describes his fears when he visits a porn arcade. He fears being seen, especially when entering or leaving. His visits conclude with an episode of masturbation and a guilty departure. The activity of the porn watcher is staring and masturbating done together, in solo simulation of interactive, socially performed arousal. These practices resemble some moments in interactive sexual performances—except there is no dialogue and no co-present partner. Masturbation to pornography is monologic, like sexual assault performed on a fictional partner. This does seem a dangerous rehearsal for a potential sex offender.

Pornography use, like ogling, is practiced as recreation by many so-called normal men. Pornography and ogling provide skill practice for each other. This association is graphic in a conversation between two college males:

[26] Field note

Joe: Hang on I gotta take a dump.

Ned: Hurry up, we're supposed to be there at four.

Joe: Dude, you got the serious library in here.

Ned: I know, check out the September issue.

Joe: This chick has the most perfect tits I've ever seen.

Ned: If I had a chick like that I would never leave the house.

Joe: Hell, I don't need the girl just give me the magazine; the magazine won't nag.

Ned: Tell me about it, Wendy (Ned's girlfriend) is always saying why don't you get rid of that stuff, it's disgusting.

Joe: What did you tell her?

Ned: I told her as long as I'm paying the bills I'll look at whatever I want. ◄

Joe: Dude you got a pretty cool girlfriend. My girlfriend would kick my ass if I brought that stuff home.

Ned: Get some balls, and hurry your ass up.

This encounter pairs Ned's interest in pornography with his interest in looking "at whatever I want." Ned claims that staring at actual women in public is a companion right to the consumption of visual pornography. Both of these rights are, in his view, supported by his earning power.

Feminist porn watcher Scott MacDonald dislikes men's street remarks, but admits that out in public: "I have to fight the urge to stare all the time." Does the consumption of visual pornography sharpen ogling skills? Do the practices of male masturbation with pornography provide practice for getting sexually aroused by women in public? How does this contribute to street remarks and to problems of sexual violence?

Some critics argue that our society supports two pornography industries, one for men and one for women.[27] Men's pornography is primarily sexually graphic pictures and films. Pornography for women takes the form of written romances. These are pornographic, it is argued, in their lack of detailed characterization and in picturing heroines for whom sexual arousal is instantaneous and overpowering. From this fictive female point of view the male appears menacing, hard, and brooding. Therefore the heroine masks her desire from the man until she can find out for sure that he loves her.

> She was being overwhelmed by sensations as she stood in the tiny cubicle on the side of the massive heavy cylinder. [A telescope!]. . . ."What do you see now, Julia?" His voice whispered just behind her neck as she kept her eye glued to the eyepiece for protection. She swallowed and tried hard to put some levity in her voice.[28]

The woman continues to look through the telescope, in part to keep from looking at the man, perhaps because her desire is so strong he will see it in her eyes. Does this passage encourage women to simultaneously covet and hide sexual arousal? Could such deception contribute to certain males' difficulties in gauging a woman's state of consent? Even civilized women are not immune from confusing sexual excitement with some element of danger.

[27] Field note (after making love)

Frank: Ahhh, that was wonderful honey, goodnight. (Kisses her)

Tina: Sweetheart, I don't mean to be rude, but (.) do we always have to have sex the *same* way?

Frank: What's wrong with the way we're doing it now?

Tina: Nothing. It's just monotonous, we kiss a little and gently caress, make love, and go to sleep.

Frank: What do you want me to do? Throw you down, chain you up and rape you over and over again?

Tina: Well . . .

When Tina complains that she finds their couple sexuality monotonous, Frank applies a stereotypical violent image to the problem. This violent stereotype is available to these consenting lovers, even though their sexual performance together has been predictable and gentle. There may be irony in Frank's extreme case formulation: "Throw you down, chain you up, and rape you." However, the woman does not reject this grisly alternative. The field worker connects this instance with her reading of a romance novel when she was in the fifth grade:

> I read it in private fearing my mother would discover me. I remember my heart quickening upon reading the so-called steamy parts. I remember when I started having sex that I wanted to feel as I did reading that book. Funny thing was that I wanted to make love sweetly and gently my first time yet once I got past the first encounter I wanted things to heat up and resemble what I had come to idealize in the romance novels, which was succumbing to the overpowering man that you hated and loved with a wantonness you never dreamed you possessed. Thus, rape from someone you loved becomes passionate lovemaking and therefore acceptable.

Tina desires, at least some of the time and within the safe frame of a stable relationship, to be treated so roughly as to imitate rape. Her professed ideal includes mixing in some fear of or hatred for her mate. Tina traces this desire to her youthful experience of romance novels.

· · ·

The event we call rape has long occupied part of the soil in which the plant of humanity has grown. So in trying to stop rapes and to allow only consenting sex, we are trying to change deeply embedded human experience. Furthermore, we are trying to change only the parts where we see overt harm attached to particular acts (e.g., rape, teen pregnancy). Meanwhile, most of us cherish the hope of achieving sexual satisfaction or even ecstasy within the framework of loving, but still slightly dangerous, relationships.

Today we throw about these issue-words: "assault," "battering," "abuse," "harassment," "rape." Each word finds its elastic terminology and its emphasis on criminalization. Criminalizing social engineering has been largely a failure in deterring crime.[29] Let us therefore not confine the discussion of harassment or of rape to a determination of which embodied enactments to punish as criminal. Let us instead discover connections between these interactive experiences and the rest of life.

If consent may be conceptualized as ongoing and not finalized at any moment, then a sexual encounter may have many consent-relevant turning points. If sexual candidates can learn not to press their attentions past indications of nonconsent, we might make progress against sexual violence.

One partial model for discourse-in-sexual performance is provided by Mara Adelman's writing on safe sex.[30] Adelman argues that the term "safe sex" is an oxymoron. Sexuality is always risky, and never interpersonally safe—even when contraception allows damage control. Adelman aims to persuade sexual partners to use condoms. She has pursued this aim, in part, by producing video role-played simulations of sexual consent that are notable for dialogue qualities:

[28] Improvisation[31]

Woman: What are you thinking about
           (Man shifts to teasing register)
Man: That you wanna make love.
Woman: Hummm. (Nods agreement)
Man: I just don't know if I (.) if I wanna go along ' ' you think. I just (.) you always put me in this position.
           (Woman laughs at his joke)
Man: You force me and I just (.) you put a lot of pressure on me to decide Emily.
           (Pause)
Man: Okay! (Woman laughs)
Man: Oh, alright, I will, I mean, you know
           (Man laughs, Woman twists his arm)
Man: Okay, twist it (.) alright, okay, I'll make love to you. I will (.) only, only this 1 year.
           (Woman laughs)
Man: Okay.
Woman: Then I'll see you next year at this time too?
Man: Perhaps, yeah, yeah. Do You?
           (Pause)
Woman: Um huh
Man: (Mumbles) Yeah, me too.
Woman: Yeah, Mmmmmmmmmm.

Man: Mmmmmmmmmm. Well (.) good! It's settled.

(They both move toward bedroom and then pause. Man hums the theme song from the film *Jaws* and pulls out a condom. Woman responds by screaming in a joking manner, sustaining the play on *Jaws*. They both laugh.)

In several ways this example models dialogic sexual consent:

- The speakers take short turns.
- The speakers check with each other at each consent-relevant moment.
- The speakers take only multiple consent, late consent, or very explicit consent as sufficient sexual intimacy—or a contraception decision.
- Consent at one moment does not guarantee consent later on.
- The speakers remain joyful and playful.
- The speakers avoid even the appearance of violence, coercion, or loss of control.

There may be no better advice for possible consenting partners than to imitate dialogic play. If you are sexually active, consider your most recent occasion of sexual performance in this light. If you plan to be sexually active in the future, consider sharing this list of dialogue characteristics with your partner as part of the process. Can we put ourselves playfully in dialogue during the interactive making of intimate consent?

5

···

Coupling as
Progressive Commitment

···

RELATIONSHIPS CAN IN SOME WAYS BE DANGEROUS, AND BECOMING A COUPLE can entail risks. Among the fairly reasonable things to fear are rape, other physical injury, venereal and other infectious diseases, the humiliation of unrequited affection, unwanted pregnancy, seduction and desertion with the attendant pain and grief, and simply making the most colossal mistake of one's life.

Science writer Melvin Konner lists some risks of becoming a member of a couple.[1] Interaction patterns during couple formation are fraught with dangers. The rules are new, the stakes seem high. The world has gone topsy-turvy. One's time is less one's own, for new coupling sucks up spare time. How long since one has seen old friends?

A new couple enters a communicative wonderland, a microculture of two persons absorbed in each other who spend much time together, grow jealous of each other, and experience growth of something mysterious: a relationship with a life of its own. A couple develops a mini-culture that grants its members special access to one another.

Most of this relationship-building is done in talk. Couple members find themselves in unfamiliar communicative terrain, performing unfamiliar social interaction at the same time as they are learning how to do it. Couple members are confused. In spite of this confusion, perhaps in part because of it, couple members mistakenly believe that they communicate quite well with one another. Novelist Laurence Durrell writes:

> Around this event, dazed and preoccupied, the lover moves examining his or her own experience; her gratitude alone, stretching away towards a mistaken donor, creates the illusion that she communicates with her fellow, but this is false. The loved object is simply one that has shared an experience at the same moment of time, narcissistically. . . .[2]

This coupling relationship is different from other friendships. It starts differently, as described in chapter 3. As couplehood forms, intense, emotion-laden experiences are focused on this two-person social unit: a couple culture with emerging traditions, memories, and rituals.[3]

Couple partners interact through a series of relational turning points to develop progressive commitment in the relationship. The interaction through which this happens seems systematically distorted by noncoupling standards, leading to overestimates of similarity between the partners. This chapter describes an anthology of turning points in the early course of coupling: allowing commitment to begin, saying "I love you," going–into public, and breaking up. Each of these moments shows couple-formation dominated by a general expectation that partners will continue to increase their accessibility to one another and their stakes in the success of the relationship. Sociologist Willard Waller describes systematically biased interaction within progressive commitment:

> [E]ach person, by a pretense of great involvement, invites the other to rapid sentiment-formation—each encourages the other to fall in love by pretending that he has already done so. If either rises to the bait, a special type of interaction ensues . . . a series of periodic crises which successively redefine the relationship on deeper levels of involvement. . . .
>
> Such affairs, in contrast to "dating," have a marked directional trend; they may be arrested on any level, or they may be broken off at any point, but they may not ordinarily be turned back to a lesser degree of involvement.[4]

Waller indicates that the processes of communication in courtship are:

- Progressive: In contrast with friendships, in which commitment may vacillate, the couple members expect commitment to increase with time. If progressive commitment is not maintained, couple members complain that the relationship is not going anywhere.

- Irreversible: When progressive commitment cannot be maintained, couples break up, rather than decreasing commitment levels.

Early coupling is often based on selective perception of selective self-presentation:

> A idealizes B and presents to her that side of his personality which is consistent with his idealized conception of her; B idealizes A and governs her behavior toward him in accordance with her false notions of his nature; the process of idealization is mutually re-enforced in such a way that it must necessarily lead to an increasing divorce from reality.[5]

Did you ever have a friend who fell in love with some jerk, yet seemed blind to the shortcomings of the loved one? Later on, a former couple member may note that the loved one had been a jerk. But while progressive commitment grows, such a thing is hard to see. Partners distort their self-presentations to please one another.

Disney's film *Beauty and the Beast* exemplifies communicative distortion during progressive commitment. As their unlikely pair-bond begins to form, the pretty young woman and the hairy ogre are pictured eating soup. He is slurping boorishly when he looks up at Belle and sees her shocked expression. Immediately, he sets down his bowl and does his clumsy best to use a spoon. After he shows this accommodation, Belle lifts her soup bowl to her lips and slurps loudly. Each imitates the other's habits as a way of celebrating similarities.

Consider this thought experiment: Suppose that you grow attracted to somebody you see several times per week. There is one style contrast between the two of you: a difference in formality of dress. You frequently dress up, but this other person is habitually informal. Here is the situation: You are RIGHT NOW making a decision about what you will wear today—a day when you will see this person. Might you dress down a bit today?

Now, consider the other person in this fantasy. Might that person dress up just a bit this same day? Consequentially both you and the other person present a false front to one another. You might even underestimate the amount that your dress styles differ. Thirty years ago I performed a survey of dating couples on a university campus. I asked each person to make agree-disagree ratings of controversial issues of the day—for example, "God is dead," "All wars are immoral." Then I asked each couple member to guess their partner's view on these issues. Partners consistently underestimated their degree of disagreement.

Interaction distortions in early courtship lend the development of romantic attachment an episodic quality, organized around turning points in progressive commitment. One series of studies asked college students to make a month-by-month graph of commitment in a couple relationship.[6] Then these people described communication events associated with upturns or downturns on the graph. A number of these events were things that happened for the first time: first date, first kiss, saying "I love you," introductions to family, or moving in together. Some of these events were chance circumstances that had relational consequences: dealing with a rival or enduring a separation. Few turning points were accomplished by talking specifically about the state of the relationship, which seems to be a taboo topic among college couple members. Some turning points reportedly occurred when one partner engineered secret tests about the relationship[7]:

[1] Baxter and Wilmot
I intentionally introduced him as my boyfriend to my best friend who came to visit and then watched how he reacted at the time and later—you know, did he seem embarrassed? Did he act upset later that I had made "us" public?

[1a]
He wants us to get married, but I don't yet. So to see if I still feel the same about it, he will joke around and say things like "Figured out yet what we'll do with the .5 child in our family of 2.5 children?" If I joke about it, he knows that I'm not ready to talk seriously about marriage yet, but also that I'm not pissed off that he keeps pushing me.

These studies point us toward the talk that accomplishes progressive commitment. Such talk is implicit, laden with hints, and rarely is the topic of the relationship specifically addressed.[8]

In the 1950s film *An Affair to Remember*, Deborah Kerr and Cary Grant meet on shipboard. They flirt, yet deny their involvement (since each is already engaged to a person not on the ship). At a stop on the trip she goes with him to visit his grandmother, and this event sparks a relational turning point. That evening, back on the ship, they kiss. We see only the bottom half of their bodies, and the kiss begins as her left hand draws his up a stair. As their bodies move together her right hand remains on the stair-rail till halfway through the kiss, when it first moves slightly to caress the rail, then rises to exit the top of the screen, apparently to enfold his body. The kiss ended, they walk down the stair, and she almost stumbles (did the boat move, or is this love?). Then they say to each other:

[2] Film: *An Affair to Remember*[9]

Terry:	We're sailing into rough seas, Nikkie.
Nikkie:	Kind of, we changed our course today.
Terry:	Mm hm?
Nikkie:	Shall I see you to your cabin?

These people are falling in love, but they do not say to one another anything like "I love you." Rather, they speak in allusive terms that allow their relationship to hover just outside explicit discussion. She introduces a nautical trope suited to their place on a ship: "We're sailing into rough seas." Nikkie responds within the metaphor: "We changed our course today." Both of these utterances denote turning points in a voyage and also turning points in relationships. These two nautical utterances signal agreement that things have changed, yet the partners will not now speak explicitly of the relationship— beyond use of the term "we." Nikkie immediately shows his perception of the relevance of this couple turning point by asking if he may escort Terry to her cabin.

Partners may avoid verbal explicitness by enacting commitment bodily. One way to do this is by kissing. Both Hollywood kissing and everyday courtship kissing can be considered as monologue (A kisses B) or as dialogue (A and B kiss each other). One scholarly description of "rounds" of kissing shows emergent dialogic form. For instance, if the man leans toward the woman in a possible pre-kiss way, and she smiles with her mouth open, the male does not follow through to kiss. However, if her mouth is closed and smiling . . . well, take a look at an abandoned kiss attempt in *An Affair to Remember* that occurs just half a minute before the movie kiss described earlier. He leans toward her, she smiles, and opens her mouth, and he stops moving toward her, even before she says "Let's walk." Such micro-dialogue in kissing shows egalitarian relational practice. Slow movement with careful reading of the other's motives increases opportunities to play with consent and to undertake only those kisses in which alignment can be ratified.

I LOVE YOU

Some dialogic features of progressive commitment can be observed in one crucial turning point in coupling: the first time new partners say "I love you" (hereafter ILY). ILY is an utterance designed to occur in pairs: ILY-ILY. ILY is like greeting (hi-hi) in that way. This pair nature of ILY shows in stable couples' telephone closings, just before goodbye.

[3] UTCL D10:2

Mark:	Everything alright?
Lillian:	Yeah.
Mark:	Ok, you sure,
Lillian:	Yeah.
Mark:	Uhmm.
Lillian:	Alright.
Mark:	I love you. ◄
Lillian:	I love you too. ◄
Mark:	Bye.
Lillian:	Bye.

This pair of ILY utterances is the very last thing before "Bye" at the end of a phone call. This utterance pair goes right together, and the second ILY adds the word "too" to show that is it the second of a series. If there is a hitch in this event the couple members may find this discomfiting.

[4] UTCL D19:2

Peg: Alright, well then I'll be here whenever you're ready (0.4) to go, so- and if anything changes, please give me a call.
Rod: I will
          (0.2)
Peg: Okay.
Rod: Okay
          (1.3)
          Buh bye
          (.)
          Love you ◄
Peg: Love you too, bye
Rod: Bye

This couple has a bit of trouble finding the slot for the ILY pair. Rod may expect Peg to volunteer ILY after his "Okay." But instead there is a silence, so Rod says "Buh bye," offering to end the call. Peg does not answer, however, so Rod quickly adds ILY, which is promptly answered.

If one of the ILY parts is missing, you can hear it missing. In one call a man complains to his fiancé that he has been unproductive at his job in a clothing store. At the end of the call she chooses an awkward moment to encourage him to sell well.

[5] UTCL D10:4

Mark: Alright
Lillian: Alright
Mark: I love you
Lillian: Sell a lot at work ◄
Mark: Huh?

Mark's "Huh" shows failure to comprehend—and this repair initiation is uttered when the expected second part of the ILY pair turns up missing.

These examples show the expectation that after a first ILY anything except a second (immediate) ILY is not anticipated. If someone says ILY and you say anything but ILY too, that something else is a marked event.[10] In one couple phone call she says

[6] UTCL D19
Peg: Do you love me?
Rod: Ye(h)s
Peg: You can't tell me though because your friends are in the room

After Peg explicitly asks for an ILY statement and Rod answers with a chuckling yes, she shows that she hears the absence of a second ILY. Peg suggests an account for that utterance's absence.

These ILY pairs and misfires each have occurred within a stable couple relationship. Yet how do couples exchange ILY utterances for the first time? In fiction, a first ILY appears swathed in mitigations, perhaps to prepare a retreat in case the other does not reciprocate.

[7] Fiction: *A Farewell to Arms*[11]
Catherine: You're sweet. You do love me, don't you?
Frederick: Don't say that again. You don't know what that does to me.
Catherine: I'll be careful then.

Catherine carefully mitigates a bid for ILY, tying it onto a compliment, and asking it as a question. She does not herself say ILY, but her willingness to do so shows in the way she puts the question. Frederick responds with meta-talk opposing the exchange of this commitment sign. Catherine, who knows how to handle a Hemingway hero, promises to "be careful" about forcing him into such talk.

The Flannery O'Connor story "Good Country People" exemplifies a combination of mitigation and prompting that may go into a declaration of love. The partners are kissing in a hayloft. He suddenly pulls away from their embrace and this dialogue ensues:

[8] Fiction: "Good Country People"[12]

Pointer: You ain't said you loved me none. You got to say that.
             (she looks outside)
             You got to say that. You got to say you love me.

Hulga: In a sense, if you use the word loosely, you might say that. But
             it's not a word I use. I don't have illusions. I'm one of those peo-
             ple who see through to nuthin.

Pointer: (frowning) You got to say it. I said it and you got to say it.

Hulga: You poor baby, it's just as well you don't understand. We are all
             damned, but some of us have taken off our blindfolds and see
             that there's nothing to see. It's a kind of salvation.

Pointer: Okay, but do you love me or don'tcher?

Hulga: Yes, in a sense. But I must tell you something. There mustn't be
             anything dishonest between us. I am thirty years old. I have a
             number of degrees.

Pointer: I don't care a thing about what all you done. I just want to
             know if you love me or don'tcher?
             (kisses her)

Hulga: Yes, yes.

Pointer: Okay then, prove it.

Pointer repeatedly pesters Hulga to say ILY, although he has not said ILY himself. Hulga mitigates and delays her response by disclosing cynical views and
academic accomplishments. He continues to pester until she agrees, but the
declarative phrase "I love you" does not actually occur.

To summarize: A first ILY pair engineers a commitment turning point
that includes:

- Mitigation in the production of the first ILY.
- Delay between the first and second ILY
- Pursuit from the initiating party. If the pair does not achieve the second ILY, this is taken to signify some important breach in the course of
  progressive commitment. A relational crisis ensues.
- If the second ILY is achieved, then something quite definite happens
  almost immediately to ratify and exploit the new commitment: In

"Good Country People," "prove it"; in *An Affair to Remember* an offer to see Terry to her cabin.

There is dialogic wisdom in these practices. The ILY turning point unfolds over the course of an encounter, leaving each partner chances to align with change. Maximum dialogue but minimal explicitness.

TIE SIGNS: BECOMING A PUBLIC COUPLE

As the internal couple culture develops through various private turning points, there are also many moments of coming–into public view. This may happen through somewhat dramatic turning points, as in this instance cited earlier in the current chapter:

[1] Baxter and Wilmot
I intentionally introduced him as my boyfriend to my best friend who came to visit and then watched how he reacted at the time and later—you know, did he seem embarrassed? Did he act upset later that I had made "us" public?

In this instance, one couple member takes a bold step, using the term "boyfriend" in introductions. This could signal a turning point in a relationship, a dramatic event that informs the man and a number of others at the same time that a coupling unit is in progress.

In many coupling relationships, however, coupleness becomes public over a variety of small events and gestures that are sometimes called "tie signs."[13] Tie signs are communication acts that give the appearance of being in public as a couple: holding hands in a public place or being seen together frequently. Some tie signs may be observable when one partner in a couple is with other people: for instance, talking incessantly of the other to your friends or showing around a picture of the other. Here is an example that appeared in another context in chapter 2.

[9] Field note (female best friends)
Kit: I'm worried that he hasn't called.

Sue:	It's only been two days.
Kit:	I know, but I want him to call me.
Sue:	He's probably freaking out
Kit:	Maybe. If nothing else, at least I got some.

Consider the tie signs that Kit gives off in this encounter. First, she indicates to Sue her consciousness that they have discussed this man before. In bringing up the man again (after only two days) Kit is showing a preoccupation with this man and the possibility that she might be interested in entering into a serious couple relationship. Also, Kit confesses sexual intimacy with this man.

Here is an example used earlier in the current chapter to exemplify how couple members say "I love you." We can now name the problem that the man faces in front of his work colleagues: To say ILY in front of them is not only a statement to his couple-mate but a public tie sign. Here is a longer fragment of that instance:

[6] UTCL D19, revisited

Rod:	Bye: Honey:
Peg:	Uhh-
Rod:	Have a good day
Peg:	Okay
Rod:	Alright
	(0.5)
Peg:	Do you love me?
Rod:	Ye(h)s
Peg:	You can't tell me though because your friends are in the room=
Rod:	=No I can say- Peggy, I love you
Peg:	Uh huh huh huh huh huh hhhhhhhhhhh
Rod:	See? Isn't that wo- Isn't that neat how it works?
Peg:	That's ne::at. Well I love you too,
Rod:	Bye.
Peg:	Bye.

In the first line of this fragment, Rod produces a tie sign of his relationship with the term of address "Honey." Peg's response, "uhh," may indicate that perhaps Rod is being abrupt, in spite of the nice term of address. So they start a more leisurely exit from the call, including Peg's prompt that pre-goodbye is a good place for an exchange of ILY. Rod gives a somewhat downgraded affirmation ("Yes" instead of return ILY). Then Peg guesses that the display of ILY as a public tie sign might not be appropriate at this moment, since Rod is at work and his friends are present. Rod responds with a public, self-conscious, and explicit tie sign. Peg reacts gushingly, and the two congratulate each other on their public display of affection.

Seen in light of these examples, a number of events that have appeared at other places in this book could be reconsidered in terms of the notion of tie signs. It seems to be a mark of the importance of courtship partnering that the line between the private relationship and the public one is continually at play. We can show this by reconsidering an instance used in chapter 3 to illustrate the beginning of a flirting episode.

[10] UTCL D8.2 You queer

Rick: Ye::ss? heh heh heh
Cara: Rick?
Rick: Ye(h)es?
Cara: You quee:r w(h)at're you doin
            (0.4)
Rick: U:h I dunno what're you doin you queer bait

The playful innuendo in this start of a conversation communicates something between the parties themselves, but it also serves as a tie sign to anyone who might be observing the encounter. Since the longer phone call of which this is part began between two others who finished off their business and then each handed the phone to a roommate, one may assume that there is an observer of this opening on either end of the line. Therefore, it may be worth considering what this telephone opening gives off to observers, as well as to the participants in the incipient flirtation. At the very least, these people are performing a certain openness to flirtation in front of their friends—and not only to one another.

Of course, such overhearers' analyses, by the bystanders at the moment, or by me, are quite fallible. Tie signs are inherently ambiguous, if only because they are often things that couple members do for each other somewhat unself-consciously, which happen to give off information to alert others. Still, we are used to relying on such judgments, albeit sometimes with comic consequences. Conversation analyst Jenny Mandelbaum tells a story about a couple

> . . . who were new in town, and accepted an informal invitation from a "friend of a friend" to attend a New Year's Eve party. The members of the couple were independent at the party, and interacted separately with other guests, meeting occasionally to "compare notes." During these occasional meetings they encountered significant difficulty in agreeing on who at the party was "with" whom: One would refer to "Joe, the big dark guy, who was with the blond woman," and the other would disagree, claiming that Joe was with a dark-haired woman. They subsequently discovered that they were both right: the event turned out to be a "mate-swapping" party.[14]

Though we can sometimes make accurate judgments about the couple-ties of strangers, we often have the advantage of some point of comparison. Tie signs are interpreted comparatively, inside the couple and out. For instance, the first time that the partner takes your hand or says "I love you," the comparison with previous signs of affection is what makes the new sign communicative.

External observers of a relationship may compare the deportment of a couple now with that of last month, or with the way people normally act in similar circumstances. If there is a subtle difference, this may trigger some new realization about the relationship. A personal example: I was with my daughter at a local sandwich shop when two acquaintances (who worked together but were each married to somebody else) entered the store to order lunch. They greeted us cheerfully, but then as we visited I noticed "something"—the only triggering tie sign I can recall is that the woman's blouse was unbuttoned one button further than was her usual style of dress. As they left the store, I guessed that they were having an affair. Subsequently they married each other.

A similar example occurs in Henry James's *The Portrait of a Lady*.[15] Isabel Archer arrives in the parlor, where her husband and a long-term woman friend are waiting, but she sees them a moment before they notice her entrance.

> Madame Merle was standing on the rug, a little way from the fire; Osmond was in a deep chair, leaning back and looking at her. Her head was erect, as usual, but her eyes were bent on his. What struck Isabel first was that he was sitting while Madame Merle stood; there was an anomaly in this that arrested her. Then she perceived that they had arrived at a desultory pause in their exchange of ideas and were musing, face to face, with the freedom of old friends who some-times exchange ideas without uttering them. There was nothing to shock in this; they were old friends in fact. But the thing made an image, lasting only a moment, like a sudden flicker of light. Their relative positions, their absorbed mutual gaze, struck her as something detected. But it was all over by the time she had fairly seen it.

Isabel first makes a comparative observation. It is unusual in that social setting for a man to sit in the presence of a standing lady. This "anomaly" strikes her forcefully, then she makes further confirming observations: Something relational is going on here, Osmond and Madame Merle give off tie signs of some intimacy.

Tie signs are observable and have consequences. Sometimes these can be quite dramatic and lead to realizations of turning points. Yet more common, and just as important to couple development, are tie signs that occur in more comfortable surroundings. One such comfortable surrounding is a couples gathering. It is especially commonplace for two or three couples to get together to eat, chat, or play a game. The very willingness of a couple to appear in such gatherings constitutes a turning point of sorts in the history of a pairing. In these settings, there are safe, comfortable opportunities to act like members of a couple. One form of tie sign in such scenes is the telling of a shared story:

[11] CD: Mandelbaum, simplified[16]

Shawn:	I was goin cra:zy today, on the- on the road.
	(0.4)
Vicki:	Well you know what he di:d?

Shawn:	Went outa my #@*# mi:nd.
Vicki:	He m(h)ade a right- It was in Santa Monica you know ha:ve- they ha:ve [all those bright
Shawn:	[Oh: @#*#
Shawn:	I made a left- left.
Vicki:	They ha:ve (.) one- way stree::ts and everythi::ng? (0.4) and then two-way streets? He ma:de- a left turn from a one-way street. (0.8) into a two-way street, (0.5) but he thought it was, he thought it was a one-way street.

Consider the detailed ensemble quality in this story, told jointly by Shawn and Vicki to their couple-friends Matthew and Nina during an informal supper at an apartment coffee table. It is a story about something embarrassing and potentially dangerous that had happened that day. The very telling of this story indicates that Shawn and Vicki had been spending some time driving around together that day. This being reported so routinely is a tie sign. Yet even more remarkable are the little signs of close-order teamwork in the story itself.

First, Shawn and Vicki team up to provide a preface for the story. Shawn makes a general statement that he was going crazy today on the road. Vicki picks up on a crazy thing that she remembers from being on the road with Shawn, and she attempts to stimulate interest in the upcoming story with the question: "Do you know what he did?" Shawn continues with strong language indicating his mental state, and then Vicki starts the actual story about the wrong turn. She begins to set the scene for the tale, and Shawn continues to act out his agitated mental state. It's as if Vicki is giving the journalistic narrative and Shawn is providing the emotional coloring with sound effects for the story. Meanwhile, Shawn corrects a detail: It was a left turn, not a right turn. Vicki seamlessly corrects this error as she spins out the narrative. The result is a shared telling of a shared experience. It creates the impression that they enacted this event together, perceived it as one, and report as one: a couple.

Telling a story together is a less dramatic turning point than the first time one holds hands or says "I love you." Yet such shared tellings and other subtle tie signs are the communicative bricks and mortar in the building of a long-term coupling.

BREAKING UP

Progressive commitment puts pressure on a relationship. In most courtships commitment cannot increase forever—especially when it is based on over-statements of common interests and styles. An example occurs in the film *Say Anything*. He and she are driving:

[12] Film: *Say Anything*[17]

He: I feel I'm gonna tell you something I I- tryin to say it, but don't want to say it, I know what you're gonna say before I say it I want to mean it. I mean it.

          (1)

He: I know you'e-

She: No, you don't have to say it

He: How do you know what I'm gonna say

She: I don't.

He: I want to say I love you ◄

          (2)

He: That's it

She: I know

          (4)

She: Lloyd, let's not start committing on this level?

He: But this is a good level.

          (2)

He: Huh?

          (4)

She: How can I let you say this

          (1.5)

He: Say what

          (5)

She: I think that we should spend some time apart

An unsuccessful proposal to escalate commitment can damage a relationship. That is one explanation for the mitigation in the first ILY. After the first (much mitigated) ILY appears, the negative response is also delayed and mitigated. She answers "I know" to acknowledge the declaration without returning it.

Finally she offers the mitigated opinion that a relational crisis has occurred: "I think we should spend some time apart."

The most ordinary resolution to courtships is a sudden termination, also known as a breakup. Breakups, like most relational turning points, are largely negotiated through talk, sometimes over a set of events. Relationship researcher Leslie Baxter offers a six-stage model of breaking up: Onset of relationship problems, the decision to exit the relationship, initiating unilateral dissolution actions, the initial reaction of the broken-up-with party, ambivalence and repair scenarios, and initiating bilateral dissolution action.[18]

A couple termination encounter (like a first flirting) can proceed by creating a disturbance, a crisis, to signal that something marked and dangerous is happening. During fictional breakup episodes the strong and usually offensive meta-talk phrase "What do you mean" appears.[19] In the play *Betrayal,* Emma and Jerry use meta-talk to pick a fight in their last scene as lovers.

[13] Fiction: *Betrayal*[20]

Jerry: I might remind you that your husband is my oldest friend.

Emma: What do you mean by that?

Jerry: I don't mean anything by it.

Emma: But what are you trying to say by saying that

Jerry: Jesus, I'm not trying to say anything.

Every utterance in this exchange is rich in metacommunication. Jerry's first utterance begins with "I might remind you that," framing a statement that could sound offensive (e.g., we have been cheating on your husband, and this hurts my friendship as well as your marriage.) Emma, who is, after all, cheating on her spouse, responds with "What do you mean by that?" challenging Jerry's claim to emotional priority on her husband. Jerry denies any deep meaning, yet Emma presses her case. Jerry's further denial is upgraded by profanity. This rough exchange creates sufficient anger to blast the couple members out of relational orbit. Here is a similar fictional example:

[14] Fiction: *Otherwise Engaged*[21]

Simon: I'd just imagined that when you did have an affair it would be with someone of more more-

Beth: What.

Simon:	Consequence overt consequence.
Beth:	He's of consequence to me.
Simon:	And that's what matters, quite.
Beth:	What did you mean, when? ◄meta-talk
Simon:	Hmmm?
Beth:	When I had an affair, you said.
Simon:	A grammatical slip, that's all, and since the hypothesis is now a fact-
Beth:	But you used the emphatic form- when I did have an affair- which implies that you positively assumed I'd have an affair. Didn't you?

Beth asks Simon (at ←meta-talk) to specify the meaning of an utterance made four turns earlier (at the beginning of this fragment). This is quite late to ask for such clarification, and Simon at first does not understand the reference. But Beth repeats the location of the offending word, "when," this time emphasizing its pronunciation. Simon's next response begins metalinguistically ("a grammatical slip") and then turns ironic (". . . now a fact."). Beth continues her grammar-based critique ("you used the emphatic form") to imply that Simon never had much faith in her. This exchange reveals partners spoiling for a confrontation and making up communicative excuses to argue.

In the following recording from a real-life breakup, similarly placed meta-talk is evident, and its placement leads to explosive consequences.

[15] UTCL D1

Sid:	I got closer t'you than I ever have t'anybody in my life.
	(2)
Alice:	I know, I think it's somethin (4) you kno:w when you always go through the comparing (2) sta:ge where (3) I don' know you just- (1)
Sid:	Comparing things you do: like smokin and drinkin
	Is that what you mean. Is that what you mean ◄meta-talk
Alice:	No? I'm saying and you hate tha:t. I know- it that's not I'm not trying to start- I'm just a-

Sid:	What are you saying I thought that's what you were sayin. ◄
Alice:	What I'm sa:ying is where y- (0.4) you start- I always find myself comparing you to other people.
	(1)
	And that's just a ha- it just somethin that your c- that I'll guess I'll do:.
	(0.3)
Sid:	What you mean. Like other guys? ◄
	(0.4)
Alice:	Yeah, I mean- I hadn been out. But- you know, mean it's jus sum'n that you do.
	(1)
Sid:	What are you sayin ◄

Sid repeatedly uses "what do you mean" to request clarification of the sense of Alice's remarks about comparing him with other guys, and this repeatedly erupts into emotional crises as understandings are checked and ruffled feelings rise. These partners subsequently note what they have illustrated—that they fight too much to stay together.

In the next instance, a dating couple shows their decision making during the actual breakup moment. These partners combine mitigating particles and meta-talk to mark the special transition that is being proposed and ratified.

[16] UTCL A32:4

Gordon:	We:ll. I got your card.
	(0.2)
Denise:	Yeah. hhhh
Gordon:	A::nd (sniff) I guess you probably read me right. It probably is what we're on. ◄meta-talk
	(0.5)
Denise:	Hang on just a second okay I'm a switch phone
Gordon:	Okay
	(long pause)
Denise:	Okay.

Gordon: I- actually w'd rather talk to you in person but I don't think I'm
            gonna be able make a meeting cause I- now have a headache
            and- fever and everything
Denise: Yeah hh
Gordon: hhhhhhh Bu:t u:m hh I think maybe I w- um would like to- stop
            really goin out, at least for right now.

The problematic nature of this phone call is raised as Gordon mentions he got a card from Denise. He does not describe the card, but his mention of it leads Denise to ask that he hold on while she switches phones.

The utterances through which this breakup is announced are multiply mitigated. Gordon's turn-beginning, "but um," seems to stall, marking what comes afterward as potentially troublesome. Next come two softening qualifiers ("I think maybe"), followed by more dysfluent delay. The utterance ends up with two more qualifiers "at least" and "for right now," which suggest the breakup could be temporary. This utterance shows how mitigating may be stacked within an utterance to create a climate of delicate softened action for which a party wishes to minimize responsibility.[22]

Turning points in the course of progressive commitment are constructed through communicative interaction. We have exemplified such interaction in descriptions of '"I love you," of the displaying of tie signs, and of breaking up. In each of these segments of coupling interaction we find systematic distortion more often than careful truthfulness. Courters begin by exaggerating similarities to each other, orienting to achieving commitment.

As couple members—those who do not break up—move along the course of progressive commitment to become members of stable long-term couples, they take increased note of individual differences between couple members. This increasing "appreciation" of difference arises as a product of the continuing duration of the relationship, as we shall see.

6

....

Coupling as a
Difference Engine

....

A TALE OF DIFFERENCE: I'M ON THE POT, PREPARING FOR A BATH. AS I GET OUT A
new roll of tissue, a little box drops on the floor. It is hotel soap. My bath
soap is almost gone, so I unwrap the soap and put it on the bathtub soap
tray. A moment later Kay shambles in and we have this exchange:

[1] Field Note

Kay: Oh you got out another soap.

Rob: Yes the other one was almost gone.

Kay: You didn't like the one I got out.

            (There is another soap on the edge of the tub. I had
            not noticed this soap.)

Rob: Well, I almost never use your big schlocky soaps.

In this brief dialogue, Kay and I have discovered and sketched out a little difference between us as members of a couple: We pursue differing tastes in
soap. Kay and I may sometimes each have a soap going and a different shampoo. We keep things in slightly different places, since she's a shower person
and I'm a tub person. I enjoy sandalwood soaps and scented shampoo; her
shampoos are organic and scent-free. My soaps may be smaller than the
Camay bars that Kay buys.

However, until this morning I'd never made a distinction about any of
this. It was only when she startled me with the notice that I got out a new
soap (which I'd done sort of by accident) and when she asked if I didn't like
her soap (which I hadn't noticed was there and might otherwise have used)

that I responded as I did. By the time I said that I didn't like her soap, I had constructed her sequence of two "statement questions" into some possible pre-reproach. All these circumstances led to my abrupt reply, in which I called her soap choice big and schlocky and stated that I "almost never" shared soap with her.

My remark about her soap being big and schlocky was the last word before Kay left the room. In this utterance I created a historical document of a difference between us, a little icon in our relational culture. Finding difference is an interactive staple in a couple relationship. Sometimes, as in this story, the partners' differences seem comic. Sometimes, as in Matisse's painting *The Conversation*, these differences between couple members come to seem more cosmic.

This interactive creation of differences between members of a couple may come about partly in reaction to the interactive construction of similarities during the early phases of progressive commitment. As couples stick together, partners share many routine yet relationship-defining moments. Partners evolve from a biased belief in their similarity toward believing that they are quite different from one another. There is something about couple interaction that serves as a difference-creating engine.[1]

To exemplify how members of a couple make perceptions of interpersonal difference, consider these two university students who consider themselves a couple and who are making a meal to share. They discuss studying for a test.

[2] Corbin DP2

Tim: My room's absolutely spotless
Ann: Why
Tim: Cause I have a test tomorrow
              (1.6)
Ann: Heh heh heh, See I'm not like that I don't do that thing, that
            clean the house- clean the room thing ◀

Tim makes a joke to his partner. The point of the joke is that he has put off studying by cleaning his room. Ann laughs at his joke, then uses it to state a perceived contrast between their personalities: "I'm not like that." You study for tests in a certain way that differs from mine. During the next few seconds this discovered contrast between study styles is documented as a personality difference.

[3] Corbin DP2

Ann: Well anyway so- u:h you haven't studied at all

(1)

Tim: No

Ann: Okay well here's the plan. (1) We're going to do chapter eight, and chapter ni:ne tonight

The difference articulated earlier is played out here. Ann outlines a study plan for the evening, indicating that she is a person who makes a list and does what is on the list. Tim and Ann go on record as having different study habits. Any daily activities can provide grounds for such contrasts.

[4] Field note

Lisa: Oh shoot my car is in a no parking zone and I'll get a ticket after 7:30 in the morning. Oh well, I'll just get up a little early and move it.

Ben: But you should move it now.

Lisa: But I can move it in the morning.

Ben: What if you oversleep and get a ticket?

Lisa: I won't oversleep

Ben: Yeah, I've heard that before. I'll wake you up so you won't get a ticket, but you should move it tonight and get it over with.

Lisa and Ben, engaged to be married, discuss a classic problem: Do a job now or put it off. Lisa decides to put it off, though Ben suggests she should move the car now. When Lisa predicts that she will not oversleep, Ben claims to have "heard that before," and offers to prompt Lisa in the morning. Ben takes the role of a person who gets things done now instead of putting things off and taking a chance.

Couple members almost inevitably contrast their dietary habits. Here is a couple talking while they make supper:

[5] Corbin DP5

Don   You don't like mushrooms, do you

Sue: Umf (no)

                (2)

Don: These are *big*.

                (1)

Sue: So what are you tryin to say?

                (0.4)

Don: You can [pick em out

Sue: [You want to stick em in it?

                (8.4)

Sue: I'd rather not uhhhh

Don: Right

                (1)

Don: I'll just put em in my own, maybe

This couple explores differences in their food tastes and negotiates how these differences should be handled: for example, pick the offending items out at the table versus cook them separately. This negotiation over tastes identifies differences between members of the couple and distills these differences into social facts.

Could coupling provide a two-person lab for difference generation? Example [6] turns upon conflict, and this time blame travels both directions. Nan attacks Bob for having said too much to friends. Bob counters that his disclosures were reasonable, but as the disagreement continues Bob reveals a different perspective than Nan's about "leaving people out."

[6] UTCL D9

Nan: You go and have to tell Brenda the whole- (1) story

Bob: But I didn't t´ll her the whole story.

                (1)

Nan: You did

                (1)

Bob: That I would call him that Valerie was excited.

                (0.3)

Nan: He's Jewish? He works at the Air Force base

Bob: Right. And he's a doctor

(1)

That's not the whole story

(1)

Nan: So how d'you- (2)

Bob: The whole story is all of background, how Valerie was dying for him

(1)

[She wants his body

Nan: [Yeah well you said that

(0.6)

Bob: Did you: give Valerie the advice I suggested

(1)

Nan: No

Bob: Are you going to?

(0.3)

Nan: No

(0.5)

Bob: I don't believe you ◀

(long pause)

Nan: You're irritable ◀

(0.5)

Bob: What?

Nan: You're irritable

Bob: Sorry I'll drink more tea

Nan: That makes you more irritable

(0.2)

Bob: T´a makes me irritable?

Nan: Mm hm it's got caffeine

(0.3)

Bob: I'm sorry

(5)

So why else are you mad at me?

(1.6)

That the only reason why you're mad at me

(1)

Nan: Yeah, it really bothered me

(1.4)

Bob: Ahhrhh then don't bring these things up with me [around

Nan: [Okay I'm

sorry I didn't mean to blabbermouth

Bob: Tchhhhhh u::::::h, well I always hate being the one left o:ut

therefore I don't like to leave out people

After Nan attacks Bob for making overcandid remarks, Bob argues that his disclosures were reasonable and asks whether Nan gave her friend some advice he'd suggested. Nan admits she has not and will not give the advice. Bob then emphasizes difference in their perspectives: "I don't believe you." Nan discredits Bob's critique by calling Bob irritable. Eventually Bob defends himself on the basis of a personal characteristic: He does not like to be left out or to leave out other people. Each move in this squabble highlights notions of individual difference to explain problems.

Couple members' discovered differences often conform to gender stereotypes, and this reinforces a general belief in sex differences. In example [7] the stereotype is that men won't ask for directions.

[7] Field note

Candy: What took you so long?

Kurt: I got lost accidentally thanks to your directions.

Candy: Did you write them down? Why didn't you stop and call me?

Kurt: Look, I found it, okay? Just be happy I'm here.

Kurt and Candy rely upon gender stereotypes to blame each other, though the gendering of the blame is not made explicit. In [8] the blame is gender-attributed to "a typical male":

[8] Field Note (couple grocery shopping)

Carla: Here's the chicken stuff and the Shake & Bake mixtures.

Jepp: I don't see the Lipton mixes though.

Carla:	Maybe it's with the soups.
Jepp:	No, I don't know why it would be there.
Carla:	Well, let's go ask someone so we can find it. I'm sure they have it somewhere.
Jepp:	No, that's okay. Let's just go. Don't worry about it.
Carla:	If you want it for dinner let's just go ask someone where it is and I'll fix it for you later.
Jepp:	No, that's okay.
Carla:	You're just like a typical male (.) You won't go and ask. This is just like you not stopping and asking for directions. ◄
Jepp:	(shocked) I can't believe you would say that.

These partners disagree about tracking down a product they would like to buy. Carla suggests asking for help to find it, but Jepp is unwilling to go to the trouble. Carla explicitly attributes the problem to a gender difference.

In example [9] an engaged couple who are making supper manage within just a few moments to articulate three domestic themes in which they differentiate themselves from each other: responsibility for a Mother's Day gift, grocery shopping, and avoiding fatty food.

[9] DP Corbin 3.1

Jen:	I have to get Mother's Day gifts ['cause I'm gonna be seeing them Sunday
Ed:	[When's Mother's Day
Jen:	Huh?
Ed:	When's Mother's Day
Jen:	Sunday
	(1)
Ed:	What ya gonna get
Jen:	So if she comes Monday I need to have her a gift
Ed:	tch!
Jen:	Well I <do:?
	(1) (Ed turns away)
	Well, and so- wan have some golden bread?
Ed:	D'you have some?

Jen: No but I can make some with the- hamburger buns

Ed: You didn't buy French bread

Jen: No I didn't buy French bread, I forgot

. . . (5 seconds omitted)

Ed: You want to share some butter

Jen: No, you can have some on yours if you want. I hate that liquid butter, that is so disgusting.

Ed: It's good.

Jen: You- no good, it's unnatural

(0.5)

And they're telling you to stop eating stuff like that- those margarine products

At the start of this segment, Jen announces that she has to shop for Mother's Day gifts. Ed does not know when Mother's Day is and seems to make fun of Jen's insistence on having at least one of the gifts ready in case of a visit ("tch"). Jen drops the gift topic and offers to make some golden bread (toast). Ed asks whether she bought French bread, and Jen says she forgot—by which she takes responsibility for food shopping. Seconds later, Ed suggests adding butter to the food, and Jen delivers a speech against fatty foods. All of this takes place in an even-tempered exchange with no hint of ruffled feelings. These partners embellish the differences between them in these ways aligned with gender stereotypes: She shops for Mother's Day gifts for both mothers, takes responsibility for buying bread, and watches out for fatty foods. He cannot remember when Mother's Day is, fishes for her shopping apology, and asks for butter.

One area that is famous for discussion of male-female difference is that of shopping for clothes. This instance was overheard in a clothing store.

[10] Field note

Woman: (holding up a dress) What do you think of this?

Man: Wow, you'd have to have some curves to wear that dress.

Woman: Who the @#*# do you think you are? You can go to @#*#, just go to @#*#.

Man: What are you talking about? What did I do?

Woman: Shut up! You're in the doghouse, mister.

This man sounds insensitive to tact in shopping talk. One of the most common idioms couples share has been labeled "sexual teasing," and this teasing often centers on appearance issues. One couple member often finds such a tease funny, whereas the other finds the tease to be discomfiting. It is rare for couple members to agree on the meaning of a tease that adds to the sensation that women and men differ in perspective.

Best-selling sociolinguist Deborah Tannen argues that male-female interaction is like intercultural communication. Men and women spring from different style-cultures, and so members of couples recurrently have difficulty understanding what the intimate other is saying. Here is one of Tannen's examples supporting that claim:

> [11] Tannen
>
> Eve had a lump removed from her breast. Shortly after the operation she told her sister that she found it upsetting to have been cut into and that looking at the stitches was distressing because they left a seam that changed the contour of her breast. Her sister said, "I know; when I had my operation I felt the same way." Eve made the same observation to her friend Karen who said "I know it's like your body has been violated." But when she told her husband Marc how she felt he said, "You could have plastic surgery to cover up the scars on your breast."[2]

Tannen summarizes the lesson of this story: " Eve wanted the gift of understanding but Marc gave her the gift of advice. He was taking the role of problem solver whereas she simply wanted confirmation of her feelings." Tannen argues that men act as objective problem solvers who see the world made up of theories and correct answers. Women, on the other hand, perceive the social world as a network of personal connections, emotions, and mutual support. In this view, communication problems are mere consequences of these male/female differences. Tannen's view is illustrated in this film scene:

> [12] Film: *White Men Can't Jump*[3]
>
> Gloria: (waking) Honey, I'm thirsty Honey? My mouth is dry.
>   (pause, he wakes)
> Billy: Hm?

	(He rises, disappears, returns with glass of water)
	There you go honey.
Gloria:	When I said I was thirsty it doesn't mean I want you to bring me a glass of water.
	(1)
Billy:	It doesn't?
	(1)
Gloria:	You're missing the whole point of me saying I'm thirsty. If I have a problem, you're not supposed to solve it. Men always think they can solve women's problems.

This fictional woman complains that she is thirsty. Like Eve's husband Marc, Gloria's man Billy reacts to his partner's disclosure by offering a solution. In both cases the woman claims to desire not a solution but empathic discussion. In both Tannen's example and this film scene, the women argue that the man's offering a solution instead of empathic listening occurs as a consequence of male-female differences. Tannen's example includes a contrast between the reaction of the husband and the reaction of Eve's female friends. This film example continues with the woman's explaining that she has read about this male-female difference in a magazine.

Identifying a couple problem as a male-female difference is part of the performance of gender. In this film scene, Gloria's summary of Tannen's argument that men and women are culturally different leads to an argument in which the partners increasingly insult each other, and the man leaves, slamming the door behind him. The last lines of the argument go like this.

[13] Film: *White Men Can't Jump*[4]

Billy:	When I say I'm thirsty it means anybody in the room has a glass of water I'd like to have a sip. When I say I want to make love, it means let's screw.
Gloria:	Exactly the kind of thing I thought you would say. Besides, I don't like the word screw, okay, I prefer make love or fuck. (.) Screwing is for carpenters.
	(He throws water at her)

Gloria: Oo:h, you're gonna get it. O::h honey hhh Hey, where you
            going?
Billy: Anywhere, to get the hell away from you (.) Psycho Chiquita
            nut case.

First, the partners articulate (as gendered) their different perceptions of saying "I'm thirsty." Then Gloria adds meta-talk to her rejoinder, criticizing his
use of the word "screw." He escalates by throwing water and leaving the
scene. His last line is an ethnic slur of his Puerto Rican partner, suggesting
that one kind of stereotypic difference in talk leads to another one.

Both Tannen's couple instance and this film one pronounce a similar
verdict: There is a communication problem because men and women are different. Are men and women really different, or do they just seem so when
couple members compare themselves carefully to one another? Here is a segment from a phone call between long-distance couple partners.

[14] Field note
Amanda: Hi honey, how was your day?
Randy: It was fine. How was yours?
Amanda: Well, it started off bad because I woke up late. Then there was
           a lot of traffic on my way to work, but once I got there my boss
           cheered me up when she said she was going to take me and
           the other new girl out to lunch. After work my mother and I
           went to work out and then we came home and ate. I am really
           ready to see this weekend.
Randy: I am ready to see you too.

Randy reflected about this fragment of conversation:

> I take it for granted that Amanda will understand what "fine" means to me. I feel
> that Amanda tells me everything that happens in order to bring me closer to
> her. . . . Amanda talks this way all day and when she calls me at night, she thinks
> that I am upset or tired because I am not as talkative. I enjoy talking to her but
> I find myself shortening my stories while she gives me the extended versions.

Randy believes that Amanda talks in much the same way all the time, a womanly way that includes details of daily events.

This position that men and women are different makes communication uninteresting except as it reflects gendered similarity or difference. My students who read Tannen's *You Just Don't Understand* as a textbook often report themselves at couple loggerheads because one member (about two-thirds of the time it is the woman) wishes a detailed supportive hearing while the other member wishes to tell brief stories or to solve a problem and move on. When a couple difference aligns with a gender stereotype, partners remember it better than when it is counter to or irrelevant to a stereotype. For instance, in examples [2], [3], and [5] in this chapter males are doing the bulk of the cooking, yet this draws no comment about differences between couple members—either from the couple members or from students who have watched the videotapes.

As couple members celebrate their differences with each other, problematic situations may tie gender stereotypes to blame of the partner. In fact, 80 percent of the examples in the first six chapters of Tannen's 1990 bestseller, including her most persuasive examples of male-female differences, depict members of couples—and moments when couple members face problems, reverses, or disappointments.

Similarly, when ABC-TV produced a two-hour show on John Gray's views about Mars and Venus, they tested his ideas only with six thirty-something married couples with children. These theories depict not an actual difference between men and women but self-reports of differences between members of middle-class married couples. Is there something about couple interaction that fabricates differences?

• • •

Couple members—our most sexist dyads—become parents. Interaction practices nurtured in courtship may be instrumental in the passing of conservative gender roles to each next generation. The family's talk provides scenes for gendering the human conversation.

Family exchanges do not simply exemplify gender relations otherwise shaped by forces outside the family but, rather, are the primordial means for negotiating, maintaining, transforming, and socializing gender identities. Certainly from the point of view of a child, routine moments of family communication are the earliest and perhaps the most profound medium for constructing gender understandings.[5]

Ethnographers Elinor Ochs and Carolyn Taylor studied narratives at family dinner tables and found parents acting out stereotypical roles in a pattern they labeled "Father knows best." In this pattern, Mom introduces narratives (hers and children's) to Dad as the primary listener and critic. Dad responds by making strong judgments, often critical of Mom. Mom plays into this situation by showing self-doubt.

[15] Ochs and Taylor[6]

Mom:	(To Jodie, age 5) You want to tell Daddy what happened to you today?
Dad:	(looking up and off) Tell me everything that happened from the moment you went in [until:
Jodie:	[I got a sho:t?
Dad:	EH (gasping) What? (Frowning)
Jodie:	I got a [sho::t
Dad:	[*no*
Jodie:	(Nods yes, facing Dad)
Dad:	Couldn't be

In this instance, Mom introduces the narrative by suggesting to Jodie that she tell Dad about something in her day. Jodie relates the event: "I got a shot." Dad reacts with mock disbelief, and this pose is held against the child's insistence upon self-understood experience.

When the Mom tells a story it also gets a teasing and critical reaction from the Dad. (Remember, this is happening in front of the children.)

[16] Ochs and Taylor[7]

Dad:	You *had* a dress right?
Mom:	(nodding yes once) Your *mo*ther bought me it (.) My mother didn't like it

> (0.4) (Mom tilts head, facing dad, as if to say, "What could I do?")

Dad: (shaking head no once) You're kidding

Mom: No

Dad: You're gonna return it?

Mom: No you can't return it (.) It wasn't too expensive (.) It was from Loehmann's
(0.8)

Mom: So what I'll probably do? (.) is wear it to the dinner the night before (.) when we go to the Marriott? ◄
(1.8) (Dad turns head away from Mom with a grimace, as if he is debating whether he is being conned, then turns and looks off)

Dad: Doesn't that sound like a (.) total: (.) w:aste?

Dad's ironic reaction to Mom's story makes her look less than competent. Mom assists in problematizing her own narrative by presenting it as a thorny problem to begin with and putting her mitigated plan in a questioning tone of voice. (See ◄)

Ochs and Taylor suggest that family narratives often follow this scenario: Mothers introduce narratives with fathers as primary recipients and evaluators. Dads react with criticism, often aimed at Moms, and Moms join in with self-criticism. Children observe this pattern and participate in it.

Men and women do not use markedly different speech patterns in setting this scenario. For instance, Dads do not talk while Moms merely support, as some writers have argued.[8] Perhaps men and women are similar, but shared customs include showing gendered difference making. Perhaps the ways that couple members communicate to each other actually *formulate* some of those differences.

• • •

What have we shown in these sketches of couple interaction? Early courtship interaction produces illusions of couple members' similarities. Partners act as they think the other expects. This leads couple members to the unrealistic belief that they are similar. As commitment increases the couple members pass through turning points toward a culture of perceived differences: One partner is typified as a night person, one is a morning person; one partner is organized, one is messy; one partner wants sex too often, the other is not demonstrative; one partner is a stickler for discipline, the other wants the kids to be friends; one partner drives too aggressively, the other too conservatively; one partner fixes cars and the other bakes cakes; one partner wants to talk over problems in a sympathetic mode, the other wants to make a guess about how to solve the problem.

Some of these contrasts may just be taken as situational or as individual differences, but some of them reinforce gender stereotypes. Perhaps it is easiest to critique your man-partner if the critique fits your stereotypes about the way men are. When gendered exceptions occur (for example, he's the one who cooks) this has no impact on the tie between cooking and gender stereotypes. As couple member differences align with cultural stereotypes that men and women are different sorts of creatures, these interaction practices support the view that women and men (in general, not just in coupling) spring from different planets.

Couple members might more accurately conclude that early couplehood creates unrealistic expectations of similarity. Furthermore, couple members might recognize the relative rarity of accurate monologic communication. Most language users seem to assume that talk-in-interaction works fine unless somebody gets a meaning wrong. It is as if you live in Austin, Texas, for a year and you think you know your way around, because you can get to work and shopping and church and half–a dozen friends' houses. Yet if you go someplace new or if you make a wrong turn, you may find that your knowledge of the city is more limited than you had guessed.

The routine repetitiveness of much everyday life seems to show talk working smoothly without our really taking notice. We come to assume that we are accurate communicators. Yet when we spend many hours per week in co-present interaction with a couple partner we meet difficult and detailed problems of understanding and collaboration.

If we understand communication as dialogue and accuracy as partial at best, then we might begin to see that coupling entails new adjustments and ongoing difficulties. However, it seems easier for most of us to conclude that our couple difficulties are monologic—and due to partners being different from each other. If we can conclude that men and women are from different planets, none of our problems are anyone's fault.

Since progressive commitment to a couple partner includes some of the most sexist things that we do as members of this culture, it is hardly surprising that those activities magnify the differences between men and women or that we explain our coupling problems in terms of sex differences.[9]

Couple members who wish to add rationality to relational interaction could observe the ways conclusion-jumping slides along couple talk—especially in encountering problems. Observe yourself as you adopt guesses about what is problematic. Can you observe yourself going from "Here's a problem that came up in communication" to "We are so different you and I?" Can you slow down that slide? Can you ponder over the details of the talk a bit longer? See if there is a way that you can muddle through the situation without necessarily setting up or hardening categories of how different you are from each other. Then continue the dialogue.

Sometimes it seems like one's mate is so different! This perception especially turns up when we learn very late of a possible difference in perception. In *The Joy Luck Club*, Amy Tan tells of an embattled couple whose marriage has become a struggle for fairness based on detailed lists of expectations. The couple is finishing supper with the wife's mother.

[17] Fiction: *The Joy Luck Club*[10]

Harold:	Who's ready for dessert? (reaching into the freezer)
Lena:	I'm full.
Mother:	Lena cannot eat ice cream.
Harold:	So it seems she's always on a diet.
Lena:	No she never eat it, she doesn't like.
	(And now Harold smiles and looks at me puzzled expecting me to translate what my mother has said.)
Lena:	It's true, I've hated ice cream almost all my life.
	(Harold looks at me as if I too were speaking Chinese and he couldn't understand.)
Harold:	Well I guess I assumed you were just trying to lose weight, oh well.

This married man has remained ignorant that his wife dislikes ice cream. It has come up a number of times that she might eat some ice cream and she has said on each occasion something like, "Oh I'm not very hungry," or "I'm watching my weight." Her husband does not know something that her mother has known since Lena was a child. She dislikes ice cream.

Is this example about couple culture? Yes, but interestingly there are other issues of culture (for example, China vs. the United States) intertwined in this story. Here is how one protagonist puts the problem:

> "At first I thought it was because I raised with all this Chinese humility," Rose said, "or that maybe it was because when you're Chinese you're supposed to accept everything, flow with the Tao and not make waves. But my therapist said, 'Why do you blame your culture, your ethnicity?' And I remembered reading an article about baby boomers how we expect the best and when we get it we worry we should have expected more because it's all diminishing returns after a certain age."[11]

In Tan's book there seems to be something about being Chinese-American that makes being a member of a U.S. couple especially difficult. Then there's an additional source of difference: one's age cohort. Baby boomers are different from earlier or later generations. How is one of these factors selected on any given occasion as explaining any particular course of action? With such a variety of choices, why do we so often choose gender as a source of problems?

If we start with the notion that men and women come from different cultures, then when something goes wrong in a couple, how will you figure out whether what went wrong is about culture difference, your generation, or a male/female difference? And what if we humans (let alone our relationships) are not just bundles of variables that determine courses of action? What if culture, personality, and gender are largely performative accomplishments?

Exciting new couple relationships are said to have chemistry. Yet the elements of this chemistry appear on no periodic chart. Human interaction bears its own pattern in embodied performances, not just in the combining of elements and variables. That is because we perform our lives in dialogic interaction. Communication patterns are relationship builders, not just consequences.

Talk about Women,
Talk about Men

TODAY, A SATURDAY IN MAY, I START PAINTING THE TRIM ON MY HOUSE. THIS IS a job I enjoy, and the cool spring breezes help the work's rhythm. Soon I find myself humming inane tunes, such as this one:

> The farmer in the dell, the farmer in the dell,
> heigh-ho the dairy-o, the farmer in the dell.
> The farmer takes a wife . . .

Suddenly I stop humming and start laughing so hard I must stop painting for a minute. I feel silly for letting this childhood ditty creep into my unguarded mind, but mostly I laugh at discovering the assumption in this rhyme that the farmer must be a male—because the farmer "takes a wife." The universe of talk is showing me something deeply ordinary. So I ask more questions about this rhyme: Did I have a picture of this farmer in my head as I sang? Well, not exactly, but something like that. Had the picture always been male, from the first mention of the farmer, or did it just become male at "The farmer takes a wife?" It was always male, and did not require the wife to make it so.

As I ponder this, I start painting again, and soon, without any bidding, the rhyme comes onto my tongue again: "The wife takes a child." Hmm, In the 1990s, the savvy language user knows that it would be better to say "The farming couple takes a child." But the traditional rhyme connects only the wife with the child. To say it the new way loses the playful rhythm.

How many hundred times have I sung, read, or heard this rhyme without stopping to consider its stereotypical presentation of male and female roles? The farmer (presumed to be a male so surely that it's unnecessary to say so—in fact, better not to say so!) acts to take a wife, who acts to take a child. Action begins with the male, who has a place in the world. In one of his acts, this male takes a wife. The wife also acts, but only within the domestic sphere, to take a child. And the wife acts only after the farmer has taken her. Before then she does not enter the story.

Like my mindless humming at the paint job, most people's usage of the English language includes forms of talk that (more or less by accident and even without malice) make women seem invisible, deemphasized, or not taken seriously. When women are talked about, certain language features seem to put women in a bad light. Both male and female speakers use features that indicate micropolitical inequalities between men and women. How do speakers use these unequally gendered features? And what are the consequences of talking differently about men than we talk about women?

Consider this fragment of a phone conversation between two men who share responsibilities for managing apartments. Dan is traveling for Thanksgiving, so he describes to a colleague how his responsibilities will be covered:

[1] UTCL L.17.3

Dan: We're gonna take off we got one of the girls here watchin the place for us

By using the expression "one of the girls," Dan indicates a person to whom he has assigned a professional responsibility. He does not state the person's name, but identifies that person only as a female living at the apartment complex. This phrase, "one of the girls here," does not help a listener recognize the particular person to whom Dan makes reference. Dan has mentioned this "girl" in a way that specifically prevents us from guessing who she might be. The word "girl" is arguably demeaning because it make the person referred to seem immature and not professional.[1]

Dan's phrase displays lexical choices within a slot in his utterance that might be filled by any of several expressions: for instance, "this kid," "a student," "this woman," or "a responsible lady." Each of these would fit into Dan's utterance in the slot occupied by "one of the girls" without changing the main speech act Dan performs—informing his colleague that someone is minding the apartments. If Dan had used "kid" or "student" in this slot these choices would not have gendered the utterance, as does "girl."

Many word choices carry gendered information. Given the variety of ways of referring to a person that the English language makes available, Dan's choice of *"girl"* might indicate something about his orientation toward women. Yet if we were to ask Dan about the use of "girl," he might find the question picky or uninteresting. Perhaps your responses are similar. Why write about Dan's usage? Because it is within just such microscopic moments that we gender our world.

Let us contrast two ways to examine Dan's utterance. First, we may ask about its main speech act, and produce a description such as informing a colleague. Second, we may examine the form of some detail in the utterance—for instance the word "girl." The main speech act in an utterance represents that speaker's primary intention. Yet that intention is rarely *all* that is occurring at that moment. A speech act, like any fabricating process, is multiconsequential.

The manager of a steel mill intends to make steel and earn money. The manufacturing of steel might also place dangerous chemicals into nearby air and water. The manager bears responsibility not only for the primary intention, but also for its accidental consequences. The manager does not try to pollute the environment, but owns unintended consequences as well as intended ones.

Similarly, when a person speaks, dozens of things happen at once, and most speakers hold only some of these events under conscious or strategic control. We experience other speech features, including habitual accent, idioms, and metaphors as bits of personality and cultural identity. When a speaker says something gendered, this may not indicate an intention to act sexist. Nevertheless, if utterances foster an impression that men and women are unequal, this activity may both indicate and sustain male-female inequality.

Harm may be done within little details of conversation. The current chapter (and the next one) describes traces of bias in our everyday gendered speech patterns, using the term "soft-core sexism" to refer to a usage (such as "girl" in example [1]) that shows gender-imbalance but does not necessarily

show an intention to slight women. To illustrate hard-core and soft-core sexist language, consider these hypothetical examples:

- This broad lacks the balls to be a manager.
- I'm not sure this little lady is management material.

The first utterance sounds blatantly sexist. The language is crass ("broad,"
"balls") and the tone is abrupt. The second utterance uses management jargon ("management material"), but the phrase "little lady" retains a demeaning overtone. Furthermore, the two utterances make the same general point,
which is that a particular female person is found unfit for a high-status job.
This pair of examples illustrates a fuzzy boundary between soft-core and
hard-core sexist talk. In soft-core sexist talk the problematic material

- is not crass in its enactment;
- is enacted as a side effect; and
- may be tolerated, because of speech habits, and because to interfere
  endangers freedom of speech.

Such items of soft-core sexist talk may become especially troublesome when
used in public:

> [2] News report[2]
> "This is the blind date stage of the campaign," said . . . Samuel L. Popkin
> of the political science faculty at the University of California at San Diego.
> "Someone tells you about a girl, but you haven't met her yet, haven't had
> a chance to check her out."

This statement sounds innocuous, like describing political races using a sports
metaphor, but the analogy here is to dating. This professor's utterance (like
Dan's utterance in example [1]) contains the world "girl," which by itself may
do little harm. Yet here this word is embedded in an extended analogy
between a political campaign and a date. Also, the word "girl" specifies a male
viewpoint, implying that all politicians are men. Is this harmful within the
male-dominated world of politics?

Let us return to Dan's utterance to consider the phrase "one of the girls." How can we determine whether these details in Dan's utterance have environmental impact, or make any difference in the world? What harm might there be to Dan's word choice, and how would we monitor such harm? One source of evidence about any utterance is the talk that occurs just afterward. Speakers show each other in subsequent utterances how they are analyzing and making use of the details of each other's talk. Here is what happens just after example [1]:

[3] UTCL L17.3

Dan: We're gonna take off we got one of the girls here watchin the place for us

        (0.2)

Jeff: Oh yeah?

Dan: D'You know Shirley, don'tcha

Jeff: Shirley, Shirley with the big whangers?

Just a few seconds after Dan mentions the name of this previously referred to "girl," Jeff refers to the same person as "Shirley with the big whangers." This physical description is one that few of us would wish applied to ourself or our sister. The description "big whangers" sounds demeaning to Shirley.

Is Jeff's demeaning usage ("big whangers") consequential to Dan's prior usage ("one of the girls")? This question cannot be answered with certainty. Jeff's utterance is more obviously demeaning than Dan's, but both are somewhat belittling, and both utterances gender Shirley.

We may contrast soft-core with hard-core sexism by comparing Dan's phrase "One of the girls" with Jeff's phrase "Shirley with the big whangers." Yet is it possible that the former phrase creates an environment in which the latter may be said?

Once Jeff's demeaning utterance is spoken, Dan and Jeff celebrate its unfairness to women.

[4] UTCL L17.3

Jeff: Shirley, Shirley with the big whangers?

      (0.4)

Dan:	Yeah.
Jeff:	[A : : w.
Dan:	[*Yeah*- uh (.) up in two o four? The bi- you know two o four.
Jeff:	Big girl, bi:g.
Dan:	We're talkin b*i*g everything's [big on her
Jeff:	[big
Dan	O:h Lord=
Jeff:	huh heh heh huh huh huh [huh huh huh huh huh
Dan:	[How sweet, how sweet
Jeff:	Indee:d, indee:d a:h yes: your- your type for sure
Dan:	Yes

Jeff's demeaning jest stimulates a period of overtly sexist speech play: "how sweet," "your type for sure." This progression is celebrated in laughter as well as in repeated choral performances of the word "big."

The impact of word choice is especially vivid in humor. When you come across a punchline, ask what makes it work. Ask what the players are celebrating. Ambiguities often provide productive points for such analysis. Here is a joke (from a 1990 joke-a-day calendar) that exemplifies how we mark ideology about women and about men.

[5] Joke Calendar
Not found in Webster's
Lady pilot: a plane Jane.

This joke plays off a dictionary format for definitions. "Lady pilot" is the term to be defined, and the definition follows: "a plane Jane." The term that makes the joke work, "plane," is an ambiguous sound. Airplane seems the primary meaning, cued by spelling of "plane," not plain, but this secondary meaning is proposed in the combination idiom "plane Jane." A plain jane is a female who might not be especially pretty or gregarious. Plain (Jane) is a pun with (air)plane, the vehicle that pilots fly.

"Pilot" is typically a man's occupation. To say "lady pilot" is to propose a marked usage, to describe an incumbent in a sex-atypical occupation. It is unusual to see a female pilot. About a woman performing a sex-atypical occupation, Samuel Johnson is supposed to have quipped that listening to a woman's preaching is like watching a dog walk on its hind legs; it is not that she does it well but that one is surprised to see it done at all. A lady pilot, like a woman preacher, is marked as atypical. Speech patterns remind us that *this* pilot is atypical. Would you ever say "man pilot," or "man preacher?" Man is assumed in words like "pilot," "preacher," "president," or "surgeon."

You may have heard this riddle: A man and his son are in a car accident. The father is killed; the child is taken to the hospital by helicopter. When they wheel this child into surgery the surgeon says, "Oh my God, this patient is my son." What is the relationship between the patient and the surgeon? When I first heard this riddle about 1980 I wondered whether the child had been adopted, or oddly positioned by divorce and step parenthood. Only after being asked to conceptualize a simpler solution did I find the more obvious probability—that this surgeon is a woman. Douglas Hofstadter discusses reactions to this story in terms of the term "default assumptions":

> Whether we light upon the answer quickly or slowly, we all have something to learn from this ingenious riddle. It reveals something very deep about how so-called *default assumptions* permeate our mental representations and channel our thoughts. A default assumption is what holds true in what you might say is the "simplest" or "most natural" or "most likely" possible model of whatever situation is under discussion. . . . But the critical thing about default assumptions— so well revealed by this story—is that they are made automatically, not as a result of consideration and elimination. You didn't explicitly ponder the point and ask yourself, "what is the most plausible sex to assign to the surgeon?" . . . You never were aware of having made any assumptions about the surgeon's sex, for if you had been, the riddle would have been easy![3]

Ordinary talk may show gendered default assumptions:

[6] Field note (overheard in elevator)

Jill: I don't know what they're doing in class today.
                I don't feel like goin'

Stan: Your *father* is paying tuition, young lady, and you . . .
                (They pass out of earshot))

Stan not only presumes that the male parent is the primary payer of tuition, but he addresses Jill as "young lady," which gives this encounter a flavor of parental discipline.

> [7] Field note (Computer support line)
>
> Carol: Thank you for calling Dell, this is Carol, how may I help you?
>
> Mike: Uh huh, (.) is this tech support?
>
> Carol: Yes it is. How may I help you?
>
> Mike: Oh, uh, wow, a female technician.

This caller seems so surprised to find a tech support phone answered by a woman that he first rechecks whether he has the correct number. The technician reassures him that he has called the correct number, then she once again asks the caller to specify the computer problem. Mike ignores this repeated request, to instead comment on having reached a sex-atypical technician.

We expect a pilot to be male; if a pilot is a woman that is exceptional. We mark the exceptional nature of a nonmale pilot by an extra modifier: "lady pilot" is the item to be defined in this fictitious dictionary. Similarly, one may say "female technician," "lady doctor," or "lady lawyer" in order to show that the woman is in an exceptional role.

The definition of "lady pilot" combines the word "plane" (which is what a pilot operates) and a woman's name. Therefore, the definition fits the term being defined. Yet the pun (plane/plain) places together within one phrase this hypothetical woman's sex-atypical occupation and her unattractive social status. This pairing comes across as a coincidence, but it is this very coincidence, and only that, that makes the joke a joke. This coincidence implies that a successful female aviator may be a social suspect. Yet that derogatory implication remains slightly out of focus, so we can laugh at the joke without making explicit its default assumptions.

This "plane Jane" joke demonstrates three themes in talk about women, compared with talk about men.

- emphasis on men,
- derogation of women, and
- notice of a woman's physical attractiveness.

Emphasis on men refers to talk that implies that men are more plentiful or important than women. "Lady pilot" indicates that an unmarked pilot is male, and thereby "pilot" emphasizes men over women. The rest of this chapter deals with this problem of emphasis.

Chapter 8 describes talk that is derogatory to women, and talk that emphasizes women's beauty. The phrase "plane Jane" carries the implication that a lady pilot carries social liabilities. Finally, this whole joke turns around connecting being a lady pilot to lacking physical attractiveness. These three issues all imply that successful women are social suspects.

This "plane Jane" joke carries linguistic traces of unfairly gendered ideology. Any real life utterance, like this joke, may carry traces of all three sorts of linguistic bias. Yet for clarity we consider these issues in isolation from one another. The present treatment concentrates on soft-core instances. Of course, hard-core sexism, blatant exclusion, and harmful insult also occur, and should draw social concern. However, there is value in examining subtler and less intended features of the ways we speak about women and men—choices as seemingly innocent as Dan's phrase, "one of the girls."

THE PROBLEM OF EMPHASIS

Some language features make it easy for speakers to emphasize males, or deemphasize women. These features invoke a world of male presence and female absence, a world in which women seem marginal while men seem central. To test the validity of each example, see if you can think of a counterexample—an example that would show something different or opposite from what the example shows.

Names

When, upon marriage, a bride changes her family name to that of the groom, her past family name has been comparatively effaced.[4] We all carry family names. Some cultures (for example, American) place family names as the final word in a person's name. Some cultures (for example, Japanese) speak the family name first. Some cultures (for example, Hispanic) put the most important family name next to last. Yet in each of these languages a man's family name has preferential status over a women's family name. If only one family name is to be specified for members of a married couple, that name is likely to be the family name held by the man prior to marriage.

A thought experiment: Suppose that you are getting married tomorrow, and that family name decisions are yours alone. Whatever you wish to do will be fine with all the others involved. Women readers: Would you change your family name to match your husband's? Would you keep your premarriage family name? Or would you seek a compromise (hyphenation, adopting a third name, etc.)? Men readers, answer the same question: How many would keep the premarriage name, how many would change, how many would compromise?

When I pose this second set of questions to the men in university classes, both men and women laugh, indicating that it is humorous to ask a man whether he is going to change his family name. What is this humor about? After the question to women, most listeners expect a *different* question to be asked of men. Did you expect me to ask if you men were going to allow your wives to keep their names? Were some of you (men and women) surprised that the same question was asked to men as to women? This illustrates a gender inequality in the use of language.

When we think about family, we may first think of the line of people with the family name that is the same as ours. To think about a mother-to-mother family line, one must think through a variety of family names. I cannot say of my maternal ancestors: "Those Hoppers were sturdy pioneers." I would have to say, "Those Butlers, Redds, Skeenes, and so on were sturdy pioneers."

A boy, knowing he comes from a long line of males bearing the name Wheelwright, for example, can identify with his forefathers: Johnny Wheelwright . . . can imagine some medieval John in whose workshop the finest wheels in the land were fashioned, a John who had a son, who had a son, who had a son, until at last Johnny Wheelwright himself was born. No line of identifiable foremothers stretches back into the past. . . .

Imagine, in contrast to Johnny Wheelwright, a hypothetical woman of today whose name is Elizabeth Jones, . . . a Woslewski whose father emigrated from Poland as a boy. . . . Elizabeth Jones' father's mother in Pennsylvania had been a Bruhofer, whose mother had been a Gruber. . . .

Thus, although Elizabeth Jones is said to have been a Fliegendorf whose people came from Schleswig-Holstein in the sixteen hundreds, fewer than 5 percent of her two thousand or so direct ancestors who were alive in that century had any connection with Schleswig-Holstein . . . The same may be said, of course, of Elizabeth Jones's brother, Ed Fliegendorf's relationship to the Fliegendorf family or Johnny Wheelwright's relationship to the bearers of his name. Yet so strong is our identification with the name we inherit at birth that we tend to forget both the rich ethnic mix most of us carry in our genes and the arbitrary definition of "family" that ultimately links us only to the male line of descent.[5]

Family names are arbitrary. None of us chooses a family name at birth. Yet a family name carries different consequences for its male and female occupants. A man's family name is emphasized more than a woman's.

In the nineteenth century most U.S. women used their husbands' full names: for example, *Mrs. Henry Stanton*. Path-breaking feminist Elizabeth Cady Stanton insisted on using her own given name and surname along with her husband's surname. Sculptor Elisabet Ney (now memorialized by a museum in Austin, Texas) was threatened by the Ku Klux Klan for her refusal to change her surname to her husband's name. Lucy Stone, throughout most of her 1855 marriage to Henry Blackwell, insisted on using only her previous family name, though she met repeated legal difficulties in doing so. Her example led to the formation of a "Lucy Stone League" in the 1920s for the purpose of encouraging women to legally maintain their surnames. "Lucy Stoners" of the 1920s included Margaret Mead, Amelia Earhart, Fannie Hurst, and Edna St. Vincent Millay. In the 1930s the practice again became rare.[6]

The way we manage married names continues to fluctuate. I have polled my classes on this question every year since 1975, when no woman in my undergraduate class would willingly change her name at marriage. By 1982 few women in the class would consider keeping their current names at marriage. In 1994, 70 percent would change family names to that of the male. This fluctuation indicates ideological fashion among college students. What remains constant is that virtually no man considers changing a surname at marriage. Family names seem derived mainly from male ancestors, which both men and women show whenever they use these names.

Given names (first names in the United States) usually mark the sex of the person, and the set of names also shows some imbalances. There are a number of women's names that seem derived from men's: Paulette, Georgette, Georgia, Pauline, Roberta, Bobbie. Many of the women's forms feature a diminutive ending such as -ette or -ine that make the labeled thing seem small as well as derived. Are there any men's names that appear to be derived from women's names, or that appear to be diminutive compared to a woman's name?

Finally, certain Anglo names such as *Leslie, Shirley,* and *Evelyn* were historically names for men. When women began to receive these names, the names became more rare among men. Were these names somehow diminished by application to women, and therefore deemed no longer suitable to men? There are now some Anglo names that seem androgynous but are mostly used for women: *Taylor, Blair, Madison.* Apparently there are nations (for example, Germany) in which names are legally prescribed to avoid gender ambiguities.

Generic "He"

Sometimes a speaker uses the pronoun "he" to refer to a person of indeterminate sex. English teachers used to tell students to use a masculine pronoun on such an occasion, since generic usage includes women by convention. The rationale is that we do not intend gender bias if we use generic terms.

The choice to say "he" when you do not necessarily refer to a man is ambiguous, or creates two meanings for the word "he":

- male individual
- referent of undetermined sex

To use "he" is to activate both of these possible meanings, and a listener must figure out which is intended. The ambiguity of words like "he" or "man" is interesting in terms of how often each of the uses occurs. One study asked (within a sample of children's books) how many of the usages of "he" were of which type. How many do you suppose were of each type? Were 90 percent of them generic, were 90 percent sex-specific, or was the breakdown about 50–50? Most of my listener-readers think near 50–50, which is a logical guess, but incorrect. Actually, 97 percent of the usages of "he" were sex-specific, not generic. Also, sex-specific "he" occurred more frequently than "she."

A generic "he" usage, then, is a marked exception, not the rule. One implication of this: When you hear "he" you expect it to be sex-specific, unless there is some clue to the contrary. Possible confusions related to these usages are captured in Lorel Scott's poem, "He or She," which reads in part:

> When I was little I had to see if he means he
> or if he means she, or if perhaps he means he or she. . . .
> The physician, he, or the gambler, he, or the
> President, he: what are we supposed to see:
> Do we read 'the President' he or she? That is how
> they say it should be. According to them,
> there's no mystery. He means he or he or she.
> Since I was a she, this was confusing to me.
> When I read he, did that mean me?[7]

Generic "he" seems ambiguous in ways that may impact the social identities of women and girls. The use of generic "he" arguably enhances sexism in talk and writing, and hence contributes to gender inequality. Generic "he" may indicate a speaker's belittling or derogatory attitude toward women: "Continual emphasis on the masculine as the unmarked conventional gender can . . . create the illusion that women have lesser rights in the moral order of speaking, an illusion shared by both men and women."[8] In other words, generic "he" unfairly emphasizes males over females, and marginalizes women.

To the degree that we use male words to talk about the human race, we could find ourselves thinking of humans primarily as males. (The farmer in the dell) The default thinking involved in generic usages is illustrated by this satirical treatment, which reverses women and men:

> Think of the future of woman which, of course, includes both women and men. . . . Recall that everything you have ever read all your life uses only female pronouns—she, her—meaning both girls and boys, both women and men. Recall

that most of the voices on radio and most of the faces on TV are women's. . . . Women are the leaders, the power centers, the prime movers. Man, whose natural role is husband and father, fulfills himself through nurturing children and making the home a refuge for women. . . .[9]

Another humorous treatment of this issue puts the generic grid imaginatively across races: black and white.

It's high time someone blew the whistle on all the silly prattle about revamping our language to suit the purposes of certain political fanatics. . . .

Most of the clamor . . . revolves around the age-old usage of the noun "white" and words built from it, such as *chairwhite, mailwhite, repairwhite, clergywhite, middlewhite, Frenchwhite, forewhite, whitepower, whiteslaughter, oneupswhiteship, straw white, whitehandle,* and so on. The negrists claim that using the word "white" . . . to talk about *all* the members of the human species is somehow degrading to blacks and reinforces racism. Therefore the libbers propose that we substitute "person" everywhere where "white" now occurs. Sensitive speakers of our secretary tongue of course find this preposterous. There is great beauty to a phrase such as "All whites are created equal."[10]

Several investigators have tried to trace the interpretations of language users who encountered generic usages versus inclusive usages.[11] Sometimes subjects were asked to read a passage and to draw (or choose from among several) pictures of what was described. Those exposed to inclusive language still drew (or chose) more males, but only by about a two-to-one ratio. When people read passages like the first one (with "he" and "man" representing everyone) such persons drew almost entirely males. Such results illustrate that words like "he" are most often understood to indicate males.

Jeffrey Stringer and I examined hundreds of instances of "he" in tape-recorded conversations to find out if generic usage occurs in talk as it sometimes does in writing.[12] We found that speakers do occasionally select "he" when referring to sex-unspecified persons in traditionally male social categories (such as pilot or surgeon). In these usages, speakers intend to refer to males, although such reference is deniable as having been generic "he." In other words, we found usages showing default assumptions that referents of "he" were actually male. These pseudogeneric "he" instances are ambiguous between sex-specific usages and a disingenuous pretense of gender-neutral "he." Most often the use of "he" appears to refer to a male-presumed occupation:

[8] Field note
S: You would have to speak with our operations manager about that.
P: Is HE available now?

(In the next few examples "HE" is capitalized for easy reading, not to show spoken emphasis.) The operations manager is female, but P refers to this stranger as "he," likely assuming that the manager is a male. If challenged, P could defend this usage as generic. Here is a related instance:

[9] Field note
Son: I saw my new doctor the other day.
Mom: What did HE say
Son: I got a prescription for my toe.

The son's doctor is female, though the mom uses "he," showing a default assumption that a doctor would be a male. The son's reply avoids the gender issue by answering the question without referring to the doctor. In this next instance Suzanne attempts to correct a pseudogeneric "he," without success.

[10] Field note
Suzanne: I was referred to your office by Doctor Sayres.
Receptionist: Is HE your primary doctor?
Suzanne: No, *she's* my rheumatologist.
Receptionist: How long have you been under HIS care?

Sometimes a recipient corrects the speaker of a pseudogeneric "he." In example [10] such a correction turns the description of a visit to a doctor into a scene of gendered controversy:

[11] Field note

Ava:	Well- what'd HE say
Bev:	He is a she- and everything's fine
Pat:	[So you went to a woman?
Ava:	[A girl doctor? Sick!
	What if she's a *lesbian*
Bev:	I'd rather have a *lesbian* check me out than a *pervert*!

Ava asks her friend Bev about a doctor's examination, using "he" to refer to the physician. Bev corrects the pronoun in her response, and two of her friends respond (in overlap) to this revelation. Pat expresses surprise that the doctor is a woman, aligning with Ava's default assumption that a physician would be male. Ava's response is more pejorative, perhaps because it was her usage that Bev had corrected. Ava criticizes the choice of a "girl doctor" as "sick," and continues by worrying that the physician might be a "lesbian."

Uses of pseudogeneric "he" may affect future actions:

[12] Field note

John:	They want me to appear in court, but I really don't want to.
Claire:	Tell them it's in the hands of your attorney and they'll have to talk to HIM.
John:	That's a good idea. I don't have an attorney, but I'll call one this afternoon and see what HE says.

John is reluctant to appear in court. Claire advises John to take the problem to an attorney, referred to as "him." John agrees to accept the advice, and John's retaining "he" may indicate an emerging plan to retain a male attorney.

The pronoun "he" also occurs in cases in which a sex-definite referent is nonhuman. Many animals have biological sex just as humans do, but an animal's sex might not be readily apparent to, or relevant to, humans. One prescribed pronoun for referring to animals or objects is "it," but this usage is rare in conversation. Instead speakers use a gender-linked pronoun to refer to animals. Most of these pronouns are masculine.

[13] NB:II:3:R:4

Lottie: Then: (.) we went down to: where we caught the big ha:libut
               yihknow: we-e- uh en: uh •hh we wo:rked *tha:t* there'n we
               fin'lly got HIM up real close to the rocks.

The speaker refers to a fish as "him." This usage seems to be a generic "him,"
but the referent is not human.

The use of gender-linked pronouns to refer to animals often follows other
gender markings in the talk. For example, consider the following interaction
about a cockroach. Could the term "COCKroach" (not roach) and the expression
"SON of bitch" have impacted the subsequent uses of masculine pronouns?

[14] UTCL J17.4

Jan: I killed that cockroach
Sid: Did you really?
Jan: Yes *sir*
Sid: That son of a bitch came back
Jan: Three ti::mes,
Sid: Guall:ee
Jan: And I kept *f*lickin HIM outta here and finally the last time I took
            my shoe off and I smashed that sucker
                       (0.3)
Sid: Good for you.
Jan: HE's *dead* now

Jan announces the killing of a cockroach, eventually referring to the insect
as "he." We can find precursors for the masculine pronoun in Jan's prior
description of the beast as a "cockroach" and a "son of a bitch."

When speakers refer to animals, there is, of course, a likelihood of an
incorrect pronoun. When this occurs, the usage may go unnoticed, or speakers may contend over the usage:

[15] Field note
M: I've been petting your cat. What's HIS name.
J: HER name is Tutti

M:	HE always runs up to me
J:	SHE loves everybody, even strangers
M:	Well HE's never tried to follow me
J:	Yeah SHE usually stays pretty close to home.

The mail carrier (M) asks the cat's name using a masculine pronoun. The cat is a female, which J (the cat's owner) indicates with an embedded correcting feminine pronoun. M shows no notice of this correction, and again uses a masculine pronoun. J observes that "she" seeks affection from friends and strangers alike. M sticks with a masculine pronoun throughout the encounter, never seeming to notice the pronoun struggle.

To summarize: Possible uses of generic "he" in conversation actually refer either to occupants of overwhelmingly male roles, or to animals. If challenged, speakers of these pronouns could claim that they made a generic reference, but the pronouns themselves communicate default assumptions that the referent is male.[13]

Though we found no unmistakable generic "he" in conversation, we did find hypercorrect usages in environments that might allow a generic "he." In example [16] a university professor is lecturing on how various peoples address a mother-in-law:

[16] Field note

K: In Arabic culture a son-in-law speaks to HIS OR HER mother-in-law with a specific type of verb form.

This speaker uses the gender-inclusive "his or her" for a sex-specific referent, "son-in-law." Such hypercorrection indicates that, even though generic "he" may be rare or absent in conversation, its use is still regarded as possible.

Generic "they" seems to be the unmarked form used in conversation when referent sex is unspecified. This construction is precisely what prescriptive grammarians have periodically cited as incorrect. Consider this office conversation in which the referent is "outsider."

[17] UTCL J20B, Wrobbel

Red: You know som:e- outsider that we don't normally recognize as

> an elmos user needs a lo:g in, some of the table corrections that
> go on, and THEY have distributed the conversions

Red refers to an unknown single and hypothetical computer user as "they." Example [18] further illustrates such unmarked use by showing how a speaker abandons generic "their" in a marked recompletion of an utterance. The scene is a suburban home on cleaning day:

[18 Field note

Kay: Somebody trashed out my freshly cleaned bathroom and did-
         n't clean up THEIR own Whiskers.
                  (pause)
         HIS own whiskers.

Kay complains about messy whiskers in a circumstance that allows no doubt about who grew the whiskers. Perhaps Kay's generic "they" softens her complaint with humorous vagueness. However, when the complaint target, who is also her addressee, does not respond vocally (the pause), Kay recompletes her utterance, substituting an emphasized *"his"* for the prior generic "their." This switch to a sex-specific pronoun turns the original tactful accusation into an on-record one.

The unmarked frequency of generic "they" in conversation suggests that grammarians originally prescribed generic "he" because most speakers already used generic "they."[14] Yet that prescription also allows certain sex-specific uses of "he," which can be possibly heard as generic. The third person singular pronoun system in English provides routine locations to gender human referents, locations in which speakers are obliged to gender-tag human referents more or less automatically, that is, without stopping to consider how such usages reinforce the importance of gender categorization. Generic "he" is part of a network of speech resources by which speakers sort referents by sex, and effortlessly emphasize men over women. Such resources include gendered terms for occupations and the retention of male surnames at marriage. These usages fit seamlessly into social-institutional arrangements such as the gendered assignment of chores to children, the gendered labeling of adult professions, and the unequal distributions of heroic figures in our stories.

The squabble over generic "he" may disguise a more important practice of gender-marking pronouns—and (in some languages) nouns and adjectives as well. It could be interesting to compare repetitive, taken-for-granted gendering procedures across a variety of speech communities.

Job Titles

If you call somebody a "salesman" you probably picture a man. If you call somebody a "saleswoman" that is marked usage, like "lady pilot." Sometimes the job title's default value of "male" is reinforced by the syllable, "-man," as in *fireman, garbage man, salesman, draftsman,* and so forth. Yet many job titles default to a male value even without this explicit linguistic marking: *lawyer, doctor, engineer, manager, president.* Any of these terms evoke the expectation that the occupant is male—as is shown in the preceding pages by the use of pseudogeneric pronouns to refer to such persons. It seems no coincidence that

- these job titles include most of the high-prestige and power occupations in our society, and
- most occupants of these high positions are male—fulfilling the stereotype and making the situation harder to either unmask or change.

There are a few job titles, mostly lower status ones, in which a female occupant is unmarked: *nurse, social worker, secretary.* These default values for job titles reflect an unfortunate degree of occupational segregation by sex in North American society. This state of affairs in the language and the world makes men look good and present whereas women look absent, marginal, or suspect. And of course, these features interact with other features (for example, pronoun use, and talk about women's accomplishments—see chapter 8) to promote occupational inequality while appearing to simply reflect it.

Representation in Fiction and Media

Who are the heroes, on TV, in children's books, and so on? There have been numerous studies of this issue over time, and some attempts to redress the problem. Thirty years ago the overwhelming majority of literary and media heroes were men, and in spite of attempts to compensate, the hero situation remains sex-imbalanced. In children's books little boys climb trees and little girls watch and worry. In spy novels the men do the fighting, thinking, investigating, and so on. This holds true across texts from the Bible to Saturday morning cartoons.

CONCLUSIONS

Men and women, in the details of talk, are portrayed as separate and unequal. This reflects no intention to slight women, but unreflective usages of traditional language forms. After a general introduction to this problem, this chapter has focused on the problem of emphasis–as represented by asymmetries in pronoun use and in surnames at marriage.

What should we do about the problem of emphasis? Proposed solutions to marriage-related naming practices have been a matter of contention for well over a century. Since 1970 a number of women and men have put themselves on the line with innovative naming practices. In the 1980s there was a backlash against such practices that largely continues today. Similarly, there has been cosmetic progress in the naming of certain titles for jobs. Terms like "salesperson," "police officer," and the like are increasingly used instead of terms including "man." However, both the stubborn facts of occupational segregation and the unmarked expectation that a doctor or lawyer is a man remain largely as they were a generation ago.

Proposed solutions for the problem of generic "he" range from the creation of totally new pronominal forms such as "shem" to the alternating use of gendered pronouns. Yet even when English speakers invent practicable linguistic solutions to these perplexities, they still experience difficulty in changing these pronoun patterns in everyday talk. Most speakers resist such changes as awkward. The most widely accepted substitute in written and spoken English is the combination "he or she," and even this usage remains controversial.

We should not overestimate the reach of grammarians' prescriptions for language practices. For example, English teachers long advised students to avoid using singular generic "they," yet that is the generic pronoun a majority of English speakers use in conversation. In recent years, some teachers and writers have prescribed greater gender fairness in pronoun use—and the results of such advocacy may be similarly modest. Such analyses tell us more about what we are like as members of a speech community than about how we should change our talk.

Still, we should not underestimate the ideological reach of unmarked language forms. Grammarians who prescribed generic "he" have not needed to prescribe something English speakers already knew without question: to use gender-specific third person pronouns whenever possible. Members' obligations within this scheme include making one's own sex routinely and unremarkably evident and deciphering the sex of conversational partners as well as that of persons described in talk. This omnipresent gender-specifying project points to cultural preoccupations about the performance of gender. Similarly, the problems of marital naming and the titles of jobs are more symptoms of sexual inequality (within a marriage or a career) than they are free-standing problems in their own right. Our spoken indications of hidden preoccupations sustain the illusion that gender is more a natural category than an ongoing accomplishment within social interaction.

Protests about these problems seem so far to outnumber the reasonable solutions. If the examples in this chapter have not persuaded you that you should change your usage, then it is probably futile to try to just be politically correct. If you are persuaded that change would be useful, do not conclude that it is simple to change. Concentrate on changing your own patterns of use, rather than finding fault in those of others. These words from the meditations of Marcus Aurelius seem to the point.

> From Alexander, the grammarian, [I learned] to refrain from faultfinding, and not in a reproachful way to chide those who uttered any barbarous or incorrect or strange sounding expression; but tactfully to introduce the very expression which they ought to have used, in the course of an answer or assent or inquiry about the thing, not about the word; or by some other suitable suggestion.[15]

This thoughtful emperor left good advice for anyone who is persuaded that we should address the imbalance between the ways we talk about men and about women.

You (as a speaking individual) may make the world a slightly fairer place for men and women if you can change some of your usages. You should be warned that changes in language habits are often difficult to achieve. It is not enough to resolve to change. Should you decide to change your speech patterns, here are some places to begin:

- Begin in your writing, or more specifically, in editing your writing. It seems futile to keep these considerations in mind as you compose a first draft, but you can look for problems of emphasis (as well as derogation of women) as you check for spelling and grammar lapses.
- Listen to a tape recording of your own speech once a year. Listen repeatedly to small bits, especially to phone conversation. This habit may help you improve details in your speaking and listening performances.
- Keep a diary of speech events that strike your ear as odd, conflicted, or just interesting. Write descriptions of events immediately upon their occurrence, using precise wording (like the field notes in this book).
- Cultivate a sense of humor about the mistakes you make in trying to change language habits. Any resolve to make a change leaves a speaker vulnerable to errors and lapses of resolve. Sometimes you reform one usage only to find yourself performing another. A university administrator of my acquaintance once began a meeting of department heads by saying: "I'd like to welcome all the chairmen and chairpersons here this morning." This administrator was making a good faith attempt to be inclusive, but he used a sex-specific form to refer to males and a sex-neutral form to refer to women. If you decide to change any feature of your speech, you will find you will make many humorous mistakes. Be patient with yourself, as well as with others.

Each of the examples discussed in this chapter reflects linguistic habits in our languages and cultures that make men seem more numerous and important than women. I attempt to give clear examples, but in real life the circumstances are rarely clear. In the definition "lady pilot, a plane jane," the words "lady pilot" point to the sense in which many words refer to males as a default value. This raises the implication that "pilot" carries an expected value of male just as does the more explicitly rendered "he" or "salesman." Women are rendered less attention than men due to such linguistic features of emphasis. Yet this is only part of the problem; another part is that the quality of attention given to men (in microfeatures of language) differs from that of attention given to women.

So women receive a discursive double whammy—the practices of emphasis make women seem marginal or absent, but then what attention women do get is largely suspect or derogatory. Linguistic attention to women is attention that makes women blameworthy. Furthermore, this blame (sometimes it seems both praise and blame) is often cast in terms of a woman's physical appearance. These are the topics of the next chapter.

8

....
Making Women
Look Bad
....

ONE EVENING IN THE EARLY 1960S I WAS WATCHING A TV VARIETY SHOW WITH my dad, who was as sweet, intelligent, and fair-minded a man as I have ever known. As a singer was introduced he commented: "Awful good-looking for a colored girl." I was appalled at this utterance and I told him so. I tried to explain that the word "colored" sounded insulting. Dad was not convinced, but he listened to me. The event stuck in my mind because it is one of the few times I have tried to correct someone's speech—let alone to correct an elder relative.

Not until many years later did I consider Dad's gendering talk in this utterance. The word "girl" may sound demeaning, but the real kicker is the speaker's presumption that a singer's looks are more worthy of comment than her voice. By accident, and intending to praise the singer, this tenderly sweet man demeaned the singer both as a person of color and as a woman. Speakers often use language resources, without malice or conscious thought, to make women look bad. Speakers, especially, do this through:

- talk that describes women in negative terms, and
- talk about women's appearance.

Ironically, our language features allow us to make women look bad, while our cultural practices obligate women to look beautiful. These two issues are connected, as are gender-differentiating talk and our belief in sex differences.

DESCRIBING WOMEN

Certain bits of English usage indicate something derogatory about a woman, or about women in general. Using these features contributes to appearances that women are lesser beings than men. Linguist Robin Lakoff illustrates the derogation of women by comparing pairs of similar words in masculine and feminine forms.[1] The feminine terms in each such pair carry comparatively negative connotations, and derogatory secondary meanings.

[1]   Lakoff, 1975

master	mistress
king	queen
sir	madam
patron	matron
bachelor	spinster
brave	squaw
tailor	seamstress
chef	cook

The word "master" and the word "mistress" are similar to each other in meaning, and in some discourse they have been used alike (as in the Christmas carol that goes "God bless the master of this house likewise the mistress too"). "Master" and "mistress" each refer to a person in a high position, or a position of authority. "Master" and "mistress" also are invoked in secondary meanings, and these are more gender-unequal than the primary ones. A "master" is an expert in some craft such as glassblowing or shoe-making. An original of a document can be called a "master copy." The first postgraduate degree is called a "master's degree." What secondary meanings emerge for "mistress"? Illicit girlfriend, or adulterer.

We arrive here at a coincidence: To make women look bad is often to make them unattractively sexual. "Sir" and "madam" are both terms of respect, but a "madam" could also be the person in charge of a bawdy house. "King" and "queen" are both titles for royalty, but "queen" has a secondary meaning of a gay man.

Word pair secondary meanings that are not explicitly sexual favor men in other ways. "Bachelor" and "spinster" both mean single adult, but "spinster" connotes a woman who chooses this lifestyle from a reduced set of options. A "bachelor" holds a job, cultivates refined tastes, and is single by choice.

"Tailor" and "seamstress" are parallel occupational labels that evoke different statuses: A "tailor" owns a store, while a "seamstress" takes sewing jobs home. Similarly, a "chef" holds a high position in a restaurant, while a "cook" stirs stews for modest wages. The secondary meanings of these feminine words make women look bad.

Sexual Terms

Studies of dictionaries indicate that there are many more words available for describing female sexuality than male sexuality—perhaps by a ratio of ten to one. Furthermore, more of the female descriptors evoke negative connotations. Julia Stanley writes of such terms in print fiction and nonfiction:

> My analysis of 220 such terms for women reveals that the only way a woman can define her sexuality with names provided by our culture is demeaning, shameful, and/or oppressively non-existent.
>
> . . . Terms like *screw, rip off, nail, shove it to her,* and *get into someone* clearly define the role of the woman as a passive object on whom the male acts out violent, sadistic fantasies.[2]

Derogatory sexual terms for women include: *ass, bimbo, bitch, concubine, courtesan, cunt, fleshpot, floozy, hag, harlot, hooker, hussy, lay, loose woman, minx, mistress, moll, nookie, nympho, paramour, piece, pig, prostitute, slattern, slut, tail, tart, tramp, trick trollop, wanton, whore.* Compare the more positive valence of the 20 or so terms for men, including: *animal, ass man, Casanova, cockhound, dirty old man, Don Juan, gigolo, letch, male whore, stud, Svengali, whoremonger.*

Test Stanley's claims with this thought exercise. List all the sexual terms you can think of in two minutes. *Do it now.* Next, re-read your list and classify each term as masculine or feminine. Finally, place a plus or minus sign next to each word, depending on whether the connotations of the word are primarily positive or negative. Most people who complete this exercise list more terms describing women than men, and rate negatively more of the sexual terms describing women. Here is another list of derogatory epithets used to describe women.

Bat, dog, chick, mutton, tart. Queen, madam, lady of pleasure, MISTRESS. *Belle-de-nuie,* woman of the streets, fruitwoman, fallen woman. Cow, vixen, bitch. Call girl, joy girl, working girl. Lady and whore are both bred to please. The old Woman image-repertoire says She is a Womb, a mere baby's pouch, or "nothing but sexuality."[3]

This postmodern rant calls attention to some ways that words make women look bad. These words work even in cases in which ambiguity veils the reference to women. Consider this popular song, which is addressed to either a girlfriend or a motor vehicle.

[2] Song: "Dirty World"[4]
He loves your sexy body.
He loves your dirty mind. . . .
You don't need no wax job.
You're smooth enough for me.
If you need your oil changed
I'll do it for you free . . .

The title of this song, "Dirty World," ambiguously refers to pornographic imagination and to engine grease under fingernails. Both a woman and a vehicle could have a "sexy body" as well as a "dirty mind" (grimy engine). This song specifies no addressee, but the singer is male, and most people hear it as a man speaking to and about his girlfriend. Both the large number of dirty words about women in our language and our willingness to hear sexual innuendoes about women promote such interpretation.

[3] Field note (college friends)
Wendy: I can't believe she messed around with him even though she knew he had a boyfriend. What a slut!
Alice: What a slut? What a bitch! Little whore bag.
Wendy: No kidding.

This sexualized vocabulary is not only useful in referring to matters of sexuality.

[4] Field note (women meet in public)

Tina: Alison!

Alison: Bitch- bitch you're wearing my shirt.

[5] Field note

Brenda: This morning some lady at the airport called me a *@#* cunt,
           cause she thought I was cutting in line.

Even in everyday occasions, sex-related insults of women are commonplace.

One genre of sexual talk, related to ogling, and to what sex offenders call "dissector," is talk about the sexually arousing portions of female bodies:

[6] UTCL A41

Don: My friend showed this picture (0.6) where the perfect woman
        was titties and a::ss and [pussy hah hah hah

Ned: [huh huh Aw ma::n, hah hah

Don: Titties and a:ss and pussy

Ned: Where's the rest of the body
                 (0.4)

Don: It was- it was cut off

Ned: hah hah

Don: She don't need- you know, you think about it that's the perfect
        woman

This instance makes explicit reference to the parts of women that form specialized objects of males' ogles, specified by familiar–but derogatory labels ("titties," "ass," "pussy"; not "breasts," etc.). These parts are described as having been "cut off," a term denoting either photo cropping or amputation. These speakers reduce the notion of woman to stereotypically desirable parts dismembered from the rest of her body. Ned and Don speak of such a reduction as perfecting a woman.

Women are so often photographed or displayed as amputated body parts in advertising that we may lose our capacity to be shocked by such representations. These practices may also be combined with other forms of social bigotry. African American feminist bell hooks tells this tale:

Friday night in a small midwestern town—I go with a group of artists and pro-
fessors to a late night dessert place. As we walk past a group of white men standing in the entry way to the place, we overhear them talking about us, saying that
my companions, who are all white, must be liberals from the college, not regu-
lar "townies," to be hanging out with a "nigger." Everyone in my group acts as
though they did not hear a word of this conversation. . . . As we enter the dessert
place they all burst into laughter and point to a row of gigantic chocolate breasts
complete with nipples—huge edible tits. They think this is a delicious idea—seeing no connection between this racialized image and the racism expressed in the
entry way.[5]

As there may be harm to pornography, there may be harm in semiporno-
graphic parodies like chocolate breasts. There surely is harm in the uncritical
acceptance of such representations—even among individuals who never
could be charged with sex offenses. The derogation of a chocolate breast
seems gratuitous, even coincidental. No woman is sexually harassed or threatened by this dessert treat (though one woman feels sexually and racially
intimidated). Alas, is it a harmless coincidence that chocolate, a favorite
dessert substance, shares a place in the color spectrum with African human
skin tones? Would a white chocolate breast have been more, or less, offensive? (A thought experiment: List the secondary meanings for the colors
white, black, yellow, red, and brown in any English dictionary, and rate them
as you rated sexual terms for men and women.)

The sexual derogation of women knows few boundaries. In contrast,
the sexual derogation of men is linguistically marked:

[7] Field note
A: You stayed with him?
B: Yeah (pause) We didn't really do anything, why?
A: I wouldn't let him touch me- he's such a male slut.

A male slut, like a lady pilot, needs gender specification to occupy this atypical role. There is no slutlike term specifically for men.

Jokes about Men and Women

Many jokes target a person who is a member of a some out-group: an ethnic minority, an aggie (from an agricultural college), or a woman.[6] Sometimes the same jokes appear about more than one of these categories. For example: Two Aggies are checking out a car's signal lights. "Go to the back of the car," says one Aggie, "and tell me if the signal light is working." The other Aggie says, "Yes it's working, no it's not, yes it's working, no it's not." Experimental comparison showed that when this joke was about two Aggies it was rated a little bit funny. With two black men it was perceived as offensive. This same joke about two women was rated as hilarious.

If speakers build a face of the alien and frightening other, this includes reference to deviant sexuality. Consider this joke I heard in more than one city during the brief 1991 war between the United States and Iraq.

[8] Field note

Q: Why do they call the camel the ship of the desert?

A: Because it's full of Iraqi seamen.

Dig into an ideological joke by examining its ambiguous term(s); here the term is seamen/semen, or sailors/seminal fluid. The implication is that members of the Iraqi culture—perhaps especially military men—practice bestiality. Someone who wears the face of the enemy in wartime is specifically eligible for slurring.

In wartime or peacetime (piece-time?) sexual slurs are readily applicable to women, especially stereotypically sexualized subcategories of women, such as blondes or cheerleaders:

[9] Field note

Scene: a restaurant kitchen, 2 males and 2 females present

Mick: Hey guys I got a joke.

Stu: What is it?

Mick: How are the Bermuda Triangle and cheerleaders alike?

Ann: Oh this sounds like a real winner! How Mick?

Mick: Well they both swallow seamen (semen) Ha ha ha

Stu: *So* true Mickey! That was a good one

Ann: That was stupid and sexist and ya'll just wish you had been with a cheerleader.

The same pun (seamen/semen) employed to create a killable enemy in war-time is used against women as standard targets of aggression. Note that this joke does not even need to specify that the unmarked form of cheerleader is female.

> [A] good deal of what we find funny in "tendentious jokes" comes from insufficient repression of our fears, that the guffaw is, in no small measure, an act of aggression prompted by those fears. In other words what scares us, we seek to make ridiculous.[7]

It is easier to tell sexual stories about women than it is about men. The language and culture are set up in ways that promote such tellings. A woman or an enemy may be slurred with bad sexuality.

Insulting Women and Their Accomplishments

In talking about human accomplishments, for example, a promotion or a prize, we may attribute the success to internal factors (skill, hard work) or to external factors (luck). Psychologist Kay Deaux found that both men and women are likely to attribute a man's success to skill or determination, but to attribute a woman's success to luck.[8] This shows up in talk:

[10] Field note

During a dart tournament last Tuesday night, a woman is playing against my boyfriend Herbert. He goes up to the board, aims, and misses all 3 shots. He turns to me, frowns, and mutters a couple of curse words indicating his frustration. His opponent's turn is next and she hits 2 triple 20s and another 20. Herbert turns to me again, swears, and says "Damn, she's getting all the shots. Talk about lucky!" It's his turn again, aims, and this time he hits a triple 20 and 2 double 20s. He turns to me, smiles, and says, "Now that's what you call skill" . . . And his opponent shouts out, "Good darts, Herbert, Good darts!"

Both Herbert male and his female opponent praise his successful shots. Nobody praises the female's skills after her successful turn. Deaux emphasizes that both men and women attribute more skill to men's success and more luck to women's.

[11] Field note
Brian: How'd you do on the history test?
Kate: I got an A.
Brian: You got an A? How the hell could you get an A—
            The test was hard as #@# !
Kate: Well, I guess I was just lucky.

Here the male indicates surprise at the woman's success, and the woman responds with two mitigating particles ("Well," "I guess") and then characterizes her own success as "just lucky." This perception can carry over from test scores to career prospects.

[12] Field note
Sarah: I'm done in August.
Roy: What are you gonna do?
Sarah: Well, I got a marketing job with General Motors.
Roy: How did you get that? (Looks shocked)
Sarah: I just interviewed with them.
Roy: Did you know anyone there?

Roy seems surprised at Sarah's job-hunting success. Sarah answers in an offhand way that downplays her achievement: "I just interviewed," indicates that Sarah did only the minimum required for an interviewee. She did not do any special research, for instance. Roy addresses the luck issue when he asks whether Sarah might "know anyone there." Roy suggests that Sarah got the job by some stroke of luck, rather than through hard work, qualifications for the job, or a successfully conducted interview.

In each of these instances, a woman's success is attributed to luck, but a man's successes are attributed to skill. What are the social costs of downplaying the accomplishments of half of humanity?

We need not wait for accomplishments to insult women. The word "woman" itself may be used as an insult. What happens to Karen when she complains to Dave that he nearly caused a serious accident?

[13] Field note

Karen: Dave, you almost hit me yesterday. You came barreling down the parking garage doing fifty.

Dave: More like seventy.

Karen: Oh, great! (sarcastic) See- you are a bad driver!

Dave: Bullshit!

Karen: Bullshit!

Dave: Bitch! ◄

Karen: Idiot!

Dave: Woman! ◄

Karen and Dave exchange a series of hostile name-callings. Dave assaults Karen with the gendered epithet, "Bitch." When Karen answers with the gender-neutral "Idiot" Dave escalates his insult by calling Karen "Woman!" This sort of insult gets circulated on bulletin boards in forms like "How to tell a businessman from a businesswoman:"

- A businessman is aggressive; a businesswoman is pushy
- He is careful about details; she is picky
- He is discreet; she is secretive

Such comparisons describe a woman's accomplishments in a negative light, while a man's accomplishments rate a complimentary vocabulary. Somewhat similarly, a game that a woman is good at might be a game worth insulting on those grounds, as in this instance from Star Trek. Two men and two women are playing poker. One of the women deals, naming a game with many wild cards.

[14] TV: *Star Trek, Next Generation*[9]

Whorf: That is a woman's game.

(pause)

Deana: Why's that.

Whorf: All these wild cards, they support a weak hand. A man's game
          has no wild cards.

Crusher: Let me get this straight. You're saying it's a woman's game
          because women are weaker than men and need more help.

Whorf: Yes.

Whorf insults the dealer's choice of game as "a woman's game" because the
game includes wild cards. Whorf suggests that with many wild cards a player
cannot calculate precise odds, and therefore winning depends on luck instead
of skill.

"Woman" is especially insulting when used to accuse males of weakness. During the 1997 football season, Patriot coach Bill Parcells was asked
about receiver Terry Glenn's recovery from an injury:

[15] News report
Glenn injured his hamstring and missed the entire exhibition season with
what Parcells insisted was a mild strain. Asked about Glenn one day at training camp, Parcells said, "She's making progress."[10]

Parcells uses the pronoun "she" to tar Glenn with womanly weakness in
recovery from an injury. Calling a man a woman has been insulting in many
cultures. Here is an example from eighteenth-century Native Americans, as
told by a nineteenth-century U.S. historian, Francis Parkman:

> The Lenape were then in a state of degrading vassalage to the Five Nations, who,
> that they might drain to the dregs the cup of humiliation, had forced them to
> assume the name of Women, and forego the use of arms.

"In Indian eyes," Parkman continues, "the name of women . . . is the last
confession of abject abasement."[11] That is, calling a warrior a woman is the
worst insult possible. Accepting the label of woman is paired with being
barred from using weapons. Woman is synonymous with weakness. The situation described occurred in the 1760s. Neither the Iroquois nor Parkman
distinguish between insulting the tribe and insulting its (male) warriors.

We seem to practice a similar insult system in America today.

[16] Field note (at a party)

Dick: Hey, where's George?

Tim: He ain't here yet. He had to pick up Fred, which will take a
          while because he is probably still primping.

Dick: Yeah, Fred is such a woman. He takes forever to get ready to
          go anywhere. Did you hear what he did to Rob?

Tim: What?

Dick: He bitch-slapped him. Rob was throwing pillows on him and
          pissed him off. Fred walked up and slapped him across the face.
          Can you believe it?

Tim: Man, Fred must have been PMSing that day.

A man, it seems can be tagged as a woman for paying excessive attention to
his appearance, and for practicing a feminine mode of hitting. The conclusion: Fred is tarred with the womanly insult of being at a characterological
low point in the menstrual cycle.

These instances should be evaluated with the specifically sexual epithets discussed previously. Together, these instances indicate a range of ways
to insult women, and to insult men by tagging them as women.

Associated with the actual term "woman" as an insult are the terms
available in English for insulting women during what could be routine references to persons or practices.

[17] Field note

Woman: Next proposal up for review is Chicks in Communication

Me: Actually it's Women in Communication

Woman: Oh, sorry I guess you're into that women's lib stuff.

The woman chairing the meeting makes a joke about the name of another
organization. Another woman corrects this usage, and draws a counterinsult.

[18] Field note

Sister: (to brother) Ed, I've got to be somewhere in 15 minutes, could
          you help Mom with the dishes

Dad:	No that's squaw work!
Brother:	(giggles)
Mom:	Hush, Tom.

This fieldworker claimed her dad was joking, but it seems unlikely that Ed helped with the dishes. Mom's response shows offense at the word "squaw," which demeans both women and Native Americans as it takes a conservative position on the sex-based distribution of domestic work.

The last examples feature recipients' disapproving reactions to insult terms. Yet such special notice is more the exception that the rule. Here, for example is the start of a story told by two women to a third—about a fourth woman, who is not present:

[19] CGH

Marie:	I thought that thing about the CHICK (.) stun that guy where she's did, went and got arrested.
Rikki:	I know, she's getting charged=
Marie:	Did I tell you that? (.) This- GIRL we met at um (0.6) where were we, Toulouse? (.) She's FROM NEW YORK, she's this BLACK GIRL . . . (CAPS added for analysis)

Here, at the outset of a story about a young woman having an altercation in a nightclub, the protagonist of the story is described by a flurry of terms: "chick," "girl," "from New York," and "black girl." Three of these terms are arguably derogatory as descriptions of a college-aged woman. However, nobody in the speech event takes notice of these descriptions in a way that allows us to assess their impact.

To summarize: There are a number of English words that characterize women negatively, compared to men. Many of these target female sexuality. Women's accomplishments also are devalued, and the word "woman" by itself can be an insult.

Words with Gendered Shadings

So far we have considered usages that specifically derogate women. Yet many commonly used words seem to lean toward the masculine or toward the feminine, carrying comparative derogations even in lightly gendered settings. For instance, the words in the Bem Sex Role Inventory (chapter 2) were developed to describe typical masculine and feminine attributes:

[20] Bem Sex Role Inventory words

masculine	feminine
self-reliant, self-sufficient	sympathetic, compassionate
defends own beliefs	shy
independent, individualistic	affectionate, loyal
assertive, aggressive	soft-spoken
forceful, dominant	tender, gentle, loves children
has strong personality	
has leadership abilities	sensitive to the needs of others
acts as a leader	eager to soothe hurt feelings
willing to take risks	does not use harsh language
competitive, athletic	yielding
analytical	cheerful
ambitious	gullible, childlike
willing to take a stand	flatterable
makes decisions easily	understanding

Masculine words emphasize power, athletic prowess, and military might. Feminine words add up to supporting others with loyalty and understanding.

A lexical study from a similar premise began with lists of the thousand most commonly used words in the English language. Subjects rated these words as masculine words, feminine words, or neither/both. Here are some common English words rated most masculine and most feminine. Guess which list is which:

[21] Borden[12]

art, beautiful, body, born, care, child, face, faith, family, feel, gave, hair, heart, home, hope, hospital, house, kind, little, love, married, morning, natural, peace, period, personal, picture, piece, pretty, red, secretary, south, social, special, summer, wish, within, young

action, analysis, army, building, chief, company, control, data, defense, direct, doctor, economic, fact, farm, firm, force, god, government, gun, hard, history, hit, income, job, law, leader, nuclear, progress, results, science, strength, tax, theory, university, work, world

Words like "military," "industrial," "authority," and "president" are rated as masculine. Words having to do with family, nurturing, limited size, and bodies are feminine. Common words in our language make available differential resources shaded toward the masculine or toward the feminine. Much that we say is made up of partly gendered words implying a bifurcated perceptual field, like a TV screen divided into a pink-shaded half and a blue-shaded half. Much that we say shades into masculinizing and feminizing.

These lists of words are not exactly something that we do. The way cultures operate, you do not have to organize things into masculine things and feminine things. As inheriting a million dollars makes one rich without personal action, the resources of our language offer a speaker an implicitly gendered world before one even begins to speak. Any utterance may include gendering talk, and many of our most common words carry gendered shadings.

Another series of studies engaged participants to list words that characterize a normal human adult. Do this—take two minutes right now to make such a list of attributes using the guide: A normal human is: . . . Next, take two minutes to list words that describe a healthy human adult female. Finally, list words that describe a healthy human adult male. *Do it now.*

The researchers found that attributes for normal human adults turn out to be the same as those for males.

[22] Broeverman et al.[13]

NORMAL MALE/ADULT	NORMAL FEMALE
independent	dependent
direct	sneaky
objective	emotional
dominant	submissive
logical	religious
adventurous	need for security
knows the way of the world	enjoys art and literature
aggressive	talkative

This state of affairs puts a female in a bind. She may set goals for herself as a normal female or as a normal competent adult, but it seems difficult to do both of these things within the same life. A male does not face that problem: To become a normal adult and a normal male is to live up to one set of self-conceptions.

This discussion has not emphasized how mass media stories, and especially advertising, distort masculine and feminine role portrayals. However, consider the beer commercials of 1996–97 in which three men watch women go by on the beach, with one of the women showing pleasure at being stared at. Then the men use their Miller can as a video rewind button to repeat view the women's passing. This ad glamorizes male ogling and female pleasure at being the object of gaze. Should females be happy that men gaze in this way? The balance of this chapter describes talk about women in terms of physical attractiveness. Such talk, like male street remarks, seems complimentary and derogatory at the same time.

THE BEAUTY MYTH

Considering the representation of women in art, critic John Berger argues that *men act or look and women appear.*[14] This is a way that we communicate differently about women than about men. A song lyric familiar to syndicated sitcom watchers describes some females as "lovely" persons whose hair is specifically praised. The man (whose surname is specified) is described only as "busy."

> [23] Song: *Brady Bunch*[15]
> Here's a story of a lovely lady
> who was bringing up three very lovely girls
> All of them had hair of gold, like their mother,
> the youngest one in curls.
> Here's the story of a man named Brady,
> busy with three boys of his own.

The "busy" man acts, the "lovely" women appear. Does the focus on women's beauty hinder women as social actors? There certainly is recurrent focus on appearance in talk about women, which Naomi Wolf labels the *beauty myth:*

The beauty myth tells a story: The quality called "beauty" objectively and universally exists. Women must want to embody it and men must want to possess women who embody it. The embodiment is an imperative for women and not for men, which situation is necessary and natural because it is biological, sexual, and evolutionary: Strong men battle for beautiful women, and beautiful women are more reproductively successful. . . .

None of this is true. "Beauty" is a currency system like the gold standard. Like any economy, it is determined by politics, and in the modern age in the West is the last, best belief system that keeps male dominance intact. In assigning value to women in a vertical hierarchy according to a culturally imposed physical standard, it is an expression of power relations in which women must unnaturally compete for resources that men have appropriated for themselves.[16]

Wolf argues that men set the terms of the beauty myth from their base of political power. The appearance of women is so widely talked about that it dwarfs all other tropes or topics about women.

[24] Field note

Sandra: You and my roommate seem to be going through the same situation right now. I should introduce you.

Mel: Is she cute?

Sandra suggests introducing Mel to her roommate because these two people share common experiences. Mel bypasses this rationale to ask the first obvious question: Is she cute?

In her book on the female teen psyche, therapist Mary Pipher ponders teens' emphasis on beauty:

Beauty is the defining characteristic for American women. It's the necessary and often sufficient condition for social success. It is important for women of all ages, but the pressure to be beautiful is most intense in early adolescence. Girls worry about their clothes, makeup, skin and hair. But most of all they worry about their weight. Peers place an enormous value on thinness.[17]

This emphasis leads to teen eating disorders, among other problems. The emphasis on beauty, even for women held up as beauty icons, has troublesome consequences. A woman can be trivialized by mention of her looks as one who appears and does not act. This seems especially to be the case if a woman shows interest in such appearances:

[25] Beach SDCL: Two Guys, simplified

W: I went out with Meli:ssa last ni:ght

T: Tuh hu: [:h?

W: [We went to u:h (0.2) In n Out? (a burger joint)

T: Uh huh

W: And uh she's all like I'm un*com*fortable in my dre:ss. ◄
            Lemme go home [and cha:nge!
                          [(shared laughter)

T: Too much cleavage?
            . . . (About 5 seconds deleted)

W: I'm like (.) totally fallin asleep in her room cause she's taken for-
            ever cha:ngin and she comes back like, How do I look, ◄
            I'm like o:h no! Like, let's not- l(h)et's not start this off on the
            wrong foot, you know? So anyways

T: I don't think she's that good loo:king do you ◄

W: Hm um

                      (0.2)

T: She's got a nice little body [but that's about it

W: [Mm hm

W: And she's got a cute little dress

The woman in this story is pictured as interested only in her appearance. If her dress seems inappropriate to an occasion (as a nice dress might be inappropriate to a burger joint) she thinks of changing her dress, not acting to change the meal site. After she changes clothes she asks for feedback on her looks. This part of the story prompts the recipient of the story to make dismissive comments on the woman's looks.

Evaluating women in terms of appearance may affect perceptions of their abilities.

[26] Field note (office)

Ed: The new group of trainees Stan hired has some real potential.

Ron: Mark and Joe are really catching on and so are those three women.

Ed: Mandy is such a hard worker, but do you think she is too much of a doll to hold her own?

Ron: Maybe she will prove us wrong

In this office setting two managers discuss a new group of trainees. Two men are named in this praise, the three women are faintly praised but not named. Ed then praises one woman, Mandy, for being a hard worker, but follows this praise by asking whether she is "too much of a doll to hold her own." One problem with evaluating women in terms of beauty is that this is negatively related to lack of professional performance expectations.

[27] Field note (office)

Tom: Did you hear? The new systems analyst will be starting on Friday.

Matt: No, who is he?

Tom: Actually he is a she and her name is Helen. And wait until you see her. She is a babe.

Matt: Hmmm, I'll be looking forward to checking her out

Hearing a technical job title (systems analyst), Matt guesses that the new employee is a male, a presumption discussed in chapter 6. It turns out that the new employee is a woman. Having stated her sex and her first name, Tom says, "Wait until you see her. She is a babe." Being a babe may become a professional liability for Helen. Matt responds that he will "be looking forward to checking her out." Will Matt examine Helen's appearance more closely than her professional skills? Might Matt consider Helen as date potential, or even as a harassment target? Helen's appearance (though Tom praises it) may handicap her professionally. A few weeks later these men (having appreciated Helen as a gaze object) might wonder whether she could be too much of a doll to hold her own. Checking her out as a babe may become more salient than checking her out as a systems analyst.

Two hundred years ago, Mary Wollstonecraft described a connection between emphasis on a woman's looks and dismissal of her useful actions.

> [M]en who, considering females rather as women than human creatures, have been more anxious to make them alluring mistresses than affectionate wives and rational mothers; and the understanding of the sex has been so bubbled by this specious homage, that the civilised women of the present century, with a few exceptions, are only anxious to inspire love, when they ought to cherish a nobler ambition.[18]

Women's powerlessness is linked to social pressures to appear in public as objects of adored beauty.

> For beauty is closely intertwined with power; the myth that married the Sleeping Beauty to Prince Charming solidifies the image. . . . A woman's beauty is of no intrinsic use to herself, but she trades her beauty for his wealth, influence, charms, strength. But it is really not a comfortable trade.[19]

Beauty provides only a slippery slope to limited power through a powerful man, and is vulnerable to fashion, aging, or the man's whim. At the same time, the emphasis on beauty takes over many discourses about women. A pop song, reborn as a movie theme, intones:

> [28] Song: "Pretty Woman"[20]
> Pretty woman walking down the street
> Pretty woman passing by
> Pretty woman stop a while and stay with me.

This text is so familiar we scarcely hear that the woman has just one characteristic, she is pretty. A bystander admires her in a sung street remark. The singer states a desire to start a relationship (respectful line?) on the basis of the woman's appearance. In the movie named after this song, the woman works as a prostitute, indicating:

- that women are objects for the male's ogling gaze, and
- that there are professional disadvantages to being evaluated in terms of appearance alone.

A scene from the film *Carnal Knowledge* opens to show a young woman dressed in white, skating to music in a public park. Audience members are invited to stare at the skater. Then slowly the camera pulls back to reveal two male friends staring at her, and saying:

[29] Film: *Carnal Knowledge*[21]

J:	Do you want her?
A:	I wouldn't kick her outta bed.
J:	Will you look at the *pair* on her.
A:	Do look at that schmuck trying to keep up with her.
J:	They're always with guys like that.
A:	That guy must be sixty if he's a day.
J:	Maybe he'll have a heart attack.
	You could save his life, get a number and #@*# her.

The male protagonists watch the skater and talk about her in terms mixing beauty and sexual availability. These men's talk supports and sharpens their looking by building sexual fantasies.

The masculine gaze plays a major role in the visual arts. Western artists have painted and sculpted female nudes for centuries. Art seems to both celebrate and promote the gazing (and talking) that these two movie protagonists practice. In any art museum, lookers both female and male find undressed representations of women in substantial numbers; nude males also occur, but less frequently and with less celebration. The male nude, like the male slut, is a marked and exceptional form.

To bring each of these art nudes into being, an artist (usually male) has ordinarily obtained the services of an actual nude woman to pose for his attentive staring during the composition. This practice is vivid in the journals of French sculptor Benvenuto Cellini. Here is Cellini's own account of the creation of his "Nymph of Fontainebleu."

I made her pose in the nude. . . . And then I had my revenge by using her sexually, mocking her and her husband. . . . What she said and did nearly drove me out of my mind, and giving into my rage, I seized her by the hair and dragged her up and down the room, beating and kicking her until I was exhausted. . . . Then I began to copy her, and in between times we enjoyed sexual pleasures. . . . [However] she provoked me so much that I had to give her the same beating, and this went on for several days, always in the same pattern, with little variation. Meanwhile I, who had won myself great honor and finished my figure, gave the orders to cast it in bronze.[22]

Cellini's model was trapped by circumstances and bound to him through a triple power relation. As a servant within his household she served his sexual needs and the requirements of his art. The male as patron, voyeur, and artist unite in the history of art nudes.[23]

The film *Camille Claudel* portrays a talented sculptor who becomes a sexually exploited model for Rodin. Early in the film, Mlle. Claudel, working as a novice in the balcony of Rodin's studio, watches as the master sculptor twists a female on a pedestal into uncomfortable positions, then sexually harasses her. Claudel assumes the voyeur position in a scene she will later enter as a participant.

Feminist legal scholar Catharine MacKinnon centers her anti-pornography scholarship around reports of brutal violence and even murder perpetrated upon females who appear in pornographic films. Such artistic activity is supported by consumers who derive pleasure by gazing lustfully in the guise of art.[24]

In horror and slasher films the object of our gaze (especially if she is sexually hungry) becomes a target for sexual violence. In *Dressed to Kill* a woman who is sexually bored with her husband unsuccessfully propositions her psychotherapist. Then she goes to an art museum and (surrounded by art nudes) lusts after a mysterious handsome man. She joins him in a cab for a steamy sex scene featuring the driver adjusting his mirror for a clearer look. Later that night, this woman is brutally murdered. The payoff for being the object of the male gaze is especially harsh if the female dares to perform her own lustful gaze.[25]

The art spectator (or film viewer) mirrors everyday ogling practices, as shown in the skating scene from *Carnal Knowledge:*

[30]   Film: *Carnal Knowledge*[26]

J: Not bad, that one. (the skater)

A: Listen, you must be getting more than your share.

J: I'd get married in a minute if I could find the right girl.

A: Bullshit artist, you and your actress friends.

J: Are you kidding Doctor, you're the one who's got the deal. I
            can- what can I say. Take your clothes off baby I want to check
            your capital gains?

                        (3)

A: I just look.

J: huh huh *Sure* you do.

A: I really do. Susan's plenty enough woman for one man.

                        (2)

A: Hey look at that.

                        (3)

J: That's Sally Joyce.

                        (1)

A: Didn't I see her on Ed Sullivan?

The tax accountant praises the skater's beauty. The doctor replies that the
accountant must get more than his share of sexual opportunity. The tax
accountant envies the doctor for working with disrobed women. The doctor
fingers his wedding ring and says: "I just look." Then immediately, he encourages his friend to look at a woman passing by pushing a stroller, finding in
this passerby a sexual object of interest of the same sort as the skater. These
ogle-and-talk episodes show these men regarding two very different women
with a similar social ogle.

The word "just" in the utterance "I just look" pretends to distinguish
the speaker-ogler from men who yell catcalls, or follow women to their cars,
or do something more menacing. "I just look" claims that action to be something harmless. I remember watching an Ed Sullivan Show in the 1950s on
which appeared a Catholic spiritual leader. His appearance came right after
that of a young woman, whom he passed as he made his entrance. The
churchman turned his head to ogle, and the audience cracked up. Ed Sullivan
said "I thought you took a vow about this sort of thing," and the priest

responded, "Just because I'm on a perpetual diet doesn't mean I can't examine the menu." That is an utterance like "I just look."

Men defend this right to ogle if it is challenged. Recently my tennis partner and I were visiting on the court after a set when he said, "Well look at that!" I followed the line of his gaze to discover a woman stretching with one leg up on a car hood. To record my disapproval I remained silent. He said, "When I stop looking you'll know I'm dead." A masculine cliché: "They'll take away my gun when they pry my cold, dead fingers off the trigger," may connect ogling and love of guns. So does a rhyme my brother learned at army boot camp: "This is my weapon, this is my gun; this one's for fighting, this one's for fun."

The discourse that defends looking bypasses the affiliation of ogling with violent acts and pornographic representations (chapter 4). Yet not all gazing at female beauty is pornographic, or even male. Women's talk about themselves and each other is frequently laden with beauty ideology.

[31] CGH

Marie: Shannon Morris looks g:orgeous have you seen her
Alice: Tell me.
Marie: She looks beautiful (0.4) beautiful like, Shannon's always been
            pretty like her face then she lost all of her weight so she was
            skinny and she still had a pretty face and she was pretty. She's
            like stunning now
Alice: Tell me why.
                 (0.4)
Marie: Her hair's like red, but with a lo:t of blonde in it?
Rikki: And it's [just so
Marie: [It's like down to here.
Rikki: And it's curly.
Marie: All curly, one length, she's thin?
Alice: Thin.
                 (0.4)
Marie: She's not skinny.
Rikki: Right. She's thin [she's this thick

Marie: [She's like ta:ll.
She's real tall looking, and she's like you look at her. She's the
type of girl that would walk down the street and you'd look like
three times. Cause she's very attractive.
                         (0.6)
Like stunning [I was in shock
Rikki: [s'lookin *so* good.

The word "stunning" centers this discussion of a local incarnation of the
beauty myth. This woman is so beautiful that passersby look at her three
times. The person who looks at Shannon is stunned, shocked.

These women show a detailed vocabulary for discussing Shannon as a
paragon of beauty: "thin" is distinguished from "skinny"; hair length is discussed in detail, as is weight loss, so that this stunning beauty is seen to have
been partly achieved. The discussion of the beautiful acquaintance then is
applied to the art of enhancing one's own personal appearance. Immediately
after the preceding fragment, Alice begins a lengthy and self-effacing assessment of her own assets in light of the ideal:

[32] CGH, continued
Marie: Like stunning [I was in shock
Rikki: [s'looking *so* good.
Alice: There's really nothing stunning about me and I've been tryin to
           figure something stunning ¡hhh like I know that I'm okay, and
           everything but I'm saying ¡hhh like there's certain people that
           you look at, and there's something that stands out with them?
           I don't think there's anything wrong with me but I don't think
           I have one thing that stands out, because the only that could
           is maybe my cheekbones? ◄
                      (1)
           But who notices cheekbones.
                      (1)
           You know?
Marie: I do.

Alice: And so my sister told me:, that I should stop wearing all- all my makeup and like do everything really lightly, and then wear bright lipstick.

(1)

That's what I been trying to do but still doesn't make me stunning

Marie: Well some people aren't stunning some people you're- are pretty.

Alice: I'm just not stunning.

Alice repeatedly pursues praise for her efforts to achieve the beauty status of "stunning." She notes that she is following her sister's makeup advice in order to look her best. Yet she still cannot achieve stunning looks. Alice puts both herself and her friends into a vulnerable position by transparently fishing for appearance compliments.

It is like that scene in Disney's *Snow White,* in which the wicked queen asks her magic mirror who is the fairest. Having heard about stunning Shannon, Alice asks her pals to reflect on her attempts to measure up to the beauty myth. Marie admits that Alice is not stunning, but grants her a consolation prize: "you're pretty." This assessment does not comfort Alice, who repeats her lament: "I'm just not stunning." The beauty myth produces few contented female contenders.

Marie and Alice go on to remember another occasion when they evaluated each other in terms of the beauty myth.

[33] CGH, continued

Marie: One time when Alice and I were earlier talking about what was the prettiest and ugliest about us, and when- I was like telling her (0.6) the- the best feature you have's like your cheekbones and all this stuff and I go what about me she goes, your best features are your eyebrows.

Alice: That is not [what I said

Marie: [It is too:

Marie refers to an earlier occasion in which She and Alice had exchanged detailed assessments of appearance features and how to improve them. That occasion had left Marie feeling wounded, she says, because the best Alice could do was to praise her eyebrows. This talk about the past indicates that these friends have shared an ongoing colloquy that spans clothing, makeup, jewelry, and cosmetic surgery. The practical project of looking good repeatedly is refocused in talk about others, as well as in interaction games to construct inventories of one's positive and negative appearance features. This candid self-evaluation points toward the unachievable goal of measuring up to the beauty myth. In pursuing this preoccupation these cosmetic esthetes spare no source of enhancement.

The practices and scenes of cosmetic criticism seem ubiquitous:

[34] Field note

Jan: Wow! She's really going for the natural look

Zoe: Yeah, she always dresses like that, T-shirt with the sleeves rolled up, some type of athletic shorts, hair in a ponytail, no makeup.

Jan: She's got a really good body.

Zoe: Yeah, she's always working out and doing some kind of exercise.

The "natural look" is not left unspecified: These onlooking critics make a list of the items of clothing needed to constitute this look. Critics also discuss these items in their own appearance, not just those of passersby. These discussions often take the form of practical advice:

[35] Field note

Rhonda: What do you think about this one?

Wendy: It looks good, but are you sure you want to wear a bikini to go waterskiing in? What if it comes off when you fall?

Rhonda: Well, hopefully I won't fall. And besides, I haven't worked my butt off at the gym just to wear a one-piece. Matt is going to be there too.

Wendy: Oh, so that's why you're so nervous.

Rhonda: I'm not nervous. I just want to look good and then we'll see what happens.

                              (Pause)

Rhonda: Do you think he'll like my navel ring, or will he think it's, uh,
            trashy?
Wendy: I don't know, I don't know him that well.
Rhonda: Oh god, maybe I should get a one-piece?

The indecisive quality of this scene grows from the women taking a number
of factors into consideration. A kind of look, the practicality for an activity
like waterskiing, the impact on a potentially interesting male of both a more
revealing swimsuit and a navel ring. The two women do not resolve this
problem; rather they turn over its possibilities and let their expertise combine
in dialog.

This sort of conversation is often portrayed as a kind of women's talk,
and something that troubles male-female intimacy.

[36] Field note
Cathy: I've gained so much weight lately
Jake: Really? I haven't noticed.
Cathy: Yeah, look, I got all this flappy stuff on my thighs and my stom-
            ach.
Jake: Oh, don't worry about it
                    (pause)
            Besides I like the flappy stuff. It makes you so nice and soft.
Cathy: You think I'm fat?
Jake: No, I don't think you're fat.
Cathy: You just said it.
Jake: No I didn't
Cathy: Yes, you did. You said I have flappy stuff.
Jake: No, you said-
Cathy: You make me feel so ugly when you say that.
Jake: You were the one who said it.
Cathy: But you agreed.

Cathy raises a beauty topic (in this case fat) in a self-doubting way. Jake gets
into interactional trouble as he reacts to an apparent request for reassurance.
As he denies the problem his credibility is challenged. As he tries to solve the

problem by being reassuring, he stands accused of having called Cathy fat. Such examples support gendered-difference mythology. What is being celebrated in this story? Perhaps that women may talk of such matters in a dialogic way—preserving indecision and face while practicing terminology and criteria. Yet a male lover's comments are received with suspicion.

In most of the examples above, women speak only of their near misses in beauty, but there is also an ugly myth.

[37] Field note

Marge: Did you see her?

Jenny: Yeah, what the hell did she do to her hair. It used to be your color, right?

Marge: Yeah, it looked so much better. The blonde looks like crap.

Jenny: (laughs) Yeah.

Marge: And she thinks she is such hot shit and she's just drop dead gorgeous. What a dumb bitch.

Jenny: (laughs) Yeah.

Jenny points out the target for her invective, and Marge volunteers a negative evaluation. The contempt for this observed woman is then turned into a failed pretension, earning the term "bitch." The association of negative appearance with other negative evaluation is exemplified in this phone chat between college men:

[38] Wool: Glenn

Stan: I was uh at my brother's wedding last weekend.

                (0.8)

Dave: There's a lot of wool at weddings. Y'know that?

Stan: I know. You wouldn't be*lie*ve all the coot that was up there.

Dave: Ho hoh khhh

Stan: They make these girls look like *dog* meat.

                (0.8)

Dave: Haw:::hhh

Stan: These girls have no (0.7) These girls look like shit down here compared to girls up there, I'm tellin ya.

Dave:	Aw *hell* yeah
	(0.9)
Dave:	Well they're *easy* to grease down here. Up there 'er a challenge

These men share an interest in the project of gazing at women (a.k.a. "girls") in a variety of environments. They compare women using reference terms applicable to wildlife and pet food ("wool," "coots," "dog meat"). The environments of women are taken for granted as subject to scrutiny.

This instance shows a mix of sexual derogation of women and orientation to the beauty myth. It is not difficult to show how the beauty myth operates in these conversations. It is a more rigorous challenge to make the connection between an emphasis on female appearance and the powerless state of women in the corporate world and in the public polity. Yet the connection seems as genuine as it is worth describing.

SHOULD WE CHANGE HOW WE TALK ABOUT WOMEN?

What have we learned from this discussion (chapters 7 and 8)?

- We talk differently about men than about women. We emphasize men over women, marginalizing women and their achievements, confining descriptions of women to stereotypical women's places. When we do talk about women, many micro speech features serve to derogate women through sexual insult. We hobble women's being taken seriously by discussing them in terms of physical appearance and describing their accomplishments as lucky rather than skillful.
- This is not just something men do to women. It is something we all do. It is not primarily that men and women speak differently in these ways, but that we all speak and listen alike. Both men and women listen differently to women than to men; both men and women speak differently about women than about men.
- Many of the ways that we talk about women and men happen out of habit or by accident. We often continue to do such things even after we try to change our habits.

These microindicators of talk about women (emphasis, derogation, and the beauty myth) combine with each other. As illustrated in the "plane Jane" joke, these uses do not appear neatly sorted into the categories raised in the past two chapters. Sex and violence issues, especially the economy of the ogle, add to the mix. We gender conversation in eclectic yet cumulative ways—one orientation sparks a next one. Each of these genderings is in some sense unfair to women and difficult to change.

These discursive practices are unfair to women in ways that may hinder the achievement of gender equity. Maybe men seem to have big egos because they have received praise, permissiveness, and patriarchal powers. Talk about men and about women displays troublesome ideology and creates bits of bad karma, drops in the bucket of inequality within the arrangement between the sexes.

We should collect information about patterns by which we treat men and women unequally or unfairly, and we should consider changing our patterns of writing and speech. Any recent change in usage, yours or someone else's, often sounds awkward to speakers and listeners alike. Any change, like any speech act, is multifaceted and creates unforeseen rhythms, new word associations, the potential for misunderstanding. We do not want to go around remarking obsessively over the ideological bias of each utterance. Yet as we develop and refine our consciousness that what we say represents us, we begin to notice that each utterance may carry undesired ideological freighting.

Any change of habitual ways of communicating is only partially under our control. Twenty years ago, when writing a textbook, I resolved to introduce gender fairness into my use of examples. Throughout the manuscript I carefully alternated examples with male and female protagonists—which did not seem that difficult since most of that text's examples were hypothetical instances. I failed to notice, however, until an editor discovered this imbalance, that thirteen straight female examples had turned on issues of physical appearance. Gleep.

Consider, if you are interested in change, the company you keep. If you try to quit smoking does it make a difference with whom you hang out? Any social partner might pull out a cigarette, and it might smell good. You might see the bulge in a friend's pocket and fall into a nicotine fit. For almost any kind of practice—name your habit—there is a speech community that supports that abuse. Who you are with makes a big difference in improving habits.

Those speakers who favor change in speaking patterns must also consider how to react when others perform potentially harmful usages. One temptation is to correct the other—yet there are few occasions in which such correction has a positive impact on the behavior of the corrected person. Furthermore, correction often leads to polarization, justification, denial, or other talk about talk. Correct others' speech sparingly. Most corrections are ineffective and cause problems of their own. Correcting details of others' writing may be useful, if circumstances make such correction appropriate. Then, be gentle. There are few activities more sexist than an accusation of sexism.

If we are concerned about the noises we make in the social world, we should give continuing consideration to the examples that have been given here. These examples show routine and familiar ways of speaking unequally about women and men. It is difficult to find examples of wording that advantage women at the expense of men. As we cast such representations within our own speech, we remake and sustain inequality between the sexes. We also sustain the notion that men and women are from different planets when we talk differently about women than about men.

9

How Men and Women Talk

IN DISNEY'S FILM *THE LITTLE MERMAID,* ARIEL STRIKES A QUESTIONABLE BARGAIN with Ursula, the sea-witch. Ariel bargains for legs, and with these a chance to become human. The mermaid wants to become human to get her man. The deal is that Ariel can stay in human form if she wins from her man a kiss of true love. The price that Ariel must pay in order to get legs is to give up her voice. Ursula the sea-witch is rather flip as she insists on this part of the bargain. She claims that men do not like women who talk anyhow. "True gentlemen avoid 'em, when they can. . . . It's she who holds her tongue, who gets her man." Ursula offers Ariel the feminine Faustian bargain—to gain success in romance she must mute her voice.[1]

To be muted is to be quieted. A musical mute is a device that is put in the throat of a trumpet to make it sound soft and whiny. Are there social pressures to systematically soften or silence women's speaking? A woman's place includes a number of nonspeaking roles, and roles where her prescribed voice is soft and whiny. Does getting a man entail muting a woman?[2]

If you get your man, do you lose your voice?

One feminist charge is that marriage is an institution designed by men and systematically unfair to women. Certainly it has proven a theme in this book that marital communication bears much of the responsibility for the perception that men are very different from women in communication style.

The muting of women also shows in the history of public speaking. Few women orators are represented in anthologies of famous speeches. This is no coincidence. In the most civilized places on earth, women have rarely been allowed to assume the public podium. In American history, women won limited public voice during anti-slavery and women's suffrage movements. Yet even today there are very few women orators and politicians. Women are less likely than men to develop a public voice. Given many centuries in which males prevented women from speaking in public, such shyness of the limelight may have become a stable feature of feminine culture. There is evidence that women avoid public speaking opportunities even now.[3]

There is also evidence that men speak more than women, not only in public but in all settings. Deborah James and Janice Drakich examined fifty-six studies of the amount of talk by males and females. Twenty-four of these studies were of formal task activities.

> Of these twenty-four studies thirteen found men to talk more than women over-
> all, and three found men to talk more in certain circumstances. . . . Only one
> study found that women talk more than men overall.[4]

These differences could be due to men's positions of status or power in formal organizations. Of sixteen studies examining amount of talk in non-task male-female dyads five found males to talk more than females overall, one found men talk more in certain circumstances, nine found no difference, and one found that women talk more.[5]

It seems likely that stereotypes about talkative women are based on a background expectation that women should talk very little, rather than on empirical evidence about female loquacity.

DO MEN INTERRUPT WOMEN?

Many investigators have studied whether women's speech is muted through the hypothesis that men interrupt women. "Interruption is an intrusion, a trampling on someone else's right to the floor, an attempt to dominate."[6] This hypothesis rings true to experience, but it is difficult to prove in concrete terms because interruption is a slippery discourse concept. To understand the difficulties let us begin with one example of an interruption from a student's experience. Mom, a professional health researcher, is teaching her daughter some biology when her husband breaks in:

[1] Field note

| Mom: | And then when the body starts to produce antibodies |
| Dad: | But before they do that they have to produce these specific cells . . . |

Mom has started a "when" clause, which projects a second clause to complete the utterance-unit. Dad breaks in to add a scientific detail, and his breaking in prevents the completion of Mom's utterance. The fieldworker wrote:

> It really, really made her mad. And the thing about dominance is that my mother has worked under my father for years, then they split up professionally. They're still married, but they no longer work together and my mother has been fighting tooth and nail to get out from under the shadow of my dad. And to stop helping him.

This man's interrupting of his wife seems to reflect power relations in their professional world—as well as their family world, and this particular interruption did some harm. Yet just what speech characteristics make this interruption interruptive? Well, one speaker (Mom) is not finished talking, when another (Dad) takes the floor. How do we find a rigorous definition to describe a large number of such instances? That is a difficult question that has perplexed dozens of researchers.

Interruption seems to be a concept about messages, but it labels enormously diverse examples. Also, one rarely applies to oneself the term interruption. Sometimes one might say "I'm sorry I interrupted you," but mostly one says, "You interrupted me," or "He interrupted her." Interruption is usually seen as a bad thing done more or less intentionally by someone else to dominate or ignore a previous speaker. *Interruption,* then, is not a concrete specific speech feature, but rather a broad interpretive category that sounds more specific than it is.[7]

Ignoring this complexity, dozens of researchers have completed studies of interruptions that have characteristics missing in the example given previously. (See figure 2.)

The definitions of interrupting vary from study to study. Still:

FIGURE 2. TECHNICAL GUIDE TO INTERRUPTION STUDIES

Three sets of criteria have evolved for characterizing instances of interruptions, though few studies employ all three.

Speech overlap. Two classic studies by West and Zimmerman tabulate only interruptions in which there is speech overlap—the second (interrupting) speaker begins to talk while the first speaker is still speaking. You can diagram a speech overlap in transcription format like this:

```
A:  xxx xxxxx xxxxx xxxxxx [ xxxxxxx
B:                         [ xxxx xxx xxx xxx
```

West and Zimmerman assume that when a speaker begins a turn unit, he or she is entitled to complete it. Therefore, if a next speaker overlaps a prior speaker's turn-in-progress—as indicated by the schematic above—then this may be considered a micropolitical overpowering of the other. Therefore, West and Zimmerman would not tabulate the instance in the story about antibodies, even though the second utterance seems interruptive of an utterance, because the instance does not include any overlap.[9]

However, West and Zimmerman do not count *all* overlaps as interruptive, but only "deep overlaps," those at least two syllables from a turn-unit boundary. For example, they would not count this instance because Carol's utterance could be heard as complete at the word "nine."

[2] UTCL D8.2

Cara: Should be around nine [or so
Rick: [Well do you have an extra *bed* in your uh (.)
       place?

This overlap occurs right at a transition-relevance place, and therefore Rick's starting up in overlap with the two final syllables of Cara's prior utterance is not really interruptive but an instance of "normal overlap." Normal overlap is rarely noticed or found to be a power issue. Yet it can be.

Facilitation. An interruption is not facilitative. The overlap cannot be just to say "Yeah," or "Uh huh," or to say the same thing as the other person. If you say "yeah," you are not trying to dominate the other person, but support him or her.

[3] UTCL J10.1
Kay: . . . You can [*write* requis [itions
Ed: [*Yeah*   [*Right*

Ed's overlaps in this instance do not override or contradict Kay's point. Ed offers something additional and facilitative, not interruptive. Tannen distinguishes supportive and nonsupportive interruptions, and argues that women do the former, and men the latter. "Whereas women's cooperative overlaps frequently annoy men by seeming to co-opt their topic, men frequently annoy women by usurping or switching the topic."[10]

Successful vs. unsuccessful interruption. The overlapping candidate-interruption drives another person from the floor in midturn. It makes a difference whether the prior speaker drops out before completing a turn unit, or apparently completes a turn unit, as in this example:

[4] UTCL F1.7
D: . . . I don't know mother lemme check my calendar I don't know what
      I'm gonna [be doing
M: [I need two more people to do phoning for Phil Gramm.

To summarize: even with these three criteria for distinguishing interruptions—criteria that require the critic to overlook many instances that participants may feel are interruptive—it still is not always clear which way to classify an example. Interruption is really a folk category, not a clear linguistic concept. Different studies count it differently. Furthermore, counting interruptions misses much of the phenomenon of interrupting—which often unfolds across many speaking turns.

> Of twenty-one studies which have compared the number of interruptions initi-
> ated by females and by males in dyadic interaction, only six . . . have found men
> to interrupt women more than the reverse. Thirteen studies have found no
> significant difference between the sexes . . . And two have found women to inter-
> rupt men more.[11]

To summarize: The hypothesis that men interrupt women has not been
proven—though it may well be true. It is not a simple matter to decide when
interrupting is taking place. These difficulties in studying interruptions
should make us cautious as we approach the issue of male-female speech differences related to social power.

STUDIES OF FEMALE-MALE SPEECH DIFFERENCES

In two and a half decades since Robin Lakoff put into modern linguistic dress
the notion that men and women speak different dialects of English, scholars
have repeatedly searched for speech differences between the sexes. These
claims carry a difficult burden of proof. In previous chapters of this volume,
I argued based upon examples that—for instance—certain language features
emphasize men over women. However, if one argues that men and women
talk differently, the standard of proof shifts from certain features in particular examples to the claim that *all* (or most) talk by men is different from all
(or most) talk by women.

For instance, to test the claim that men speak more than women
(thereby showing and maintaining micropolitical dominance) one must find
a way to tally speech features to document this general pattern within a large
and carefully chosen sample of talk. In spite of these difficulties, many investigators have rushed to the argument that men and women speak differently—probably because the notion of male-female speech differences seems
so plausible.

Several scholars claim that women's speech contains powerless features
that mitigate each woman's social power. Despite the widespread appeal of
this thesis, it has been supported and refuted by equal numbers of studies.
Clearly, most speakers *believe* men's speech to be different from women's. That
belief, along with ways we talk about women and perform sexuality, sustains

our perceptions of genderlects. Numerous studies in the 1970s described features alleged–or reported to distinguish men's and women's speech.[12]

- *Quantity of talk.* Men are reported to talk more than women, in male-female interaction at least; and men interrupt women. This constitutes micropolitical domination of the floor.
- *Questions.* Women are reported to ask more questions than men, especially tag questions and questions that are grammatical statements except for rising terminal pitch. Men say: "Dinner at six." Women say: "Dinner at six, all right?" or "Dinner at six?" The women's forms give the recipient more options; the men's forms limit the others' options.
- *Qualifiers.* Women are reported to clutter their speech with qualifying particles and disclaimers, thereby hedging the force of utterances. Men say: "I'm against the tax reform bill." Women say: "I'm no expert, but I think I'm sort of against the tax bill."
- *Politeness.* Women's speech is reported to be polite and supportive, carrying the burden of keeping interaction going. Men's speech is blunt, self-assertive, and political. Women say "uh huh," and follow up on men's topics, but this is not reciprocated.[13]

Genderlect sociolinguists is the 1970s claimed to have discovered in gender a new source of dialect variation. These researchers argued that women's use of these features contributes to their own political victimization. The most-recommended short-term solution to such problems is for women to take assertiveness training—even though there has been limited evidence that women are less assertive than men.[14]

Most of these early genderlect studies used self-report data, and written rather than spoken stimuli. Some researchers were discerning enough to describe such work as studying *folklinguistics,* or how people *believe* men and women speak. Other writers confused stereotypes with evidence. Most English speakers *do* report their belief that men and women use different language patterns. However, evidence taken from tape recordings of natural talk rarely confirms that men and women speak distinct dialects.[15]

To the extent that actual male-female speech differences exist, these differences show only weak association with power. Men, for instance, may actually use more nonstandard pronunciation or grammar, and have smaller vocabularies and lower voices than women.[16] These differences are widely believed in, but few researchers have examined them rigorously because they seem remote from the issues of male dominance that fuel the research.

The sex dialects literature evolved into the powerless speech literature during the 1980s. Researchers did not find that women use hedges, question forms, or polite speech. Instead, they found that persons holding little power use these features: inexperienced court witnesses, unemployed persons, assembly line workers, uneducated persons.[17] If women use these features more, this reflects social position more than gender.[18] It is not too surprising that there are more powerless women than men; but powerless men use the same features. The features do not seem to be specifically gendered.

Powerless speech hypotheses improve upon stereotype-based positions because they may be tested in details from actual speech samples. These studies also emphasize that women sound powerless because gendered social practices keep them in subordinate positions.

One problem with most genderlect research is that it remains insensitive to the addressee in coproducing discourse. Linguist Dede Brouwer, who studied ticket purchasing at a Dutch railway station, argues that we may be "on the wrong track" if we look only for male-female differences in speech patterns. Her studies actually showed more message variation associated with sex of addressee than with sex of speaker—especially in use of politeness markers such as "please," or in use of modal auxiliaries (e.g., could, should).[19]

Certain features of most utterances change with different recipients. This insight broadens the genderlect issue by suggesting that speech pattern should be studied not just as a characteristic of female speakers, but as stuff that emerges within three sex-relevant dyads: male-male, female-male, and male-female. Larger groups of speaker-listeners create added complications.

There also may be connections between the recipient's role in genderlects and certain *speech evaluation research,* which communication researcher Anthony Mulac has labeled a gender-linked language effect.[20] This effect emerges in contrasts in ratings of male and female language samples. Most of these samples come from monolog situations, and in most studies the samples are rated in written form only. Raters cannot tell male from female samples, but somehow various projective ratings do distinguish male from female monologs. Males and females are rated differently in esthetic quality (females higher) and in dynamism (males higher). In some studies, women's speech is rated higher in status, which runs somewhat counter to language and power theories. Mulac also argues that, although no single feature distinguishes male from female speech patterns in his stimulus material, a statistical combination of over a dozen features does allow such predictability. Mulac argues that this combination of findings shows clear, if subtle, male-female speech differences that lead to differing evaluations. Yet perhaps his ingenious set of studies shows something less than this: When raters make evaluative decisions about writing, they may utilize gender stereotypes in this task.

One speech evaluation study used matched guise procedures to distinguish evaluative consequences of female speech features (sex-dialect hypothesis) from the evaluative consequences of attributing speech to a female (stereotype hypothesis).[21] Results slightly favored the latter hypothesis—that identifying a speaker as female leads to rating speech as attractive, and identifying a speaker as male leads to evaluating the speech as dynamic.

These diverse approaches suggest the need to study the impact of speaker sex on speech features in a way that allows us to compare it with sex of addressee. May we compare what the *same* person would say when speaking to a male and when speaking to a female? May we, conversely, compare how similarly male and female speakers speak *to one and the same addressee?* May we compare these against other variables, such as social status?

A STUDY OF LANGUAGE, POWER, AND GENDER

We did such a study of tape-recorded telephone calls to a healthcare information service.[22] Callers were half men and half women. Therefore, these materials included recordings of (female) information specialists talking to men and talking to women in very similar circumstances (allowing us to ask how speakers adapt to sex of addressee). This same sample revealed male and female callers talking to the same addressee (the information specialist), allowing tests of hypotheses about speaker sex.

Further, we compared callers' speech to that of the information specialists, who hold information power and are experienced in this speech event. We calculated quantitative measures associated with each of three independent variables: sex of speaker, sex of addressee, and speaker power.

Dependent variables included four sets of language features: quantity of speech, questions, qualifiers, and indicators of politeness. Some specifics on these measures:

- *Quantity*—We compared the number of syllables spoken by each partner. We also tabulated deep interruptions as a ratio of *successful* interruptions over total interruption attempts.
- *Questions*—We tabulated questions, separating tag questions and all other questions.
- *Qualifiers*—We distinguished qualifiers that *shield* the speaker's state of uncertainty (e.g., I think, I'm not sure) from those that *approximate* speech content (e.g., maybe, sort of).[23]
- *Politeness*—We tabulated these indicators of politeness: salutations by name or title, expressions of gratitude, modal auxiliaries (e.g., might, could), the particle "uh huh," and praise.[24] Table 9.1 shows the number of instances of each speech feature—according to speaker, addressee and role (information power).

To summarize table 2: The role difference between callers and information specialists was associated with more contrasts than either notion of genderlect—connected with speaker or connected with addressee. Some of the apparent gender differences (e.g., males say "uh huh"), appear to contradict the findings predicted in the powerless speech literature. A tabular summary shows that genderlect variations pale before power as a predictor of speech variation.

- *Sex of speaker* (speech patterns of male vs. female callers)
  — Quantity: No differences
  — Questions: No differences
  — Qualifiers: No differences
  — Politeness: Males use more *uh huhs* (70/24).
- *Sex of addressee* (talk to male vs. female callers)
  — Quantity: No differences
  — Questions: Females may be asked more tag questions (13/5).

TABLE 2. GENDER-RELEVANT FEATURES BY
SEX OF SPEAKER, SEX OF ADDRESSEE, AND SPEAKER ROLE

SPEECH FEATURES	SEX OF SPEAKER		SEX OF ADDRESSEE		SPEAKER ROLE	
	MALE	FEMALE	MALE	FEMALE	INFO.SPEC.	CALLER
Quantity						
syllables	3,899	4,148	6,053	6,016	12,069	8,047
interruptions	5/9	4/10	5/5	9/10	14/15	9/19
Questions						
tags	3	6	5	13	18	9
others	18	18	58	58	116	36
Qualifiers						
self-limits	13	12	10	8	18	25
approximators	14	13	17	23	40	27
Politeness						
modals	23	31	81	61	142	54
salutations	4	2	0	5	5	6
gratitude	13	17	7	4	11	30
uh huh	70	24	51	42	93	94
praise	2	2	17	1	18	4

— Qualifiers: No differences

— Politeness: Males receive more praise (17/1).

— Females receive more salutations (5/0).

- *Information Power* (information specialists vs. callers)

    — Quantity: Information specialists speak 60 percent of the time. A high percentage of information specialists' interruptive overlaps succeed.

    — Questions: Information specialists ask more questions (145/35).

    — Qualifiers: No differences

    — Politeness: Information specialists use more modal auxiliaries (142/54).

    — Information specialists give more praise (18/4).

    — Callers more frequently express gratitude (30/11).

Few powerless language features are used differently due to sex of speaker or recipient. The differences that do appear are either counter to predictions (males' "uh huh" use) or cannot be interpreted due to small numbers of occurrences. Some of these features, however, do correlate with speaker power. The quantity variables differed in the predicted direction, but questions differed in the opposite direction of predictions, as did modal auxiliary use and use of praise. The powerless speech hypothesis, in some complex form, can be supported. However, it must be separated from the genderlect hypothesis. These results agree with a summary of speech evaluation research by social psychologists Ng and Bradac:

> Lakoff's claim is that women . . . have been socialized into a low-power role and that a part of this role entails using a style of speech labeled the *feminine register*. The language features representing this register are very similar to the features representing the low-power style. . . . [T]here is some reason to believe that males and females . . . differ to some extent in their use of language, albeit in ways differing from the style suggested by Lakoff. . . . It seems likely, however, that situational factors such as communicator role are stronger influences on language production than is language per se. . . .
>
> Even though objective linguistic differences appear to be small and their relationship to objective differences in power unclear, there appear to be widely shared, strong beliefs or stereotypes about how men and women talk.[25]

Although self-report studies have indicated female-male speech differences associated with power, close examination of discourse features from tape recordings supports only "powerless speech" hypotheses—not genderlect hypotheses. Perhaps genderlects are products of stereotyping. More likely, gendering occurs in ways that do not make distinctive use of power-relevant features. Powerful people, most of whom are men, may have multiple grounds for how they talk. Studies of power in language should take these directions:

- Studies such as the one reported here should be replicated across larger and more varied records of naturally occurring speech samples. Sex of speaker and of recipient should not necessarily be the only focus for curiosity. Kinds of power (e.g., information, position, status) should be systematically investigated. Results will not be simple, and may not clarify the issue of male-female speech differences.

- Genderlects must be addressed in terms of power issues. Most genderlect research to date has tabulated males' and females' use of speech features presuming equal social power.
- We should find ways to integrate genderlects with issues of courtship, marriage, and the family. Since these are highly gendered settings, such talk may show more of the distinctive properties of genderlects than turn up elsewhere.
- Certain modes of talking that we consider masculine may actually be features of monologue/dialogue. This issue is discussed in the remaining pages of this current chapter.

IN A DIFFERENT VOICE

Another version of the genderlect hypothesis has become widespread in the 1990s: Men speak in the voice of public rationality and women in the voice of relational sensitivity. This concept may be traced to Carol Gilligan's 1982 book, *In a Different Voice*.[26] Gilligan's topic is the moral development of children. This work grows from the theories of cognitive psychologist Jean Piaget, who pictured human cognitive and social development occurring in stages. Gilligan joined a team of researchers who had been studying how children use moral prescriptions as guides to action. One mark of such development is that older children learn to take into account more than one moral issue at a time. The child first masters absolute rules for action, but later learns that certain rules contradict others. An adult is able to state two contradictory rules that apply to a situation and then choose which one is most salient to the current moment.

To illustrate this skill, let us consider one of the problems that researchers have posed to children of various ages: Heinz's dilemma. Heinz's wife is ill and will die unless she receives a very expensive medicine that they cannot afford. Heinz realizes that he could steal the drug and probably not get caught. The question: Should Heinz steal the drug? This problem poses two value statements (you should not steal, and you should help a loved one in need), then forces a choice between them. According to Piaget's theory, an adult, or an older child, should be able to verbalize these conflicting value statements, then choose between them.

In the early studies in this tradition, results for boys seemed quite clear and supported Piaget's theory, but girls' development seemed less clear. Perhaps for this reason these researchers studied only boys for many years. Gilligan asked whether studies of girls might show a different picture of development. Her interview studies found that girls and women resisted answering the Heinz's dilemma as posed. Rather than choosing between the two abstract values (not stealing, helping a loved one) girls suggested talking things over with the druggist, or with people from social agencies. Girls, claims Gilligan, approach such problems with a *relational voice*. Women see life as a network of relationships with people. Males (and also science and government) view life as physical and factual. Life has right and wrong answers. Men perceive life in terms of rules and hierarchy, whereas females are concerned about a network of relationships. Women, it is argued, calculate the personal and social costs of any course of action. Women also discuss a problem with others rather than searching alone for an objective solution. Deborah Tannen labels this female pattern *rapport talk,* which she distinguishes from the male pattern of *report talk.*[27]

I stated one problem with Tannen's position in chapter 6: Her most compelling evidence is examples from couple members. If there are any sex differences in couples, these might grow as much from the way couple culture develops as from the nature of males and females in general. A second problem emerges when we consider the notion of dialogue (chapters 1, 4) as primarily a sex difference. Undoubtedly, social stereotypes link femininity to relationship and dialog—and link men to monologue and content. How far can we go from there toward saying that men and women actually do speak in these different modes?

Investigators who rely on self-report data confirm this view that men are monologic and women are relational-dialogic. How we may test this idea in samples of naturally occurring talk is a more difficult problem. We need to determine the features by which we can identify these two forms of talk and find out how discrete they are from each other. Are there really two ways of talking, or just two ways of analyzing any talk? Can we list the features that count as monologue vs. dialogue? (Is this only a male way to put the issue?)

To the extent that there may be actual (and not just stereotypical) evidence of male-female speech differences in the relational dimension, these arise out of all-female groups, compared with all-male groups. Marjorie Goodwin gives examples related to this contrast in her studies of African American boys' and girls' play groups.[28] Boys, she argues, play competitively and hierarchically. Their directives express personal desires:

[5] Goodwin, 1980

Michael: Gimme th pliers!

Poochie: (Gives pliers to Michael.)

Juju: Terry would you go hurry up and get it!

Terry: No. I'm not going in there. I don't feel like it.

Aggravated directives receive aggravated responses; mitigated requests receive mitigated responses—except from the leader of the group, who is likely to give an aggravated response to a mitigated request. This is one way that boys show their pecking order.

Girls, argues Goodwin, indicate joint participation in play groups. Their directives use collective wording and project future collaborative activities:

[6] Goodwin, 1980

Sharon: Come on. Let's turn back y'all so we can safe keep em.
            Come on. Let's go find some.

Girls use on-record hostility only when there are breaches of etiquette—or when they play in mixed boy-girl groups. This last point is worth emphasis. Girls can and do compete with boys in an assertive environment. The girls can interact in the masculine voice, but the boys seem not to be bilingual in the girls' style.

In the business world it is sometimes charged that women are too relational, not political enough. Goodwin finds that the boys are disadvantaged in terms of communication skills. Girls can do things in both the relational voice and the directive voice.[29] This is one model for tomorrow's manager: to have control of both monologic and dialogic voices. Are monologue and dialogue intrinsically marked for gender, or is this only a product of stereo-types that insist on gendering a dimension in talk?

HOW MUCH DIFFERENCE MAKES A DIFFERENCE?

In the 1970s, and again in the 1990s, scholars have claimed that men and women speak differently. These positions entail that the sexes are different to begin with, and must communicate interculturally. Popular science publications now feature arguments that men's and women's brains are different. This is being used to support the notion that women are holistic, while men are left-brain rational.

There is also currently an attempt being made to put language and gender issues in terms of race, class, situation, and so on. This is undoubtedly important, but no one has yet figured out how to assemble detailed evidence to show how such factors work together. Studies in the 1990s do give some consideration of the moment-to-moment achievement of gendering practices. This promising development provides the subject of the next chapter.

Is difference always a problem for communication? Clearly if monolingual speakers of English and Chinese try to talk philosophy, they will experience problems in understanding. Yet it is much less obvious what grows from minor speech differences, such as the regional difference between dialects spoken in Boston and Dallas, or the difference between the speech of Caucasians and African Americans, or the suspected-but-not-well-proven male-female speech differences. We do not know much about how small differences impact talk, except as they engage stereotypes that become embedded in subsequent talk. Do two speakers who differ in use of a dozen or twenty features—out of a language-scape of thousands of words and hundreds of grammar rules—face inevitable misunderstanding? I do not think so, unless we speak to each other in an environment of suspicion or rely too much upon monologue assumptions about how communication works.

We create gender in our communicative performances—of courtship and family building, or sexuality and violence, and of how we talk about women and men. If scholars should finally isolate subtle female-male speech differences, these may prove of minor importance compared to factors such as talk about women or couple talk.

How Gender Creeps into Talk

I FIRST HEARD THIS JOKE WHEN I WAS THIRTEEN: A THERAPIST ADMINISTERS A word association test, and each time the therapist says a stimulus-word the patient responds: "sex." After a while the therapist says, "It sounds like you have sex on the brain." The patient replies, "You're the one saying all the dirty words." This patient, enmeshed in sexualizing each stimulus, still misses the gendering work inherent in each test response.

Like the patient in this joke, most speakers perform gender in talk while believing that gender is something that happens to people. The performance of gender seems to efface itself and leave the appearance of a natural category. How do we do this?

We do it in part by using a vast array of resources for talking about gender. Almost anything that comes up in social interaction can become gendered by some of the language features discussed in this book. The ease with which gender is available in creating discourse can be illustrated by a newspaper cartoon published in October 1997, when the weather phenomenon called "El Niño" was getting a great deal of press.[1] The cartoon chronicles six supposed vernacular uses of this term in social talk:

PANEL 1: Teenaged girl exclaimes to male friend, "I got pierced and my dad went, like, El Niño."

PANEL 2: Bumpersticker "El Niño Happens"

PANEL 3: Unshown speaker says, "Mother's Here!" Middle-aged male groans, "El Niño-in-Law."

PANEL 4: Man holding out baby with a leaking diaper to woman, "OOPHH . . . El Niño!"

PANEL 5: Two male sportscasters, one whispers to the other, "Mary's career is El Niño."

PANEL 6: A couple laying in bed, the woman says, "Not tonight dear, I have El Niño."

Five of the supposed uses of "El Niño" are gender-marked, and each presents some difficulty in male-female interaction. The panels 1 and 3 both chronicle problems communicating with an older relative of a different sex. In panels 4, 5, and 6 the references are to a dirty diaper (and a man's inability to change it), to a violent sexual assault ending a sportscaster's career, and to a woman's refusing a sexual invitation. This cartoon is about coining new words into a language. The cartoon implies that five out of six linguistic innovations are gendered. Gender is easily available for linguistic invention and improvisation.

• • •

This book has detailed the performances by which speakers gender social scenes. Much gendering talk (e.g., gendered pronouns, sexual innuendo) may pass without speakers' explicit notice. Linguistic anthropologist Elinor Ochs, who has studied gender in several cultures, writes that "Few features of language directly and exclusively index gender."[2] Rather, gender creeps into talk across multiple utterances spoken by more than one person.

How do we act to weave gender into talk? One answer to this question is quite simple, if startling: *We mark gender in the same ways that we mark many issues or problems.* Across various topics in this volume, several discourse markers recur in our descriptions of gendered talk.

- ambiguities
- repair-initiations
- meta-talk
- noticings
- terms of address and reference
- mitigations

AMBIGUITIES

Words with multiple meanings have many uses in gendering social scenes. Many sexual words carry nonsexual primary meanings—*coming, doing it, aroused*. Almost any kind of word can be made into a gendered reference, as illustrated by this example from chapter 6.

> [1] Joke Calendar—Not found in Webster's
> Lady pilot, a plane jane.

The ambiguity of the word "plane" (plain) pairs a sex-atypical occupation with social undesirability. Ambiguity is often recognized (and sometimes created) in the next utterance after the ambiguous word, as in this example of sexual innuendo from chapter 3.

> [2] Film: *Pretty Woman*[3]
> He: Hundred dollars an hour (1) pretty stiff
>   (While driving she puts one hand in his lap)
> She: No, no:. But it's got potential.

Sometimes, sexual ambiguity is more sequential than lexical, as in this example from chapter 4.[4]

> [3] UTCL A12 (following rude staring)
> Woman: What's *your* problem
> Man #1:   We think you're really cute ◄
> Man #2:   You're upset at us ◄

In this instance two responses to a question appear in speech overlap, one orienting to a respectful line and one to a disrespectful line in males' harassment. There is no ambiguous word, just two different directions charted in a next utterance—thereby showing ambiguity in the prior acts.

REPAIR-INITIATION

A repair-initiation is a brief time-out from the course of talk to indicate inter-action problems—criticism, disagreement, or misunderstanding.[5] This instance appears in chapter 3.

[4] Film: *The Presidio*[6]

Nina: Is it hard?

                       (1.0)

Jay: Is what hard ◄

                       (2.4)   (she turns head in double-take)

Nina: Being a policeman

                       (0.4)

Jay: O:hhhh yeah. hh

Jay's question-repeat points to a possible ambiguity in Nina's utterance, "Is it hard?" and thereby stimulates sexual innuendo. The repair-initiation sus-pends the prior course of talk until the issue is resolved, and often sparks interaction troubles.

META-TALK

Meta-talk interrupts the course of interaction in order to comment on the talk itself.[7] The form of talk is always important to interaction, yet rarely draws explicit attention. To say "What do you mean" or "You said that wrong" is to stop the flow of normal conversation and specify the form of talk as a topic.

Speakers use meta-talk to show they are upset or offended. Meta-talk accompanies (and precipitates) disturbances in conversation. Where there is argument and upheaval, one finds meta-talk. Garfinkel used meta-talk in his "breaching" studies in order to bewilder a conversation partner.[8]

[5] Field note: Garfinkel, 1967

S: How are you?

E: How am I in regard to what? My health, my finances, my peace
             of mind?   ◄meta talk

S: (Red in the face and suddenly out of control)
            Look! I was just trying to be polite. Frankly I don't give a damn
            how you are.

Speaker E, in questioning some deeper sense behind a routine utterance, enrages a conversation-partner. Here is a gendered example from chapter 3.

[6] Film: *The Presidio*[9]
Jay: I'm inspector Jay Austin, San Francisco Police Department.
             We're here-
Nina: You didn't do that right ◄

"You didn't do that right" is a confrontive utterance seemingly calculated to elicit trouble. Meta-talk can be found in many instances of gender trouble, and it often leads to further trouble in its wake.

NOTICING

Noticing refers to talk that calls attention to something. Noticing may bring gender-relevant problems or information to focused attention.[10] Consider an example in which two birdwatchers talk about a singing bird. Cissy refers to that bird as "he." Then, after a pause, Cissy notices that she does not know this bird's sex.

[7] Film: *Strangers in Good Company*[11]
Cissy: He was- he was so pla:in, wasn't he
                          (1)
Cissy: I'm saying he, it might be a she ◄

As Cissy calls explicit attention to her prior use of a masculine pronoun to indicate a singing bird of unknown sex, she acknowledges that uncritical use of the pronoun "he" may be problematic to a listener. Gender-inclusiveness also underlies this next example:

[8] UTCL D6.2

Brandon: And what's Shipe Park named after.

(0.4)

Some guy name Shipe?

Kate: Or a lady. Or a lady named Shipe? ◄

Kate notices that Brandon may have presupposed (in saying "guy") that the park in which they are talking had been named after a male.

In examples [7] and [8] an utterance makes gender an increased focus of attention. Noticing gender places at center stage some issues that already may be present on the scene but have not previously been explicit in talk.

MITIGATION

Sometimes gender may be marked by words that weaken or qualify the utterance's force. Here is an example of mitigation that appeared in chapter 2:

[9] Field note, American Sign Language

Mandy: Who are you asking to the dance on Saturday?

Alice: I think I might ask Brian. ◄

Asked a direct question about her plans, Alice responds with two mitigating particles "I think" and "I might" before she names an individual.

Mitigation may take the form of starting to say something controversial, then correcting the utterance in midstream to say something less pointed:

[10] Film: *Strangers in Good Company*[12]

Mary: I'm a lesbian, I don't really like tuh- ◄

Cissy: Oh

Mary: Men don't interest me all that much ◄

In this film example Mary discloses her sexual preference to Cissy and adds a descriptive sentence to add further detail: "I don't really like tuh-" This sentence could be completed in any number of ways that might amplify what being a lesbian is like for Mary: for example, ". . . sleep with men," or ". . . be intimate with men." Mary says none of these but instead breaks off in mid-sentence and then completes the thought with a statement of attitude: "men don't interest me all that much." This statement of general disinterest in men softens the expression of disinterest in men and makes it seem less sexual. Mary also adds the phrase "all that much," implying that her not preferring men is just a matter of degree. By this array of devices Mary softens the potentially offensive character of disclosing her sexual orientation.

Responses to questions and other assertive speech acts are mitigated when the answers show disagreements or criticism. Mitigation appears at difficult moments in the human conversation:

[11] Field note

Hal: Listen, do you have feelings for me or not?

Mary: You know how much I value our friendship, and how wonder-
          ful of a person that I think that you are. It is just that, right now,
          I am in a weird phase. I'm not really emotionally together
          enough to be with someone else right now. I just got out of a
          long relationship, and I am not ready to start a new one.

Hal: Yeah, but do you have feelings for me or not.

Mary: As a friend, of course I do, (.) but as more than a friend, I really
          can't say. I mean no, I guess not.

Hal's question is embarrassingly direct, vulnerable, and suspicious. Mary's first answer begins by affirming Hal as a friend, and then she makes three excuses explaining why she does not want to practice romantic intimacy now. Hal brushes all this aside and repeats his yes-or-no question. Mary again affirms friendly feelings but then says, "as more than a friend, I really can't say." This is a "maybe" response that points toward "no." Then, finally, she says no, adding the qualified "I guess not."

TERMS OF ADDRESS AND PERSON-REFERENCE

Terms of address are what you call someone to whom you speak: for example, Doctor Jones, Ms. Jones, Ma'am, Leslie Jones, Leslie, Les, Girlfriend—

these might all be terms that you could use for one person. The choice among these terms, in roughly the order listed, indicates a continuum from formality/respect to informality/intimacy. We especially notice terms of address when someone corrects a usage.

[12] Field note
Student: Hey, Mr. Booker, I have to ask you a question.
Professor: It's *Dr.* Booker sir, and who might you be?

This student chooses a relatively formal term of address, but the professor makes clear in the immediate correction that a student should use a more specific term of respect. Terms of address have become contested: Masculine *Mr.* is not quite equivalent to *Miss* or *Mrs.*, so in recent years some speakers have adopted the term *Ms.* This usage shows something about the user as well as about the user's expectations of the person addressed.

Various terms are also available in situations in which a speaker *makes reference* to a person. Some reference terms specify a referent's sex but little else.

[13] Some Girl
Marie: I'm sitting at the club, and Dan and Robby and all them were sitting around the bar:? And u:m- and I was just standing next to Dan they're all talking and Robby was talking about some girl . . . ◄

Marie begins to tell a story in which she makes reference to two males by first name, and some others are not named: "and all of them." These people are pictured in the narrative as talking about another unnamed person, "some girl." This range of namings helps us to understand some relationships indicated in Marie's story.

IMPLICATIONS OF THESE TERMS

The previously listed terms of address and person references. recur in more than one kind of gendered talk (e.g., courtship interaction, sexist talk, genderlects). Furthermore, each of these features finds other functions besides marking gender. In conversation we use many of the same features to mark gender trouble as we use to mark different sorts of problems. Gender is unique only for the frequency with which gender problems in talk arise and achieve notice.

These discourse particles mark or indicate some trouble or problem but do not specify it precisely. That job remains for conversation partners in talk that follows these particles. These terms serve only as entry points for analyses—for social actors as well as for those of us who try to understand our own actions. We must also examine how these features (and others) trace out sequences and episodes in which gender creeps into talk.

Episodes in Which Gender Creeps into Talk

Gendering of talk rarely happens all at once, nor does gendering occur as primarily the work of a single speaker. Once something is marked or noticed in conversational interaction, this social fact is thereby added to the stack of stuff piled in the center of any encounter. A speaker can find any such resource and turn talk toward it.[13] Therefore, to study the importance of a gendered noticing we may examine how themes rendered in the noticing turn are extended in subsequent gender-marked interaction.

Detailing the performances by which gender is successively indexed across multiple speaking turns may help us understand gender's contextual "omnirelevance"—the sense that gendering talk might apply to any concept or moment.[14] This sense grows up not only because speakers are all gendered beings, but also because speakers mix various kinds of gendering practices (e.g., gendered references to absent persons, gender-inclusive language) within each single social scene.

Not all gendering activity appears explicitly in talk. Nevertheless there are advantages to describing those instances in which gender is explicitly indexed.[15] In this example Cara uses the explicitly gendered reference term "lady" and then both conversation partners make subsequent use of this gendered resource:

[14] D8.2
Rick: Why. Do you know the instructor heh heh

Cara:	No. Instructor's a lady ◄
Rick:	Oh- well do you know her
Cara:	Do I know her
Rick:	Yeah
Cara:	I mean I know her,
Rick:	O:h hh Oh you know her. hih
Cara:	But I don't know her.
Rick:	You don't- hah hah
Cara:	You know hih hih
Rick:	I wouldn't know ho

Subsequent to Cara's use of the term "lady," the talk teeters toward gender issues. These partners construct an innuendo-laden play episode focusing on repetitions of the word "know" that invoke the carnal sense of that word as a subtext for flirtation.

Explicitly gendered reference also occurs immediately subsequent to Cissy's gendered noticing of a pronoun "he" in [7].

[7] Film: *Strangers in Good Company*[16]

Cissy:	I'm saying he, it might be a she, huh huh huh
Mary:	it sings it's a he.
Cissy:	Oh, oh is it really?
Mary:	They are very few female birds that sing,
	which is one of those ¡hhh sa:d things.
Cissy:	Oh, I didn't know that?

Cissy indicates that she is unsure of the singing bird's sex and also acknowledges that her use of the pronoun "he" might be considered inappropriate. At the same time she casts herself as a bird-watching novice, Cissy shows herself to be sympathetic to arguments against the generic "he." Mary immediately demonstrates her own bird-watching expertise as she informs Cissy that singing birds are, in fact, ordinarily males. Thus, Cissy's noticing of her pronoun usage turns out to lead to quite a bit more talk about gender.

In this instance from chapter 8, Matt presumes that a new systems analyst will be a male. In responding to Matt's pronoun mistake, Tom begins to introduce gender-unfair speculation about the new employee.

[15] Field note (office)

Tom: Did you hear? The new systems analyst will be starting on
            Friday.

Matt: No, who is he?

Tom: Actually he is a she and her name is Helen. And wait until you
            see her. She is a babe.

Matt: Hmmm, I'll be looking forward to checking her out

Is it possible that the pronoun problem opens the way for Matt and Tom to consider Helen's looks more than her professional qualifications?

Example [8] is a speech event that displays gendered contention. Brandon seems at first to accept Kate's noticing/correction, "Yeah." But after a short pause, he adds a third item to the list of possible namesakes: "Or a dog named Shipe."

[8] UTCL D6.2

Brandon: What's Shipe Park named after
                        (0.4)
            Some guy named Shipe?

Kate: Or a lady. Or a lady named Shipe? ◄

Brandon: Yeah
                        (0.5)
            Or a dog named Shipe

The phrase "Or a dog named shipe" comes off as a wisecrack. By it Brandon has constructed a series of three categories of namesakes for a park: *guy, lady, dog*. The third item in this series makes the list ludicrous. Brandon suggests that he will grant that it is possible to name a park after a lady if Kate admits it is possible to name one after a dog. What is the point of this irony in response to Kate's correction? Is Brandon defending his usage of "guy" or indicating that Kate's correction was out of line? His utterance places those possibilities on the table without having to go on record about them.

Having considered some consequences of gendered noticing, let us next consider its antecedents. How is a scene prepared in which gendered noticing is appropriate? An announcement may have greatest impact if a speaker saves it until something in the conversation seems to touch it off. Noticings of gender index prior moments as already having been gendered. The bird-watcher, Cissy, in example [7] indexes recent utterances as she notices a pronoun:

[7] Film: *Strangers in Good Company*[17]

Mary:	Look in: (0.6) it's at the very top of one a those ba:re ¡hh bushes there.
Cissy:	<O::h.
	(long pause)
Mary:	I've lost him. ◄
Cissy:	Pardon?
Mary:	I've lost the one that [was singing
Cissy:	[<Yes, huh huh, and uh- he was- he was so pla:in, wasn't he ◄
	(1)
Cissy:	I'm saying he, it might be a she,

Cissy's noticing self-corrects her immediate prior utterance, in which she had referred to the bird as "he." Mary had referred to this same bird as "him" just moments before, sandwiching this reference between two others in referring to the bird as "it" and "the one that was singing." Perhaps such alternating use of gendered and gender-neutral references sets up a contrast between sex-specific (or generic) and sex-neutral usage in referring to an animal. Gender issues creep gradually into the talk in this episode through an action series of three phases: peripheral use, noticing, and extension. The creeping toward gender's salience is clear in this example:

[16] Field note

Jill:	I've signed up for one of those informal classes about car maintenance and repair.
Pip:	That's a good idea. A lot of women can really learn a lot from these classes
	(short pause)
Pip:	Well, I guess there's a lot of guys who can learn from 'em too.

Jill announces that she has enrolled in a class. Pip introduces gender by the phrase "a lot of women" in her response. This phrase presupposes that this class is particularly relevant to women. Pip subsequently corrects that very presupposition, indicating sensitivity to possible offense given by raising a gender stereotype.

Sometimes noticing evokes contention, as when it is packaged as other-correction. Let us consider how Cara's use of "lady" in example [14] looks back to prior talk:

[14] D8.2 (Preview to noticing)
Cara: Yeah, I'm gonna get an A in the class. (0.2)
           For sure (0.2) eh huh hah hah ¡hhh
Rick: Why. Do you know the instructor hheh heh
Cara: No. Instructor's a lady ◄

Cara notices gender in a backward-looking way. Cara denies Rick's accusation on the grounds that the "instructor's a lady." This response displays Cara's analysis that Rick's suggestion already presumed the instructor was a male and that Cara would flirt with a male teacher to improve her grade. Cara's denial claims that "a lady" is an ineligible recipient for her (heterosexual) flirtations.

Gendered noticing is facilitated by the status of gender as omnirelevant in social interaction—as illustrated in the El Niño cartoon. Gender's omnirelevance has many roots. Most participants in every human culture consider the self and other(s) to be persons exhibiting one sex. Most of us dress and groom ourselves to make it evident that we enact only one sex, and throughout much of the lifespan this includes sexual enactment. Furthermore, gender-indexical resources occur in talk even when gender identity does not seem central to the course of interaction, including gendered pronouns (she), given names (Sallie), and terms of address and reference (sir, lady). Additionally, many sexual acts are named in ambiguous words with nonsexual uses: "arouse," "excited," "intercourse," "climax," "coming." Then there are the uses of words that usually describe feminine appearance (e.g., beautiful, stunning, stacked) or feminine sexuality (e.g., bitch, slut, tease). Any speaker may index gendered identity at almost any time, whereas many important and noticeable issues—poverty, justice, or patience, for example—may be occasioned only in more limited circumstances. The availability of such a variety of address, references, and ambiguous words increases both the ease of locating gendered pre-texts in any scene and the ease of making gender off-handedly noticed.

Since a language is a work of art produced by large numbers of artists across many generations, these varied resources for gendering show a long-standing community preoccupation with gendered projects. Given this preoccupation, it should not surprise us that many spoken usages turn attention toward gender. Of course there are also noticings that turn in other directions. In fact, it seems that many turn-marking devices—address terms, disagreements, corrections, and so on—may mark various issues as of contextual relevance to a present social situation. Ways of occasioning gender are not in principle different than ways of occasioning anything else: ethnicity, social power, tardiness, tact, and so on.

Gender creeps into talk through a series of utterance-events:

- peripheral gendered activity
- gendered noticing
- extending gender's relevance

Following this series we may see how an early utterance provides contextual slotting for fuller renderings of gender-marked talk. Early utterances that use gender implicitly may make the situation safe for later utterances that can be damaging. This principle was illustrated as a possibility in chapter 6 with this instance:

[17] UTCL L17.3

Dan: We're gonna take off we got one of the girls here watchin the place for us

(0.2)

Jeff: Oh yeah?

Dan: D'You know Shirley, don'tcha

Jeff: Shirley, Shirley with the big- whangers?

This instance suggests how an offhand and implicit gender marking such as the phrase "one of the girls" provides openings for the sexist body description that follows. This example also illustrates that gender trouble may be interactionally produced within a nest of other issues, such as doing one's job or indicating that you know who Shirley is. A deep understanding of such events must indicate gender's salience among other issues.

• • •

With these descriptions of how gender creeps into talk we may return to the question with which we began this volume—as well as the current chapter: How is it that gendering social scenes seems "natural" to us as we fail to notice our own moment-to-moment gendering work? Answers to this question include:

- Sex-sexuality-gender, because everybody participates in it, may be used to explain actions.
- Gender's omnirelevance is facilitated by an immense array of language resources for indexing gender in talk.
- Ways of occasioning gender may be similar to ways of occasioning other situated dimensions of context: for example, ethnicity, authority, hurrying, colluding, and so on.
- Our gendering accomplishments appear as ongoing, improvised, embodied performances. Gender seems to make itself evident as it creeps into talk, yet we are the puppets who pull our own strings.
- One array of ways to occasion gender is within a series of actions showing peripheral orientation, noticing, and extending. This series allows gender to creep into our talk rather than to be framed as one speaker's explicit rhetorical project.

In examining the uses of these resources throughout the current volume we have often emphasized the indexing of different dimensions of gendering: for example, the use of sexist language particles; the invocation of male/female differences; and the language of flirtation and courtship. Yet in the gendered noticing series we have examined, these analyzably different dimensions often are indexed within the same series. A noticing of a sexist particle may lead to discussions of sexual practices or to flirtatious innuendo. The various gendered practices discussed in separate chapters of this book actually are rather uncritically mixed together within speech events. This makes all of us speakers a bit like the patient who sees sex everywhere—because we have developed so many devices for perceiving and marking gender's relevancies. Any gender-relevant speech serves as an opening for almost any other gender-relevant speech. (Perhaps a majority of examples begin with implicit usages or gendered pronouns, then move to more marked usages involving derogation or flirtation, but I cannot reach a definite conclusion about this.)

● ● ●

Since we recurrently gender contexts in a variety of ways, and since gender indicators also mark many aspects of context, we rarely notice how we use these features to gender our social world. The subtlety with which we weave gendering into talk creates the appearance that gender's relevance creeps up on speakers—that is, it is just a natural thing that happens to us, rather than a social performance.

It is not the differences between men and women that evoke the serial performances detailed in this chapter. Rather, it is the similarity of all speakers in utilizing the materials of the language and culture. If we wish to change the world to provide a more level playing field for men and women, we might develop greater awareness of these gendering performances and seek to bring them into a greater degree of self-control. I am optimistic that this can and should be done but believe it to be the work of multiple generations of speakers, both women and men.

··

Leveling the
Playing Field

··

HOW DO WE ADDRESS "THE RELATIONSHIP BETWEEN GENDER INEQUALITY AND the language practices of a society"?[1] Principled and repetitive inequality seems un-American. Yet gendered performances continue in part because these performances efface themselves into appearances of doing something natural. How can we level the playing field in such circumstances? How do we take the issues discussed previously and point them toward applications in the worlds of careers, couple-making, and family interaction?

I would like to have written this chapter around success stories, reports of occasions in which speakers talk in ways that make or preserve a level playing field. I have found these stories hard to come by, which suggests one or more of the following:

- There are more problems than successes in gendering talk.
- We still have a long way to go in gaining control over gendering talk before success stories can be commonplace.
- People remember and report stories of problems, or of inequality; but since individual equality is presumed in U.S. society, it does not attract our attention.

Perhaps one measure of progress against the problems of gendering talk would be to not find any such problems—because they are not there, not because we are naive.

Perhaps we may chart some progress in the fact that we now hear the kinds of stories reported throughout this book as stories about gender troubles,

stories that relate to the many-tentacled problem of the uneven playing field
we call gender inequality. While puzzling through the writing of this chapter
I have sent phone messages and e-mails to friends and colleagues for their
ideas about how to proceed. Here is one response from ethnographer Kristine
Fitch:

[1] Field Note: Fitch
Leveling the playing field as a chapter in your gender book . . . I have a
thought on that, with two stories to go along. First the two moments:
Guilford sent me a letter suggesting I go to local bookstores and encourage them to order my book, local author, etc. I went to the one with the
espresso bar upstairs and had this conversation with the woman behind the
counter:

Me: I'm uh looking for- I need to talk to someone in charge of
         ordering books. I've uh written a book and the publisher sug-
         gested
Her: Children's books? Well we have several people who order
         books, the one in charge is that guy back there whose name is
         Hanks, but then we have other people in charge of specialized
         areas, like children's books.

         I walked away puzzled over the bad taste in my mouth;
         Daena was there and put it into words. "Aside from your gen-
         der what led her to assume it was a children's book you'd writ-
         ten?" I didn't go back and pose the question to the clerk.

         The second event happened at a nice lunch reception for
         people who had taken part in various internationally oriented
         programs. There was chatting afterwards and a guy, maybe
         fifty, faculty, stopped and asked about the award I got (the
         global scholar thing that gives me two semesters off). I told him
         the basics and he said congrats it sounds wonderful, and then
         as he turned to go added "I'd have sworn you were an under-
         grad." The conventional-response slot in my head said, "This is
         a compliment, smile brilliantly and say thank you," which I did,
         but then I chewed on it the rest of the day. Why exactly is this

supposed to be a compliment, in the context of a status-based
system in which the undergrads are at the bottom of the stack?[2]

Like most of the stories that come to mind as we consider a gender-level
playing field, these are stories of perceived unequal treatment, not stories of
solutions. These stories may be read in terms of the categories in the present
book but only incompletely. These two stories are slightly suspicious in tone,
and each story connects gender with issues of status and respect. Another feature of these two stories is that they each occur at a first encounter with a
stranger.

Consider Fitch's second story, the story of a compliment from a fellow
academic during a discussion of her recent hard-earned scholarly honor. The
compliment seems to follow other praise about her work, and it is delivered
en passant at the encounter's close. In form, it is an appearance compliment—a polite cousin of street remarks (chapter 4) that could be studied for
the sexual undertone frequently implicit in such remarks. In content this
compliment is a non sequitur in a conversation about professional accomplishment. Does this compliment detract from the attribution of professional
success to skill or hard work (chapter 6)? It is hard to say. Certainly the compliment shifts the footing of the talk from professional to personal, in the
context of man-to-woman talk. Fitch responds in a polite and womanly way,
thanking him for noticing that she is young-looking. Then the rest of the day
she frets about the compliment and about her response. The man who delivered the compliment never learns of the trouble ensuing from the remark—
which is another pattern typical in minor episodes of sexual violence or
insinuation.

Is the remark made a problem due to Fitch's feminist consciousness?
What good does the perception of such a problem do if there is no likely resolution? Could the perception of a problem in the past help Fitch to respond
better next time? (Could a more suspicious response: for example, "I'd never
make that youthful-appearance mistake with you!" construct a better, fairer
world?) Would this compliment experience help Fitch to watch out for this
guy in the future? (And might she miss some opportunity to learn from this
man in being paranoid about sexual aggression or political incorrectness?)
Finally, Fitch pairs this story with a status dimension—that her youthfulness

allows the male professor to place her in a low-status category (undergraduates). To what extent is this a shrewd critical observation, and to what extent is it primarily suspicious?

Fitch's first story, about the double mention of children's books during her brief encounter with a bookstore employee, is more difficult to read in terms of the categories raised in the present book. Fitch, and her overhearing colleague, understand that she has been perceived as an author of a children's book, and they interpret this moment as an expression of gender bias by that employee. The gender imputation is more implicit than in the story about the compliment, and in fact Fitch admits she did not put this observation into words until her colleague did so. The gendered nature of taking Fitch for a children's book author (if that is what happened) fits neatly into no category discussed in the current volume. Children's author may be a stance associated with a woman, but the talk shows no sexual innuendo, biased family communication, or talk about a woman as a sexual being or as an object of beauty. Perhaps it carries an implication that it would be a feminine stance to be a part-time writer while being a mom or holding some other kind of job—and this could be taken as a slur by a well-published academic scholar (who is also a mom).

However, these nongendered possibilities may also be considered: Perhaps five out of ten requests for bookstore publicity come from children's authors. That is, the employee may be responding to other things instead of (or in addition to) seeing a well-dressed, youngish, Anglo woman self-identifying as an author. Another possibility: That children's books require special treatment for such requests, and therefore the children's book possibility is dealt with first, no matter which author appears. Or perhaps the children's book person is not in the store right now, and the employee wants to postpone the process if Fitch should turn out to be a children's author. None of these possibilities are of staggering likelihood, but there is some firm possibility that gender is only a trace element in this encounter. We never find out about all the other possibilities, for something seems to terminate the encounter unsuccessfully before it gets very far. (Only these first utterances are recorded here.) This observation returns us to the mild sense of paranoia in both these narratives. Like an African American who frets about probable discrimination in job interviews, Fitch is perhaps too prepared by life to give a gender cast to interpreting narratives about interaction problems. Where is the correct balance between keen communicative acuity and becoming habitually suspicious of others?

UNEVEN ENVIRONMENTS

Gender troubles seem especially to surface in four kinds of environments: at first meetings with a stranger, in the professions, in single-sex enclaves, and in the family. For slightly varying reasons, each of these settings operates under constraints of gendering talk. That is, there are normal pressures toward gender marking and conservatism in each of these environments. The reasons for persistent gender troubles differ in each of these environments, yet each environment's way of working points to the persistence of gendering problems. Taken together, these environments probably make up a majority of all the interaction we do—and this helps us to understand why there are so many puzzles and difficulties problematizing any wish to level the playing field.

Family and Couple Interaction

In chapters 3 to 6 I claim that dating is in principle a sexist activity at the level of partner selection, that sexual innuendo is a prominent way to initiate flirting and to differentiate potential courtship from other kinds of talk, that flirting talk bears disturbing similarities to coercive talk attendant to sexual violence, that couple development through progressive commitment highlights the uniqueness of male-female interaction in ways that are magnified as couple members begin to collect differences between them and to gender those differences. The constraints of being a couple and juggling the demands of children and careers provide plenty of opportunities to emphasize male-female difference as an explanation for troubles that appear in daily routines. In all these ways, courtship and family environments promote gendering talk and the assignment of interaction problems to gender troubles.

Some experts see couple and family problems as a simple outgrowth of sex differences. For example, Deborah Tannen and John Gray have produced bestsellers about sex differences in which most of the examples are drawn from marriage. Yet a good deal of such difference is performed through the detailed enactment of couple formation. It is coupling that creates the appearance of male-female difference more than it is male-female difference that creates couple problems.

First Encounters

Many examples in this book take place in first meetings between strangers: the two Fitch stories above, for instance; the examples of street remarks in chapter 4; and the instances of pronoun mistakes in chapter 6. A few instances may enhance the discussion to follow:

[2] Field note (Computer support line)
Carol: Thank you for calling Dell, this is Carol, how may I help you?
Mike: Uh huh, (.) is this tech support?
Carol: Yes it is. How may I help you?
Mike: Oh. Uh, wow, a female technician.

[3] Field note
S: You would have to speak with our operations manager about that.
P: Is HE available now?

[4] Field note
He: Pardon me, I hope you don't find this offensive, or take this the wrong way, but you have great legs.
She: (embarrassed giggle) Thank you.
He: Whatever you do to stay in shape, keep it up (walks away)

[5] Film: *Thelma and Louise*[3]
Harlan: Now what are a couple a kewpie dolls like you doin in a place like this.
Louise: h h h Mindin our own business Why don't you try:.
Thelma: Uh we left town t'ave a weekend cause we wanted to try and have some fun.

These four events have in common with most first encounters the feature of high uncertainty about the other (as discussed in chapter 3). The actors have very little information about each other as individuals. This increases the possibility that one will proceed either to say something very bland, or that gender stereotypes will fuel guesses about strategic choices. In the first two instances, the initiator of an institutional encounter presumes that the target for the talk will be male, and these initiators are surprised at what ensues. In the last two examples a man approaches a woman with a compliment on appearance, a compliment that women may accept with a smile even before thinking it over. These properties echo the two Fitch stories.

To level the playing field about such instances we must examine our default assumptions about strangers and choose our delivery of appearance compliments with increased discretion and discernment.

An aside: Certain studies of interaction, for example, one famous study of interruption, are based upon laboratory simulations in which strangers come together and talk for a few minutes in undirected ways. It would be hardly surprising that gender differentiations might be accentuated at such moments.

Single-Sex Speech Events

The addressee of talk may influence its form as much as the speaker does, and all-male or all-female conversations sometimes take gendered formats. For example:

[6] Goodwin, 1980
Michael: Gimme th pliers!
Poochie: (Gives pliers to Michael.)

[7] Goodwin, 1980
Sharon: Come on. Let's turn back y'all so we can safe keep em. Come on. Let's go find some.

These are contrasting styles of boys' and girls' directives in play groups, as studied by Marjorie Goodwin.[4] Girls use collaborative language, where boys' talk is more confrontational and hierarchical. Yet when girls and boys play together in the same scene, girls are as confrontational as boys.

Single-sex groupings of speakers also may produce some uniquely marked talk about women's appearance:

[8] CGH
Alice: And so my sister told me:, that I should stop wearing al- all my makeup and like do everything really lightly, and then wear bright lipstick.
                             (1)
            That's what I been trying to do but still doesn't make me stunning
Marie: Well some people aren't stunning some people your- are pretty.
Alice: I'm just not stunning.

[9] Wool: Glenn
Dave: There's a lot of wool at weddings. Y'know that?
Stan: I know. You wouldn't believe all the coot that was up there.
Dave: Ho hoh khhh
Stan: They make these girls look like *dog* meat.
                             (0.8)
Dave: Haw:::hhh
Stan: These girls have no (0.7) These girls look like shit down here compared to girls up there, I'm tellin ya.

These last two instances are rather extreme examples (from chapter 8) of making women look bad with talk about appearance. The first is from a conversation among three women friends with no men present and is part of a painfully frank assessment of Alice's attempts to look stunningly beautiful. The "wool" segment is from a sexist conversation between two males, which seems a safe environment for a certain demeaning style of talk about women as sex objects.

    It seems that single-sex environments, from jazzercise classes to monasteries to locker rooms, provide settings to emphasize sexual differentiation. Within a one-sex setting, participants may find gender to be of easy relevance to talk.

As one way of indicating the influence of single-sex enclaves, consider sports. The dominant spectator sports in the United States—soccer, football, boxing, and baseball—are played at the highest level entirely in men's leagues. Certain other sports, such as basketball, gymnastics, and tennis, offer world-class competition for both men and women but only on a rigidly separate basis. Try to imagine a sport of the twenty-first century in which men and women compete as equals—individually or as members of mixed-sex teams. Such sports will be invented in some egalitarian future and probably will become as popular as current mass-media sports. Yet I have posed this question again and again to groups of college students, and nobody so far has been able to envision the shape of such a sport. That failure of imagination is among the clearest indications of how much our social worlds must evolve before the male-female playing field becomes level.

Professional Interaction

Most of us like to believe in a possible professional world in which gender discrimination would vanish, in which men and women would work as information-age equals, cooperating together, competing fairly. Most of the time, most of us believe that there is more professional and educational opportunity for women than there used to be. How do we continue to trip up on issues of gender and language in the workplace?

In some of the ways we might most expect to see professional progress, it escapes us. There are still some men's occupations (physician, accountant, manager, engineer) and some women's occupations (teacher, nurse, secretary, social worker). When you say the words for male-typical occupations, you see a man—even though some women hold these jobs. If you want to see a woman you mark the usage: lady lawyer, lady engineer, female scientist. A woman in a sex-atypical occupation is a sexual suspect: A lady pilot is a plane jane!

This shows up in "he" mistakes for managers and doctors:

[3] Field note
S: You would have to speak with our operations manager about that.
P: Is HE available now?

[10] Field note
Suzanne: I was referred to your office by Doctor Sayres.
Receptionist: Is HE your primary doctor?
Suzanne: No, *she's* my rheumatologist.
Receptionist: How long have you been under HIS care?

What causes the continuing imbalance between men's and women's positions in the world of the professions? One problem is that women frequently do not get adequate credit for professional accomplishments.

[11] Field note
Sarah: I'm done in August.
Roy: What are you gonna do?
Sarah: Well, I got a marketing job with General Motors.
Roy: How did you get that? (Looks shocked)
Sarah: I just interviewed with them.
Roy: Did you know anyone there?

[12] Field note
Ed: The new group of trainees Stan hired has some real potential.
Ron: Mark and Joe are really catching on and so are those three women.
Ed: Mandy is such a hard worker, but do you think she is too much of a doll to hold her own?

Some critics charge that women's speech is not political enough or assertive enough to compete in the professions. This charge amounts to the claim that women's speech is dialogic and relational. Yet Marjorie Goodwin's study of boys' and girls' play groups (chapter 9) suggests that boys' and girls' play groups use directive speech differently. When girls play with boys they can be blunt and assertive. Yet the boys can perform only their aggressive style. If there is a verbal disadvantage in these groups, it is the boys who are disadvantaged. By analogy, men in professional organizations are disadvantaged if all they know how to do is be objective, blunt, and impolite.

Sociologist Rosabeth Kanter argues that gender trouble in the corporation does not emerge from behavioral differences between men and women but because of differences in opportunity.[5] To have opportunity to move up is the most important feature of career success. If you are a high-opportunity professional, the way you act is a function of that. People who are stuck at a job with no possibility of promotion may be rules-oriented or anti-authority in communication style. Most such people are women, but the style is a function of organizational position, not of sex differences between men and women. People who are stuck at first-level supervision, for instance, often have trouble delegating responsibility and may use fear to motivate subordinates.

However, the few women who do move up the hierarchy face a different problem, the problem of being a token. Kanter defines "token" as a minority member in a "skewed group"—a work group where fewer than 15 percent of the members have the minority characteristic. The reason for the classification (e.g., sex, ethnicity) does not matter to the communication in a token-dominant situation. If you are a token, you feel especially visible.

With increased visibility there are certain opportunities. If I want people to remember my name, token status can be helpful. There are also some special vulnerabilities to token status, however. If you have not already done so, I recommend that you find a situation in which you are a token on some characteristic. I have experienced male-token status in dance and jazzercise classes. I feel clumsy in a group of dancers exercising before a mirror when I am the tallest person in the room. If I turn the wrong way, others may cluck or chuckle. If I perform reasonably well, I may be chosen for overblown praise. It takes up a lot of energy being a token. There is a special sense of being vulnerably visible that some people thrive on—and still find a strain. Some women similarly thrive as token managers. Yet Kanter argues that tokenism is self-perpetuating.

Suppose that a woman manager goes to a meeting with seven men managers. During this meeting she takes on a confrontation and loses. What might be made of that event, given that she is so visible? What if she takes on the same confrontation and wins? People will say, "She is not like other women." If she fails in this situation, it stands as proof for the stereotype that women cannot function at this level. If she succeeds, it is taken as exceptional.

The problem with token status is that the stereotype does not come up for reexamination. When it comes time to hire the next manager, it does not matter if the woman now working as a manager is a success or a failure, people still believe that women are not successful at this level.

Kanter describes four roles that high-opportunity women are stereotyped into.

1. *Seductress.* This vamp may have slept her way to the top.
2. *Pet.* This girl is to be patted on the head. She is everyone's little sis: supportive, enthusiastic, cheerful. But who can take her seriously?
3. *Mom.* This woman is seen as a caretaker who is so essential at her job that she is unpromotable.
4. *Iron Maiden.* This woman is crusty, tough, ugly, and asexual.

An interesting feature of these roles is that nobody seen as occupying them is a good candidate for higher promotion. The seductress is unethical, the pet is impulsive, the mom is too valuable where she is, and nobody wants to work for the iron maiden. So these stereotypes interact with failures to credit women for their accomplishments to make barriers to the promotability of women—the glass ceiling.

Kanter argues in favor of quotas in job categories for women and other underrepresented groups. Another suggested resolution to problems of the opportunity glass ceiling is that young professionals seek mentor relationships with highly placed older people in their organization. This kind of relationship can provide advice and support about the culture of the organization. The downside, for women professionals, is that most mentor candidates are men, and there are stereotype-based reasons for being suspicious of relationships between younger women and older men. Some people also report that mentor relationships often lead to disillusionment over the years. The best advice seems to be to seek mentoring relationships with as many experienced persons as possible, so as to limit the problems of depending on just one mentor.

Another vulnerability that is increasingly perceived as a threat to the promise of a level playing field in the professions is the mixing of work and sexuality. Such mixing becomes almost inevitable in the world of the workaholic—a world in which most of us spend the majority of our waking hours in a professional setting. If one is going to flirt anywhere, it may happen at work. However, there are at least two categories of problems related to this: sexual harassment and the conflict between work and courtship. This double vision is related to the similarity between flirting and sexual violence:

[7] Field Note (at a work party)
Donna: Hey William, the Shiner keg is having problems. I keep playing with the adjuster but it keeps coming out mostly foam.
William: I'll show you how to give good head.

[14] Field note (at work in restaurant)
Shelly: Hey Derrick, can I have a bun?
Derrick: Do you want the left or the right?

There is today a growing recognition that office romances, even consensual ones, can cause serious professional problems.[6] Professional life can be quite lengthy, and both flirtation and couple making generate many brief amorous relationships after which the former flirters would like to be away from one another. In these situations, professional effectiveness can be impaired and one of the people (usually the less powerful person, therefore usually the woman) may lose professionally from this difficulty.

Even the determination to treat men and women as equals can get lost in the day-to-day routines that differentially credit women and men with accomplishments, that give birth to possibly flirtatious (possibly harassing) double entendres, and that have different expectations for the promotability of women and men. There is great hope for a level playing field in professional environments, but there is still a very long way to go in making this dream into reality.

• • •

Journalist Susan Faludi, in her book *Backlash*, cautions us against a simple belief in progress.[7] (Faludi notes that the first Miss America Pageant was held the year after women won the vote.) Why does this side-stepping progress occur? Is there some plot against women? I do not think so. Nor do I believe that men and women speak very differently. Rather, women and men listen similarly. That is, both men and women listen differently to women than we do to men. Both men and women are vulnerable to stereotypes and other social pressures of life in families, professional settings, single-sex enclaves, and first encounters. If something is not going quite as we wish, we have a limited number of options for setting things right. None of them work very well in establishing the elusive level playing field.

- Correcting. When we correct another person's speech we add a problem, the problem of correction, as we treat the problem we correct. Sometimes there is no net gain in this process.
- Implying. Sometimes there is something indirect that can be said. Of course, if you are a woman, you may draw suspicion of being typically feminine and sneaky by leaving implications of impropriety.
- Pro-acting. Looking ahead and avoiding trouble spots by early warning. This is the best thing to do when you know how to do it, for example, don't use noninclusive language, or, learn to anticipate when a certain kind of fight is coming.
- Considering alternative explanations while counting to ten. When something goes wrong, do not be too positive that gender troubles are the best explanation. Sometimes another, more innocent, explanation will become evident.

In fact, we are creating our problems each moment. We are not completely victims of our culture and our personality, however; we might be able to do something about it. We tend to think too quickly. Something went wrong—whose fault is it? Can we substitute the question: What is going on here, and what's the next best thing for us to do?

When something goes wrong, watch yourself sliding toward a hypothesis about why it went wrong. See if you can slow down that slide. See if you can observe the details of the talk just a bit longer. See if you can mull these details a bit before you decide how different you are from someone else.

• • •

Here is a joke I got off the Internet in the spring of 1998. The heading of the joke is "the difference between men and women." A man was driving down a winding mountain road when a woman in a convertible passed him. She waved one hand frantically at him and shouted, "Pig!" He answered "Bitch." He rounded the next curve and slammed into a thousand-pound pig.

This is a story about a man's failure to hear a woman as an equal player on a level playing field. He saw her not as another human but as a woman. When she yelled "Pig"—intended as a road warning to a fellow motorist—he heard this as an insult, part of the ongoing war over feminist responses to an unlevel playing field. His response was a feminine insult term.

This joke pictures the male as unable to hear an evident warning from a woman but rather able only to process her talk as being from a woman. If anything, his arousal over this gender trouble makes him less, not more, aware of the trouble about which she warned him. Feminism itself may be heard as such a warning: Make the field more even and we may be able to operate as equals. If the response to this warning is competitive or ideological, we may face bigger trouble around the next bend.

One implication of this joke appears in its title: the difference between women and men. On the surface the joke is not about any male-female difference, certainly not a difference in dialect or speech style. Reflection suggests this difference, however: the woman, seeing a problem, is willing to warn anyone about it; but the man, hearing a woman speak anything that might be heard as gender trouble, perceives such a distorted message that he soon runs into trouble. The implied difference is that women are willing to act on the faith that a level playing field is possible, but men systematically mishear attempts to do so. The truth, I have suggested during this volume, seems more complex. Women and men both are likely to mis-hear women, to the detriment not only of women but of the entire speech community.

⑫

....

Return to
Laughter

....

ALBERT CAMUS WROTE A MIDCENTURY PHILOSOPHICAL ESSAY ON THE DILEMMAS of Sisyphus. Sisyphus is a character in Dante's Hell whose torment is to roll a heavy boulder up a hill, only to watch helplessly as the boulder rolls back down again. Then Sisyphus must push the boulder uphill again, with the same consequence, for eternity. Camus casts a terrible sociological fable on the futility of work.

Camus resolves this problem by focusing on a fictional interlude in Sisyphus's story. Right after the boulder begins to roll down the hill, and in full sight of the meaningless labor ahead, Sisyphus enjoys a moment of respite, a moment when he is not pushing, a time when he is somehow greater than his rock. At that moment, Camus imagines Sisyphus laughing. That redemptive laughter gives Sisyphus the strength to get up and do what needs to be done. Or at least to do what must be done again as it has been done before, but with increased understanding and compassion.[1]

Considering the futilities of authentic action in the world of gendering talk, I admire the tenacity of Sisyphus's laugh. A bit less often, I am able to return to laughter as the rolling boulder of "natural" gender undoes my attempts at visualizing rational action on a level playing field. There is a fleeting and partial escape from recurrent problems in a redemptive interlude of laughter. Today as a happily married cancer patient celebrating my first grandchild, I understand this point with greater compassion for self and others than I did ten years ago—when I stood like the man in Matisse's "Conversation," looking at the gendered other across a colorful window.

Can laughter redeem some of our reflexive performances of gender? Can even midlife marrieds share amusement at their predicaments in the arrangement between the sexes? Can the object of a vile street remark laugh the laugh of Sisyphus? Can both the feminist and the neorepublican laugh about political correctness in the language of James Finn Gardner's portrayal of little Red Riding Hood?

> On the way to Grandma's house, Red Riding Hood was accosted by a wolf, who asked her what was in her basket. She replied, "Some healthful snacks for my grandmother, who is certainly capable of taking care of herself as a mature adult."
>
> The wolf said, "you know, my dear, it isn't safe for a little girl to walk through the woods alone."
>
> Red Riding Hood said, "I find your sexist remark offensive in the extreme, but I will ignore it because of your traditional status as an outcast from society.[2]

This text permits reading by both the advocates of changing language habits and those who oppose such changes as ridiculous. What response to a recurrent problem shows more strength and compassion than an invitation to laughter?

To put the problem this way is to admit that I cannot figure out how to end this book. Another summary is superfluous. One more argument will not convert you, unless you "got it" long ago. To add a series of prescriptions for interaction also seems unnecessarily repetitive of what you have already read. If you've got it, you are already performing some of it. Maybe it's time for one more sexual joke, this one on men:

> Q: Why does it take over a million sperm to fertilize a single egg?
> A: The little guys won't ask for directions.

This joke turns a stereotype on itself and dissolves it as we laugh. Maybe that is because the joke is on the powerful party, and yet the stereotype seems incidental to imbalances of power.

• • •

One problem with the division of thinking reflected by the chapters in this book is that certain fragments of data relevant to the puzzles of gender in talk have been omitted due to lack of fit within any of the chapter headings. The treatment of male-female speech differences in chapter 9, for example, gives attention mainly to ideas relevant to language and power hypotheses. We must remain alert to gendering talk that fits none of the preconceived categories of our theories. Throughout the current project, I have collected, yet rarely written about, instances of talk that struck my intuitions as gendered— but for no particular reason. I exemplify this ragged edge of analysis with some discussion of the laughter of women and men.

Tarzan and Jane: Courtship and Difference

Sometimes I hear someone laugh and reflect: That sounded like a feminine kind of laughing. In some cases, this intuition seems stimulated by a particularly marked and raucous laughter that goes on for some time, often at a high pitch. Conversation analyst Gail Jefferson, the foremost contemporary expert on how we laugh, suspects that a woman (interacting with a man) will accept a man's invitation to laugh more often than a man will accept a woman's invitation to laugh.[3] She tested this notion quantitatively and found, as have most investigators of male-female difference speech patterns, few and mixed indications of such differences. Still, however, she argues that in certain cases gender and laughter are connected in a way that contributes to and grows from gender stereotypes. She writes of these possibilities using the terms "Tarzan" and "Jane" to emphasize the reflexive relations of her hunches to stereotypes.

Jefferson, who invented the conversation transcription system used to describe tape-recorded speech samples in this book, insists on transcribing every spoken syllable in recordings of talk, including nonword vocalizations such as laugh tokens. When transcribed this way, some laughter shows itself to be shared laughter or laughter in which more than one person joins, usually answering an invitation by the speaker of some laughable utterance. In two-party conversation the speaker of the laughable adds laugh tokens in order to invite the other to share.

[1] UTCL A10.14

Rick: I called up- immediately after work, I said, what the *@#* Billy
           man, you're *pissin* me off hah hah
Jessy: Huh huh huh

Rick finishes a story and laughs. Jessy immediately joins in the laughter, sharing her judgment of the punchline's funniness.

About a third of all first laughs are shared. Sometimes, following apparent invitations to laugh, the conversation partner declines the invitation:

[2] UTCL A10.2

Joy: Let us know whether you can (0.4) take all of us to a movie or
           n(h)ot hih hih
Pete: Okay, I will do that.

Joy playfully instructs Pete to call that weekend and take a group of her
friends to a movie. Joy laughs after this apparent mock proposition. Pete,
however, plays it straight, apparently agreeing to call but not sharing the
laughter.

Many laughs are not apparently performed in order to be shared. For
example, some laughter expresses mocking or derision at the other. Some
laughter expresses self-deprecation or self-criticism. Most usually, a social
partner does not share these laughs. The old rhyme: "Laugh and the world
laughs with you" is only partly true.

With that background, Jefferson argues that Janes are "laugh receptive"
to Tarzans, but Tarzans are "laugh resistant" to Janes. Specifically:

- A Jane will join a Tarzan's laughter even when she does not see any-
  thing to laugh about, *except*
  —A Jane will not join a Tarzan's laughter if he's disagreeing with her,
    and
  —A Jane will not join a Tarzan's laughter if he talks about a trouble he's
    having
- A Tarzan will not join a Jane's laughter if he does not see what's funny,
  except

—A Tarzan will share laughter during flirting

—A Tarzan will join in a Jane's laughter if she is talking about a trouble she's having.

In other words, Jefferson argues that there are stereotypical positions for men and women out of which they share laughter with a member of the opposite sex. Phillip Glenn, Erica Hofmann, and I found that Jefferson's claims describe laughter shared by dating partners better than laughter shared by other male-female pairs.[4] Laughter in courtship also occurs more often in the service of ridicule than that of affiliation. Female courters invite laughter more than males, and most often invite laughter at self! Courting men laugh at the expense of women more often than the reverse, and women frequently join in laughter at self.

This suggests an unequal political economy of humor within courtship. These findings echo the patterns of female criticism in family dinner narratives studied by Ochs and Taylor (chapter 6). Above all, this repeats the suspicion that links the myth of gendered difference in stereotypes about intimate sexual couples.

Even when laugh partners are not members of a sexual couple, practices of flirting raised by laughter can be used for a variety of nonamorous purposes—including racist put-downs.

PAUL AND DYAN: GENDER/ETHNICITY

Consider a unique laughter-laced episode that occurred on a televised talk show broadcast on the North American Univision Network. The show's bilingual host, comedian Paul Rodriguez, skillfully interviews guests who speak Spanish and guests who do not, such as actress Dyan Cannon, for a largely bilingual audience. In her interview Dyan displays a number of partially informed opinions about Hispanic language and culture, culminating in an assertion that Hispanic men show their feelings more than Anglos. Paul disagrees, citing his own frustrations with machismo mythology, especially the "myth of the Latin lover." This utterance sparks a sex-play episode in which Dyan enacts a stereotyped blonde flirt role in which laughter helps her to pin an ethnic slur on Paul. A videotape of this scene shows that

- The woman (Dyan) laughs more than the man (Paul) during this highly gendered episode,
- Dyan uses laughter to perform the role of a sexy blonde,
- Dyan uses this sexy persona to launch flirtatious sexual teases at Paul, and
- These sexual teases help Dyan prevail in an argument about Latino sociology as she manipulates Paul to assume a stereotyped role of "the Latin lover."

Here is a transcript of this laughter-laced segment:

[3] *Paul Rodriquez Show*[5]

Dyan: I think that your audience [Hispanic] men show their feelings more [than Anglos]. Do you think so?

Paul: No, I disagree with you, I think- I think we especially Hispanic men are saddled with something that we inherited from our *parents*, from our- specially from our *fathers*, this machi:smo stuff we have to live up to uh to- to an image that we- just like for example you know the- the Myth of the Latin lover how we're endlessly cra:ving for love, and- and you go *all* night long, uh [look,

Dyan: [Sounds good to me: huh huh huh huh huh
[huh huh huh huh huh huh huh huh hah

Paul: [Well let me tell you Dyan, *we're goo:d* now,
[don't get us wro::ng, you know-

Dyan: [hah hah hah hah hah hah hah hah

Audience: (Laughter, whistles ◄   )

Dyan: [hah ha ha ha, hah hah hah hah hah hah

Paul: [<huh- uh huh you kno:w
But- but all night lo: ng, come o:n.

Dyan: Oh- oh [ho hoh hah huh huh huh huh huh huh huh

Paul: [Only- three, four ho:urs, oka:y.

Dyan:	huh huh huh huh huh huh huh huh
	[huh huh huh huh huh huh huh
Paul:	[You know, even *I* could do that, huh huh
Dyan:	hhuh huh hah hah huh-
	O::h, I *bet* you could go all night lo:ng, Paul.
Audience:	(gasp) OO<OO [OO ◀
Dyan:	[huh [huh hah hah hah hah
Paul:	[Yeah I could,

After Dyan poses the culturally naive hypothesis that Hispanic men are more expressive than Anglos, Paul sketches some burdens that machismo stereotypes place upon Hispanic males. His sociological seriousness shows in the words "image" and "myth." His statement includes the first-person plural pronoun "we," which claims firsthand experience in these burdens. Yet late in the utterance, Paul shifts focus from machismo in general to one example: stereotypes about Latino sexual performance. He exaggerates his intonation of the cliché phrase "all night long," and rolls his eyes. Paul's formulation of male sexual adequacy goes over the top, although he packages this utterance to project a coming punchline ("look").

Dyan interrupts this turn unit to project a surprising and approving uptake on his sexual cliché. "Sounds good to me" cuts across Paul's serious discussion of a negative aspect of cultural stereotyping by responding as if Paul had been bragging. This response casts Dyan as a sexually experienced woman who might appreciate a man's extreme virile performance. Dyan uses a singular pronoun, "me," to shift Paul's speaking on behalf of Latinos ("we") toward a more personal focus. Dyan's tease reframes Paul's sociological discussion as sexual innuendo. Dyan casts herself in a sexpot role by displaying this willfully thick mishearing, and she laughs right afterward.

[3] *Paul Rodriquez Show*[6]

Paul:	the myth of the La:tin lover how we're endlessly cra:ving for
	love, and- and you go *all* night long,
	uh [look,

Dyan: [Sounds good to me: huh huh huh huh huh
            [huh huh huh huh huh huh huh huh
Paul: [Well let me tell you Dyan, *we're goo:d* now,

Paul responds by building on Dyan's tease, repeating her term "good" with a twist into positive self-assessment of Latinos' sexual prowess: "We're good now," he brags.

Pushed by Dyan's flirting and laughter, Paul is manipulated to perform the very sex-role stereotype he had just been at pains to deny. He brags that he is capable of performing for three or four hours. Dyan responds with her loudest laughter of the segment, showing mock arousal at Paul's assessment of his Latin virility. Then Dyan acts like she is bargaining: "I bet you could go all night long." Dyan works blonde stereotypes to critique Paul's sexual performance—and to insist that he be the best that he can be at actualizing her ethnic-sexual stereotype.

Paul's last word is a complete capitulation: "Yeah I could," which literally accepts what he first denied. Paul has actualized his own stereotype. This segment shows Dyan wielding a combination of race, gender, and culture to defend her racist characterization of Hispanic men delivered to a Hispanic man on national TV. Is this a dark side of laughter? Is this kind of power-reversal judo on the laughter patterns found in courtship?

This segment should make us cautious about assuming that gender stereotypes such as "sexy blonde" inevitably work against women in discourse. In this instance Dyan's stereotypical self-casting is part of a ploy to win an argument.

DIDJU HEAR THE ONE ABOUT GENDER?

A humorist once remarked: It ain't what we don't know that hurts us, it's what we know that t'ain't so. So it may be with regard to male-female differences in communication. It may be that our stereotypes about sex differences mediate in our performances as gendered beings—creating sex/gender differences where they need not be. This is part of the arrangement between the sexes.

How different are men and women as communicators? We do not really know, but research claiming such differences remains inconclusive. Meanwhile, most of us, as members of a culture, believe that such differences exist, and we come to expect gendered misunderstandings as routine occurrences in social life. These natural differences, it is widely believed, just happen to us.

In contrast with this view, I argue that speakers create a good deal of the gendering in talk:

- by reenacting stereotypes about male-female differences;
- by engaging in dating and courtship, then forwarding these sexist relational practices into family formation;
- by talking differently about women than about men;
- by treating men and women differently as conversation partners; and
- by allowing women to enjoy only second-class power, status, and economic clout in many social and institutional settings.

All of these practices have been going on for a long time and within many cultures. This gendering has become institutionalized in languages as grammaticalized gender, as semantic asymmetries in descriptive terms applied to men and women, as default assumptions about the status of females—and more. Gender's omnirelevance is shown in the subtle ways that gendered markings creep into talk and by the ways that talk about one facet of gender may lead to talk about another facet—with no sense of transition occurring.

These issues are before us and provide a project for any imagined future. We can make some progress, but the task of readapting to gender in talk is one that will not resolve our most serious problems in one self-improvement binge. I remain optimistic that three or four generations of hard-headed negotiation and truth-telling could lead to a more fairly gendered world. This is not a taken-for-granted conclusion. We could just as easily fumble the tenuous gains of recent generations, especially if we insist on believing that men and women are socially different critters. Attaining male-female parity and finding mostly healthy ways to express sexuality—these are many-faceted tasks. We should approach these tasks with great seriousness and with our most cosmic sense of humor.

Notes

Chapter 1: Gendering the Conversation

1. J. Gray, *Women Are from Venus, Men Are from Mars: A Practical Guide for Improving Communication and Getting What You Want in Your Relationships* (New York: HarperCollins, 1992). D. Tannen, *You Just Don't Understand: Women and Men in Conversation* (New York: William Morrow and Company, 1990).
2. D. Harraway, *Simians, Cyborgs, and Women* (London: Routledge, 1991), 72.
3. J. M. Atkinson and J. C. Heritage, eds., *Structures of Social Action: Studies in Conversation Analysis,* (Cambridge: Cambridge University Press, 1984). Transcribing symbols used are a simplified form of a format used for conversation analysis devised by Gail Jefferson.
4. *Pretty Woman,* directed by G. Marshall, Touchstone Pictures/Silver Screen Partners IV, 1990.

Chapter 2: The Arrangement between the Sexes

1. W. Waller, "The Rating and Dating Complex," in *On the Family, Education, and War,* ed. W. Waller (Chicago: University of Chicago Press, 1970), 169–80.
2. See D. Scheibel, "Faking Identity in Clubland: The Communicative Performance of 'Fake ID,'" *Text and Performance Quarterly* 12 (1992): 160–75, for a detailed discussion of old dating norms in present-day colleges.
3. *The Women,* written by C. B. Luce, directed by H. Stromburg, featuring an all-woman cast, 1939.
4. E. Goffman, "The Arrangement between the Sexes," *Theory and Society* 4 (1977): 301–32.
5. Ibid., 311

6. J. Butler, "Performative Acts and Gender Constitution," in *Performing Feminisms,* ed. S. Case (Baltimore: Johns Hopkins University Press, 1990), 270–82.

7. Goffman, "Arrangement between the Sexes," 302.

8. Ibid.

9. See, for example, D. Graddol and J. Swann in *Gender Voices* (Oxford: Basil Blackwell, 1989).

10. H. Garfinkel discusses this at length in *Studies in Ethnomethodology* (Englewood Cliffs, N.J.: Prentice-Hall, 1967).

11. N. Barley, *The Innocent Anthropologist: Notes from a Mud Hut* (New York: Holt, 1992), 53, 57.

12. See E. O. Laumann, J. H. Gagnon, R. T. Michael, and S. Michaels for their discussion of research on human sexual behavior in *Sexual Practices in the United States* (Chicago: University of Chicago Press, 1994).

13. S. Bem, "The Measurement of Psychological Androgyny," *Journal of Consulting and Clinical Psychology* 42 (1974): 155–62.

14. M. Crawford, *Talking Difference: On Gender and Language* (Thousand Oaks, Calif.: Sage, 1995).

15. Butler, "Performative Acts and Gender Constitution," 270–82.

16. U. Le Guin, *The Left Hand of Darkness* (New York: Ace Books, 1969), 90–92.

17. Ibid., 93.

18. D. Baron, *Grammar and Gender* (New Haven, Conn.: Yale University Press, 1986). See also G. G. Corbett, *Gender* (Cambridge: Cambridge University Press, 1991); and W. A. Foley, *The Papuan Languages of New Guinea* (Cambridge: Cambridge University Press, 1986).

19. See J. T. Wood and W. B. Pearce for this discussion of the term "sexist" in "Sexists, Racists, and Other Classes of Classifiers: Form and Function '. . . ist' Accusations," *Quarterly Journal of Speech* 66 (1980): 239–50.

20. C. A. MacKinnon discusses U.S. courts' criteria for judging sexist discrimination claims in *Only Words* (Cambridge, Mass.: Harvard University Press, 1993).

21. See K. K. Campbell for her analysis of nineteenth-century feminists in "Stanton's 'The Solitude of Self': A Rationale for Feminism," *Quarterly Journal of Speech* 66 (1980): 304–12.

Chapter 3: Flirting

1. See P. Watzlawick, J. Beavin, and D. Jackson for their discussion of content and relationship communication in *The Pragmatics of Human Communication* (New York: Norton, 1967).

2. E. Schegloff, "Preliminaries to Preliminaries: 'Can I Ask You a Question?'" *Sociological Inquiry* 50 (1980): 115.

3. R. Hopper, *Telephone Conversation* (Bloomington: Indiana University Press, 1992), 71–97.

4. E. Goffman used the term "civil inattention" in *Behavior in Public Places: Notes on the Social Organization of Gatherings* (New York: Free Press of Glencoe, 1963).

5. E. Goffman, "The Arrangement between the Sexes," *Theory and Society* 4 (1977): 309.

6. See discussions of uncertainty reduction by C. Berger and R. Calabrese, "Some Explorations in Initial Interaction and Beyond: Toward a Developmental Theory of Interpersonal Communication," *Human Communication Research* 1 (1975): 99–112; M. Knapp, *Social Intercourse: From Greeting to Goodbye* (Boston: Allyn and Bacon, 1978); and C. Berger and J. Bradac, *Language and Social Knowledge: Uncertainty in Interpersonal Relations* (London: Arnold, 1982).

7. "Baby, Baby." Written/performed by A. Grant; Heart in motion album, Age to Age Music, 1991. From the CD liner: "This song is dedicated to Millie, whose six-week-old face was my inspiration."

8. *Bambi,* directed by D. Hand and P. Pearce, Walt Disney Productions, 1942.

9. M. C. Bateson, "Joint Performance across Cultures: Improvisation in a Persian Garden," *Text and Performance Quarterly* 13 (1993): 115.

10. "Hit Me with Your Best Shot," E. Schwartz, ATV Music Corp., BMI; Singer: P. Benetar, Crimes of Passion album (1980).

11. E. Berscheid and E. Walster, "A Little Bit About Love," in *Foundations of Interpersonal Attraction,* ed. T. L. Huston (New York: Academic Press, 1974), 355–80.

12. E. Segal, *Love Story* (New York: Signet, 1970), 2–3.

13. See D. Schiffrin's discussion of meta-talk in "Meta-talk: Organizational and Evaluative Brackets in Discourse," *Sociological Inquiry* 50 (1980): 199–236.

14. W. Shakespeare, *Much Ado about Nothing,* ed. Peter Holland (New York: Penguin Books, Inc., 1958/1971/1999).

15. *Clueless,* directed by A. Heckerling, Paramount Pictures Corporation, 1995.

16. *Sweet Dreams,* HBO Home Video, 1985.

17. *The Presidio,* directed by P. Hyams, Paramount Pictures Corporation, 1988.

18. Ibid.

19. Ibid.

20. "The Tennis Song," from City of Angels Music by C. Coleman, Lyrics by D. Zippel. Recording CBS CK 46067, 1989.

21. *Pretty Woman,* directed by G. Marshall, Touchstone Pictures/Silver Screen Partners IV, 1990.

22. Segal, *Love Story.*

23. Shakespeare, *Much Ado about Nothing.*

24. G. Bateson, "A Theory of Play and Fantasy," in *Steps to an Ecology of Mind* (San Francisco: Chandler, 1970), 177–93; and R. Hopper and P. Glenn, "Repetition and Play in Conversation," in *Perspectives on Repetition,* vol. 2, ed. B. Johnstone (Norwood, N.J.: Ablex, 1993), 29–40.

Chapter 4: Hey Baby, You Bitch

1. See the discussion of the relationship between violence and flirtation in S. Lloyd, "The Darkside of Courtship: Violence and Sexual Exploitation," *Family Relations* 40 (1991): 14–20; and M. Roth, "Transforming the Rape Culture that Lives in My Skull," in *Transforming a Rape Culture,* ed. E. Buchwald, P. R. Fletcher, and M. Roth (Minneapolis, Minn.: Milkweed Editions, 1993), 405–15.

2. Many problems of sexual violence are not addressed here. There is no discussion of child abuse (see M. Sniffen, "Most Sex Offenders Target Kids, Study Says," *Austin American Statesman,* 4 March 1996), of occasions in which men are victims, of surgical mutilation, of murder of wives, of female infanticides, of dowry murder (see J. T. Wood, "Our Stories: Communication Professionals' Narratives of Sexual Harassment," *Journal of Applied Communication Research* 20 [1993]: 363–90), or of marital violence (see P. Harvey and P. Gow, *Sex and Violence: Issues in Representation and Experience* [London: Routledge, 1994]).

3. See H. Sacks's analysis of invitations and rejections in "On the Preferences for Agreement and Contiguity in Sequences in Conversation," in *Talk and Social Organization,* ed. G. Button and J. R. E. Lee (Avon: Multilingual Matters Limited, 1987), 54–69.

4. Ibid.

5. "Maybe I Mean Yes." H. Dunn, C. Waters, and T. Shapiro. Holly Dunn's Greatest Hits album, Warner Brothers Records, 1991.

6. See R. Hopper's and C. LeBaron's discussion of narratives of sex offenders in "The Interactive Construction of Leadership in Group Therapy" (paper presented at the Annual Convention of the International Communication Association, Montreal, Canada, May 1996).

7. J. Curtis reports this in her research on a sexual battering intervention program in "Manufacturing Consent: Discourses of Masculinity in a Battering Intervention Program," unpublished manuscript (1995).

8. Ibid.

9. The following three excerpts from narratives of sexual harrassment are from J. T. Wood, "Our Stories: Communication Professionals' Narratives of Sexual Harassment," 363–90.

10. M. Motley and H. Reeder, "Unwanted Escalation of Sexual Intimacy: Male and Female Perceptions of Connotations and Relational Consequences of Resistance Messages," *Communication Monographs* 62 (1995): 355–82. See also C. Muehlenhard, "Misinterpreted Dating Behaviors and the Risk of Date Rape," in *Violence in Dating Relationships: Emerging Social Issues,* ed. M. Pirog-Good and J. Stets (Westport, Conn.: Praeger, 1989), 241–56; and C. Muehlenhard and L. Hollabaugh, "Do Women Sometimes Say No When They Mean Yes? The Prevalence and Correlates of Women's Token Resistance to Sex," *Journal of Personality and Social Psychology* 54, no. 5 (1988): 872–79. (Table is simplified from Motley and Reeder, "Unwanted Escalation," 363.)

11. See D. Hicks and P. Glenn, "The Pragmatics of Sexual Harassment: Two Devices for Creating a 'Hostile Environment,'" in *The Lynching of Language: Gender, Politics and Power in the Hill-Thomas Hearings,* ed. S. Ragan, D. Bystrom, L. L. Kaid, and C. S. Beck (Chicago: University of Illinois Press, 1996), 228.

12. See C. B. Gardner, "Passing By: Street Remarks, Address Rights, and The Urban Female," *Sociological Inquiry* 50 (1980): 336.

13. *Thelma and Louise,* directed by R. Scott, MGM-Pathe Communications Company, 1991.

14. *Tootsie,* directed by S. Pollack, Columbia Pictures Industries, Inc., 1982.

15. Ibid.

16. *Thelma and Louise.*

17. Ibid.

18. C. Paglia, *Sexual Personae: Art and Decadence from Nefertiti to Emily Dickinson* (New York: Yale University Press, 1990).

19. *The Quest for Fire,* directed by J-J Annaud, ICC, 1984.

20. J. A. Senchea, "Gendered Constructions of Sexuality in Adolescent Girls' Talk" (Ph.D. diss., University of Iowa, 1998).

21. Hopper and LeBaron, "The Interactive Construction of Leadership in Group Therapy"; and R. Hopper and C. LeBaron, "The Interactive Deception of Detection in Group Therapy" (paper presented at the Annual Convention of the National Communication Association, San Antonio, Texas, November 1997).

22. N. Malamuth and L. Brown, "Sexually Aggressive Men's Perceptions of Women's Communications: Testing Three Explanations," *Journal of Personality and Social Psychology* 67 (1994): 699–712.

23. See, for example, M. Roth's work on sexuality as rape, "Transforming the Rape Culture That Lives in My Skull," 413.

24. C. Ralston, "Public Passions," in *Penthouse Variations* (1991): 75, 78.

25. See, for example, M. Allen, T. Emmers, L. Gebhardt, and M. Giery in their analysis of the link between pornography and rape, "Exposure to Pornography and Acceptance of Rape Myths," *Journal of Communication* 45, no. 1 (1995): 5–26.

26. S. MacDonald, "Confessions of a Feminist Porn Watcher," *Film Quarterly* 36, no. 3 (1983): 49.

27. See, for example, A. B. Snitow's discussion of women and pornography in "Mass Market Romance: Pornography for Women Is Different." In *Powers of Desire: The Politics of Sexuality,* ed. A. B. Snitow, C. Stansell, and S. Thompson (New York: Monthly Review Press, 1983), 245–63.

28. S. Paulos, *Till Morning's Light,* Candlelight Ecstasy Romance Series (New York: Dell Publishing Corp., 1985), 46–47.

29. See M. Foucault's analysis of criminalizing social problems in *Discipline and Punish: The Birth of the Prison,* trans. A. Sheridan (New York: Pantheon Books, 1977).

30. M. Adelman, "Play and Incongruity: Framing Safe-Sex Talk," *Health Communication* 1 (1991): 148–49.

31. Ibid.

Chapter 5: Coupling as Progressive Commitment

1. M. Konner, *The Tangled Wing: Biological Constraints on the Human Spirit* (New York: Holt, Rinehart and Winston, 1983), 263.

2. L. Durrell, *Justine* (London: Penguin, 1957), 37.

3. See J. T. Wood's discussion of couple culture in "Communication and Relational Culture: Bases for the Study of Human Relationships," *Communication Quarterly* 30 (1982): 76.

4. W. Waller, "The Rating and Dating Complex," in *On the Family, Education, and War: Selected Writings*, ed. Willard W. Waller (Chicago: University of Chicago Press, 1970), 179; first published in *American Sociological Review* 2 (October 1937): 727–34.

5. Ibid, 180.

6. See C. Bolton's work on relationship development for a discussion of these studies in "Mate Selection as the Development of a Relationship," *Marriage and Family Living* 23, no. 3 (1961): 235.

7. See L. Baxter and W. Wilmot for their research on secret tests, "Secret Tests: Social Strategies for Acquiring Information about the State of the Relationship," *Human Communication Research* 11 (1984): 171–201.

8. In addition to Baxter and Wilmot (1984), see also L. Baxter and W. Wilmot, "Taboo Topics in Close Relationships," *Journal of Social and Personal Relationships* 2 (1985): 253–69; and L. Baxter and C. Bullis, "Turning Points in Developing Romantic Relationships," *Human Communication Research* 12 (1986): 469–93.

9. *An Affair to Remember,* directed by L. McCarey, Twentieth Century-Fox Film Corporation, 1957.

10. See H. Sacks's discussion of missing adjacency pairs in "On the Preferences for Agreement and Contiguity in Sequences in Conversation," in *Talk and Social Organization,* ed. G. Button and J. R. E. Lee (Avon: Multilingual Matters Limited, 1987), 54–69.

11. E. Hemingway, *A Farewell to Arms* (New York: Charles Scribner, 1929), 91.

12. F. O'Connor, "Good Country People," in *A Good Man Is Hard to Find and Other Stories* (New York: Harcourt, Brace, and World, Inc., 1955), 287–88.

13. E. Goffman discusses "tie signs" in *Relations in Public: Microstudies of the Public Order* (New York: Basic Books, Inc., 1971).

14. J. Mandelbaum, "Couples Sharing Stories," *Communication Quarterly* 35 (1987): 147.

15. H. James, *The Portrait of a Lady* (London: Penguin, 1969), 164–65. (Quoted in Goffman, *Relations in Public,* 201.)

16. This example is from J. Mandelbaum's (1987) research on shared stories.

17. *Say Anything,* directed by C. Crowe, Twentieth Century Fox Home Entertainment, 1989.

18. L. Baxter, "Trajectories of Relationship Disengagement," *Journal of Social and Personal Relationships* 1 (1984): 29–48.

19. S. Ragan and R. Hopper discuss fictional break-up episodes in "Ways to Leave Your Lover," *Communication Quarterly* 32 (1984): 310–17.

20. Play fragment from H. Pinter's *Betrayal* (New York: Grove Press, 1978; as analyzed by S. Ragan and R. Hopper, 1984).

21. Play fragment from S. Gray's *Otherwise Engaged and Other Plays* (New York: Viking, 1975; as analyzed by S. Ragan and R. Hopper, 1984).

22. R. Hopper and K. Drummond discuss how mitigation may be stacked with an utterance in their analysis of a relational turning point in "Emergent Goals at a Relational Turning Point: The Case of Gordon and Denise," *Journal of Language and Social Psychology* 9 (1990): 39–65.

Chapter 6: Coupling as a Difference Engine

1. See a discussion of relationship relevant events in the work of D. Goldsmith and L. Baxter, "Constituting Relationships in Talk: A Taxonomy of Speech Events in Social and Personal Relationships," *Human Communication Research* 23 (1996): 87–114; S. Duck, D. Rutt, M. Hurst, and H. Strejc, "Some Evident Truths about Conversations in Everyday Relationships: All Communications Are Not Created Equal," *Human Communication Research* 18 (1991): 228–67; and S. Sigman, "Handling the Discontinuous Aspects of Continuous Social Relationships: Toward Research on the Persistence of Social Forms," *Communication Theory* 1 (1991): 106–27.

2. D. Tannen, *You Just Don't Understand: Women and Men in Conversation* (New York: William Morrow and Company, 1990), 49–50.

3. *White Men Can't Jump*, directed by R. Shelton, Finger Roll Productions, Inc; Twentieth Century-Fox Film Corporation, 1992.

4. Ibid.

5. See E. Ochs's and C. Taylor's discussion of family talk in dinnertime narratives in "The 'Father Knows Best' Dynamic in Dinnertime Narratives," in *Gender Articulated: Language and The Socially Constructed Self,* ed. K. Hall and M. Bucholtz (New York: Routledge, 1995), 98.

6. Ibid, 101.

7. Ibid, 108–9.

8. S. Blum-Kulka discusses sex roles in family discourse in *Dinner Talk: Cultural*

Patterns of Sociability and Socialization in Family Discourse (Mahwah, N.J.: Lawrence Erlbaum, 1997).

9. J. M. Gottman discusses sex differences and couples' problems in *Marital Interaction: Experimental Investigations* (New York: Academic Press, 1979).

10. A. Tan, *The Joy Luck Club* (New York: Putnam, 1989), 162.

11. Ibid., 156.

Chapter 7: Talk about Women, Talk about Men

1. R. Lakoff discusses the demeaning connotation of "girl" in *Language and Woman's Place* (New York: Harper and Row, 1975).

2. W. A. Apple uses this dating analogy in discussing political campaigns in "Feel-Good Celebration Does Not a Presidential Election Make," *New York Times*, 14 August 1996, A13.

3. D. R. Hofstadter, *Metamagical Themes: Questing for the Essence of Mind and Pattern* (New York: Basic Books, 1985), 137.

4. D. Carbaugh discusses this concept in *Situating Selves: The Communication of Social Identities in American Scenes* (Albany: State University of New York Press, 1996).

5. C. Miller and K. Swift talk about family naming practices in *Words and Women* (Garden City, N.Y.: Anchor Press, 1976), 9–10.

6. For a discussion of the history of women's adoption of their husbands' names, see S. Kupper, *Surnames for Women: A Decision-Making Guide* (Jefferson, N.C.: McFarland and Company, 1990), 11–14.

7. L. Scott, "He or She," *Text and Performance Quarterly* 13 (1993): 184–85.

8. P. Mühlhäusler and R. Harré, *Pronouns and People: The Linguistic Construction of Social and Personal Identity* (Cambridge, Mass.: Basil Blackwell, 1990), 229.

9. T. Wells, "Woman—Which Includes Man, of Course," in *Exploring Contemporary Male-Female Roles: A Facilitator's Guide,* ed. C. G. Carney and S. L. McMahon (San Francisco, Calif.: Jossey Bass, 1977), 28–29.

10. Hofstadter, *Metamagical Themes*, 159.

11. Among these investigators, see F. Khosroshahi, "Penguins Don't Care but Women Do: A Social Identity Analysis of a Whorfian Problem," *Language in Society* 18 (1989): 505–25; and C. Miller and K. Swift, *Words and Women* (Garden City, N.Y.: Anchor Press, 1976).

12. J. Stringer and R. Hopper, "Generic 'He' in Conversation," *Quarterly Journal of Speech* 84 (1998): 209–21.

13. A. Graham discusses the so-called generic "he" further in "The Making of a Nonsexist Dictionary," in *Language and Sex,* ed. B. Thorne and N. Henley (Boston: Heinle and Heinle Publishers, 1975), 57–63.

14. See A. Bodine, "Androcentrism in Prescriptive Grammar: Singular 'They,' Sex-Indefinite 'He' and 'He or She,'" *Language in Society* 4 (1975): 131; and D. E. Baron, *Grammar and Gender* (New Haven, Conn.: Yale University Press, 1986), 196.

15. Marcus Aurelius, *Marcus Aurelius and His Times* (Roslyn, N.Y.: Walter J. Black, Inc., 1945), 13.

Chapter 8: Making Women Look Bad

1. R. Lakoff, *Language and Woman's Place* (New York: Harper and Row, 1975).

2. J. P. Stanley, "Paradigmatic Woman: The Prostitute," in *Papers in Language Variation: Samla-Ads Collection,* ed. D. L. Shores and C. P. Hines (Tuscaloosa: University of Alabama Press, 1977), 305–6.

3. T. Minh-ha, *Woman, Native, Other: Writing Post-Coloniality and Feminism* (Bloomington: Indiana University Press, 1989), 96.

4. "Dirty World," The Traveling Wilburys, Warner Brothers, 1988.

5. b. hooks, *Black Looks: Race and Representation* (Boston: South End Press, 1992), 61.

6. N. J. Wrather and M. Sanches discuss racist and sexist humor in "The Acceptability of Racist and Sexist Humor" (paper presented at the Annual Meeting of the Speech Communication Association, November 1978).

7. M. Jacobson, "Let Your Laughter Be Your Guide," *Esquire,* August 1988, 49.

8. See K. Deaux and J. Taynor, "Evaluation of Male and Female Ability: Bias Works Two Ways," *Psychological Reports* 32 (1973): 261–62; and K. Deaux and T. Emswiller, "Explanations of Successful Performance on Sex-Linked Tasks: What Is Skill for the Male Is Luck for the Female," *Journal of Personality and Social Psychology* 29, no. 1 (1974): 80–85.

9. *Star Trek: Next Generation,* created by Gene Roddenberry, 1987, Paramount Pictures.

10. "NFL Notes," *Austin American Statesman,* 28 August 1996.

11. F. Parkman, *The Conspiracy of Pontiac,* 8th ed., vol. 1 (Boston: Little Brown and Co., 1875), 30–31.

12. George Bordon, "The Perceived Sexuality of American English," mimeo, n.d.

13. See I. Broverman, D. Broverman, F. Clarkson, P. Rosencrantz, and S. Vogel, "Sex-Role Stereotypes and Clinical Judgments of Mental Health," *Journal of Consulting*

and Clinical Psychology 34, no. 1 (1970): 1–7; and Inge Broverman, S. Vogel, D. Broverman, F. Clarkson, and P. Rosencrantz, "Sex-Role Stereotypes: A Current Appraisal," *Journal of Social Issues* 28, no. 2 (1972): 63.

14. See J. Berger for his discussion of how men "act" and women "appear" in *Ways of Seeing* (New York: Viking Penguin, 1973).

15. "The Brady Bunch" musical theme.

16. N. Wolf , *The Beauty Myth: How Images of Beauty Are Used against Women* (New York: W. Morrow, 1991), 12.

17. M. B. Pipher, *Reviving Ophelia: Saving the Selves of Adolescent Girls* (New York, Putnam, 1994), 183.

18. M. Wollstonecraft, *A Vindication of the Rights of Woman* (New York: Alfred A. Knopf, 1992), 1. (First published 1792.)

19. R. Lakoff and R. Scherr, *Face Value: The Politics of Beauty* (New York: Routledge, 1984), 18–19.

20. *Pretty Woman,* directed by G. Marshall, Touchstone Pictures/Silver Screen Partners IV, 1990.

21. *Carnal Knowledge,* directed by M. Nichols, Icarus Productions, 1971.

22. N. Vickers discusses this in "The Mistress in the Masterpiece," in *The Poetics of Gender: Gender and Culture Series,* ed. N. K. Miller (New York: Columbia University Press, 1986), 22–23.

23. Ibid, 36.

24. C. MacKinnon, *Only Words* (Cambridge, Mass.: Harvard University Press, 1993), 55.

25. C. J. Clover discusses sexual violence in horror and slasher films in "Her Body, Himself: Gender in the Slasher Film," in *Gender, Race and Class in Media: A Critical Text-Reader,* ed. G. Dines and J. M. Humez (Thousand Oaks, Calif.: Sage, 1995), 169–83.

26. *Carnal Knowledge.*

Chapter 9: How Men and Women Talk

1. *The Little Mermaid,* directed by R. Clements, Walt Disney Productions/ Silver Screen Partners IV, songs by H. Ashman and A. Menken, 1989. For a discussion of this see E. Bell, L. Haas, and L. Sells, *From Mouse to Mermaid: The Politics of Film, Gender and Culture* (Bloomington: Indiana University Press, 1995).

2. C. Kramarae discussed "muted women" in *Women and Men Speaking: Frameworks for Analysis* (Rowley, Mass.: Newbury House Publishers, 1982).

3. See D. Tannen for her comments on women's avoidance of the public podium in *You Just Don't Understand: Women and Men in Conversation* (New York: William Morrow and Company, 1990).

4. D. James and J. Drakich, "Gender Differences in Amount of Talk: Critical Review of Research," in *Gender and Conversational Interaction*, ed. D. Tannen (New York: Oxford, 1993), 289.

5. Ibid., 296.

6. D. Tannen discusses implications of interruptions in *You Just Don't Understand*, 189.

7. For more analysis of interruptions see A. Bennett, "Interruptions and the Interpretation of Conversation," in *Discourse Processes* 4 (1981): 171–88.

8. For their discussion of speech overlap see C. West and D. Zimmerman, "Small Insults: A Study of Interruptions in Cross-Sex Conversations between Unacquainted Persons," in *Language, Gender and Society*, ed. B. Thorne, C. Kramarae, and N. Henley (Boston, Mass.: Heinle and Heinle Publishers, 1983).

9. H. Sacks, E. Schegloff, and G. Jefferson discuss interruptions extensively in "A Simplest Systematics for the Organization of Turn-Taking for Conversation," *Language* 50 (1974): 696–735. (Also appears in *Studies on the Organization of Conversational Interaction*, ed. J. Schenkein [New York: Academic Press, 1978], 7–56.)

10. Tannen, *You Just Don't Understand*, 212.

11. D. James and S. Clarke, "Women, Men, and Interruptions: A Critical Review," in *Gender and Conversational Interaction*, ed. D. Tannen (New York: Oxford, 1993), 231. For additional research on interruptions and various definitions thereof, see Kathryn Dindia, "The Effects of Sex of Subject and Sex of Partner on Interruptions," *Human Communication Research* 13 (1987): 345–71; Robert Hopper, *Telephone Conversation* (Bloomington: Indiana University Press, 1992); and Candace West, "Against Our Will: Male Interruptions of Females in Cross Sex Conversation," *Annals of the New York Academy of Sciences* 327 (1979): 81–97.

12. For example, see *Language and Sex*, ed. B. Thorne and N. Henley (Boston, Mass.: Heinle and Heinle Publishers, Inc., 1975), 105–29; and *Language, Gender and Society*, ed. B. Thorne, C. Kramarae, and N. Henley (Boston, Mass.: Heinle and Heinle Publishers, Inc., 1983).

13. P. Fishman reported the nonreciprocal nature of topic extension in "Interaction: The Work Women Do," *Social Problems* 26 (1978): 397–406; revised version in

Language, Gender and Society, ed. B. Thorne, C. Kramarae, and N. Henley (Boston, Mass.: Heinle and Heinle Publishers, Inc., 1983), yet this finding has not been replicated, even in other studies of married couples. For example, see S. Blum-Kulka, *Dinner Talk: Cultural Patterns of Sociability and Socialization in Family Discourse* (Mahwah, N.J.: Lawrence Erlbaum, 1997), 83.

14. M. Crawford discusses the issue of women's assertiveness in *Talking Difference: On Gender and Language* (Thousand Oaks, Calif.: Sage, 1995), 58.

15. See, for example, research that rarely confirms genderlect hypotheses by C. Kramer, "Women's Speech: Separate but Unequal?" *Quarterly Journal of Speech* 60 (1974): 14–24; A. Haas, "Male and Female Spoken Language Differences: Stereotypes and Evidence," *Psychological Bulletin* 86, no. 3 (1979): 616–26; and G. N. Garcia and S. F. Frosh, "Sex, Color, and Money: Who's Perceiving What? OR Men and Women: Where Did All the Differences Go To?" in *The Sociology of the Language of American Women,* ed. B. L. Dubois and I. Crouch (San Antonio, Tex.: Trinity University Press, 1976), 63–71.

16. See discussions of men's and women's speech differences in D. Graddol and J. Swann, *Gender Voices* (Oxford: Basil Blackwell, 1989); and D. Brouwer, *Gender Variation in Dutch: A Sociolinguistic Study of Amsterdam Speech* (Hawthorne, N.Y.: Mouton de Gruyter, 1989).

17. Research in language and power is seen in studies by W. O'Barr and B. Atkins, "'Women's Language' or 'Powerless Language,'" in *Women and Language in Literature and Society,* ed. S. McConnell-Ginet, R. Borker, and N. Furman (New York: Praeger, 1980), 93–110; B. Erickson, E. A. Lind, B. Johnson, and W. O'Barr, "Speech Style and Impression Formation in a Court Setting: The Effects of 'Powerful' and 'Powerless' Speech," *Journal of Experimental Social Psychology* 14 (1978): 266–79; and J. Conley and W. O'Barr, *Rules versus Relationships* (Chicago: University of Chicago Press, 1990).

18. Women's use of powerless speech has been studied by S. Ng and J. Bradac, *Power in Language: Verbal Communication and Social Influence* (Newbury Park, Calif.: Sage, 1993); R. M. Kanter, *Men and Women of the Corporation* (New York: Basic Books, 1977); and D. J. Maltz and R. Borker, "A Cultural Approach to Male-Female Miscommunication," in *Language and Social Identity,* ed. J. J. Gumperz (Cambridge: Cambridge University Press, 1982), 196–216.

19. For example, see D. Brouwer, M. Gerritsen, and D. De Haan, "Speech Differences between Women and Men: On the Wrong Track?" *Language in Society* 8 (1979):

33–50; and D. Brouwer, "The Influence of the Addressee's Sex on Politeness in Language Use," *Linguistics* 20 (1982): 697–711.

20. For studies of gender-linked language effect, see A. Mulac and T. L. Lundell, "An Empirical Test of the Gender-Linked Language Effect in a Public Speaking Setting," *Language and Speech* 25, no. 3 (1982): 243–56; A. Mulac, L. L. Torberg, and J. Bradac, "Male/Female Language Differences and Attributional Consequences in a Public Speaking Situation," *Communication Monographs* 53 (1986): 115–29; A. Mulac, L. Studley, J. Wiemann, and J. Bradac, "Male-Female Gaze in the Same-Sex and Mixed-Sex Dyads: Gender-Linked Differences and Mutual Influence," *Human Communication Research* 13 (1987): 323–44; A. Mulac, J. Wiemann, S. Widenmann, and T. Gibson, "Male/Female Language Differences and Effects in Same-Sex and Mixed-Sex Dyads: The Gender-Linked Language Effect," *Communication Monographs* 55 (1988): 315–35; S. Ng, and J. Bradac, *Power in Language: Verbal Communication and Social Influence* (Newbury Park, Calif.: Sage, 1993); and A. Mulac, "The Gender-Linked Language Effect: Do Language Differences Really Make a Difference?" in *Sex Differences and Similarities in Communication: Critical Essays and Empirical Investigations of Sex and Gender in Interaction,* ed. D. J. Canary and K. Dindia (Mahwah, N.J.: Lawrence Erlbaum, 1998).

21. S. Lawrence, N. Stucky, and R. Hopper, "The Effects of Sex Dialects and Sex Stereotypes on Speech Evaluations," *Journal of Language and Social Psychology* 9 (1990): 209–24.

22. R. Hopper, and J. Hsu, "Do We Speak Genderlects?" (paper presented at the International Communication Association, Miami, Florida, May 1992).

23. In the previous study (Hopper and Hsu), qualifiers were distinguished according to procedures used by E. Prince, J. Frader, and C. Bosk, "On Hedging in Physician-Physician Discourse," in *Linguistics and the Professions: Proceedings of the Second Annual Delaware Symposium on Language Studies,* ed. R. J. DiPietro (Norwood, N.J.: Ablex Publishing Corp., 1982).

24. In the study (Hopper and Hsu), politeness indicators were tabulated according to the procedures of D. Brouwer, "The Influence of the Addressee's Sex on Politeness in Language Use," *Linguistics* 20 (1982): 697–711; and J. Holmes, *Women, Men and Politeness* (New York: Longman, 1995).

25. S. Ng, and J. Bradac, *Power in Language: Verbal Communication and Social Influence* (Newbury Park, Calif.: Sage, 1993), 46–47.

26. C. Gilligan, *In a Different Voice* (Cambridge: Harvard University Press, 1982, 1993).

27. D. Tannen discusses rapport talk and report talk in *You Just Don't Understand*.

28. See M. H. Goodwin's studies of boys' and girls' play groups, including "Directive-Response Speech Sequences in Girls' and Boys' Task Activities," in *Women and Language in Literature and Society*, ed. S. McConnell-Ginet, R. Borker, and N. Furman (New York: Praeger, 1980), 158–59; *He-Said-She-Said: Talk as Social Organization among Black Children* (Bloomington: Indiana University Press, 1990); and "Tactical Uses of Stories: Participation Frameworks within Boys' and Girls' Disputes," in *Gender and Conversational Interaction*, ed. D. Tannen (New York: Oxford University Press, 1993), 110–43.

29. M. H. Goodwin, "Directive-Response Speech Sequences in Girls' and Boys' Task Activities," 165.

Chapter 10: How Gender Creeps into Talk

1. W. Handelsman, "El Niño Finds its Way into the American Vernacular," Tribune Media Services (printed in *Austin American Statesman*, 5 October 1997).

2. E. Ochs, "Indexing Gender," in *Rethinking Context: Language as an Interactive Phenomenon*, ed. A. Duranti and C. Goodwin (Cambridge: Cambridge University Press, 1992), 340.

3. *Pretty Woman*, directed by G. Marshall, Touchstone Pictures/Silver Screen Partners IV, 1990.

4. For a thorough analysis of conversational ambiguity, see E. Schegloff, "On Some Questions and Ambiguities in Conversation," in *Talk and Social Structure: Studies in Conversational Analysis*, ed. J. M. Atkinson and J. Heritage (Cambridge: Cambridge University Press, 1984), 28–52.

5. See E. Schegloff's, G. Jefferson's, and H. Sacks's study of repair initiation in "The Preference for Self-Correction in the Organization of Repair in Conversation," *Language* 3 (1977): 361–82.

6. *The Presidio*, directed by P. Hyams, Paramount Pictures Corporation, 1988.

7. D. Schiffrin writes extensively of meta-talk in "Meta-Talk: Organizational and Evaluative Brackets in Discourse," *Sociological Inquiry* 50 (1980): 199–236.

8. H. Garfinkel, *Studies in Ethnomethodology* (Englewood Cliffs, N.J.: Prentice-Hall, 1967), 44.

9. *The Presidio*.

10. H. Sacks discusses noticing in *Lectures on Conversation*, ed. G. Jefferson (Oxford: Basil Blackwell, 1992), 2:87–93.

11. *Strangers in Good Company,* directed by C. Scott, National Film Board of Canada, 1990.

12. Ibid.

13. See H. Sacks, *Lectures on Conversation,* 2:93.

14. H. Garfinkel and H. Sacks discuss the "omni-relevance" of gender in H. Garfinkel, *Studies in Ethnomethodology,* 112; and H. Sacks, *Lectures on conversation,* 2:515–16, 594–97.

15. See the following for a discussion of this notion: J. Mandelbaum, "Beyond Mundane Reasoning: Conversation Analysis and Context," *Research in Language and Social Interaction* 24 (1991): 331–48; E. Schegloff, "Reflections on Talk and Social Structure," in *Talk and Social Structure: Studies in Ethnomethodology and Conversation Analysis,* ed. D. Boden and D. H. Zimmerman (Cambridge: Polity Press, 1991), 44–71; and in *Structures of Social Action: Studies in Conversation Analysis,* ed. J. M. Atkinson and J. Heritage (Cambridge: Cambridge University Press, 1984).

16. *Strangers in Good Company.*

17. Ibid.

Chapter 11: Leveling the Playing Field

1. C. West, M. Lazar, and C. Kramarae, "Gender in Discourse," in *Discourse as Social Interaction. Series in Discourse Studies: A Multidisciplinary Introduction,* ed. T. A. Van Dijk (Thousand Oaks, Calif.: Sage, 1997), 119–43. See also D. Cameron, *Feminism and Linguistic Theory* (New York: St. Martin's Press, 1985).

2. K. Fitch, *Speaking Relationally: Culture, Communication, and Interpersonal Connection* (New York: Guilford, 1998).

3. Thelma and Louise, directed by R. Scott, MGM-Pathe Communications Company, 1991.

4. M. H. Goodwin, "Directive-Response Speech Sequences in Girls' and Boys' Task Activities," in *Women and Language in Literature and Society,* ed. S. McConnell-Ginet, R. Borker, and N. Furman (New York: Praeger, 1980), 165.

5. R. M. Kanter, *Men and Women of the Corporation* (New York: Basic Books, 1977).

6. P. Weiss discusses problems of office romance in "Don't Even Think about It (The Cupid Cops Are Watching)," *New York Times Magazine,* 3 May 1998, 43–60.

7. S. Faludi, *Backlash: The Undeclared War against American Women* (New York: Anchor Doubleday, 1991).

Chapter 12: Return to Laughter

1. A. Camus, *The Myth of Sisyphus and Other Essays,* translated from French by J. O'Brien (New York: Knopf, 1969).

2. J. F. Gardner, *Politically Correct Bedtime Stories* (New York: MacMillan Publishing Company, 1994), 2.

3. G. Jefferson, "A Note on Laughter in 'Male-Female' Interaction," unpublished manuscript, 1994, UTCL, University of Texas at Austin.

4. P. Glenn, E. Hofmann, and R. Hopper, "Woman, Laughter, Man: Gender and the Sequential Organization of Laughter" (paper presented at the American Association for Applied Linguistics, Chicago, March 1996).

5. For more discussion of the D. Cannon and P. Rodriguez interview, see R. Hopper, "Episode Trajectory in Conversational Play," in *Situated Order: Studies in the Social Organization of Talk and Embodied Activities,* ed. P. Ten Have and G. Psathas (Washington, D.C.: University Press of America, 1995).